ELECTRONICS COOLING

Edited by **S M Sohel Murshed**

Electronics Cooling
http://dx.doi.org/10.5772/61407
Edited by S M Sohel Murshed

Contributors
Chan Byon, Mohamed Elnaggar, Ezzaldeen Edwan, Wei-Keng Lin, S M Sohel Murshed, Soheil Soleimanikutanaei, Yiding Cao, Olubunmi Popoola, Mohammad Reza Safaei, Mostafa Safdari Shadloo, Mahidzal Dahari, Marjan Goodarzi, Omid Ali Akbari, Jian Qu, Qian Wang, Haruhiko Ohta, Yasuhisa Shinmoto, Daisuke Yamamoto

Published by InTech
Janeza Trdine 9, 51000 Rijeka, Croatia

Publishing Process Manager Dajana Pemac
Technical Editor InTech DTP team
Cover InTech Design team

First published June, 2016
Printed in Croatia

Additional hard copies can be obtained from orders@intechopen.com

Electronics Cooling, Edited by S M Sohel Murshed
p. cm.
Print ISBN 978-953-51-2405-4
Online ISBN 978-953-51-2406-1

For EU product safety concerns:
IN TECH d.o.o., Prolaz Marije Krucifikse Kozulić 3, 51000 Rijeka, Croatia,
info@intechopen.com or visit our website at intechopen.com.

Meet the editor

Professor S. M. Sohel Murshed was born in Bangladesh and is currently with the University of Lisbon, Portugal. He obtained his PhD in Mechanical and Aerospace Engineering from Nanyang Technological University of Singapore in 2007 and then worked as postdoctoral fellow at universities in Singapore and USA. He has so far authored/co-authored 4 books, 16 book-chapters, and over 100 papers in leading international journals and conferences and has Google Scholar citations of 2670. He is a Portugal national delegate of the management committee of a European COST action. He is an editor of *Journal of Nanofluids* since 2012 and editorial board member of few other international journals. His main research interests include nanofluids, nanoscale heat transfer, microfluidics, advanced energy, and cooling technologies.

Contents

Preface

Recent developments in electronics and semiconductor technologies and the continued miniaturization have resulted in very high increase in power density for high performance chips and devices. Although impressive progress has been made during the past decades, there remain serious technical challenges in thermal management of electronic devices as the conventional cooling approaches are increasingly falling short in meeting the ever-increasing cooling demand of high-heat flux generating electronics.

Featuring contributions from internationally renowned academics and researchers in the field, this book covers various key electronics cooling approaches, including conventional and advanced ones.

This book starts with an introductory chapter overviewing available conventional and emerging cooling methods as well as coolants such as nanofluids for electronics cooling.

The second chapter introduces an innovative cooling method using boiling heat transfer to immiscible liquid mixtures and also presents and discusses experimental findings.

The third chapter covers the knowledge and state-of-art technologies in regard to heat pipe and phase change heat transfer, which are very essential for reliable operation of ultra-high heat flux generating electronic devices.

The fourth chapter presents application of heat pipe systems for computer cooling. It also reviews studies on the types of heat pipes and their applications in electronics cooling particularly computer cooling.

The fifth chapter presents the operating principles, heat transfer characteristics, and fabrication process of MEMS-based micro-grooved heat pipes and further reports some promising and innovatory applications of MEMS-based micro heat pipes.

The sixth chapter presents an extensive numerical study on the performance evaluation of laminar mixed convection heat transfer of nanofluids and microchannel for the electronics cooling application.

The seventh chapter provides insight into experimental, numerical, and analytical studies on the reciprocating-mechanism driven heat loop (RMDHL) cooling technology for power electronic systems. This chapter also clarifies the fundamental physics behind the working mechanism of RMDHLs and derives a working criterion as guidance for the design of a RMDHL.

The final chapter pertains to the theoretical derivation for the estimation of the junction temperature of package chip, which is very important in order to design any integrated circuit.

This book is intended to be a useful source and guide to researchers, engineers, postgraduate students, and academics in the fields of thermal management and cooling technologies as well as for people working in the electronics and semiconductors industries.

I would like to thank all the authors for their high-quality contributions and the staffs from the publisher for providing continuous support, which have made possible the successful and timely completion of this book.

This book is dedicated to my wife Romana Afroz for her unconditional love, constant support, and selfless care.

S M Sohel Murshed
University of Lisbon
Lisbon, Portugal

Chapter 1

Introductory Chapter: Electronics Cooling—An Overview

S M Sohel Murshed

Additional information is available at the end of the chapter

http://dx.doi.org/10.5772/63321

1. Introduction

Recent development in semiconductor and other other mini- and micro-scale electronic technologies and continued miniaturization have led to very high increase in power density for high-performance chips. Although impressive progress has been made during the past decades, there remain serious technical challenges in thermal management and control of electronics devices or microprocessors. The two main challenges are: adequate removal of ever increasing heat flux and highly non-uniform power dissipation. According to a report of the International Electronics Manufacturing Initiative (iNEMI) Technology Roadmap [1], the maximum projected power dissipation from high-performance microprocessor chips will reach about 360 W by 2020. In fact, the micro- and power-electronics industries are facing the challenge of removing very high heat flux of around 300 W/cm^2 while maintaining the temperature below 85°C [2]. Furthermore, due to increasing integration of devices, the power dissipation on the chip or device is getting highly non-uniform as a peak chip heat flux can be several times that of the surrounding area.

Conventional cooling approaches are increasingly falling apart to deal with the high cooling demand and thermal management challenges of emerging electronic devices. Thus, high-performance chips or devices need innovative techniques, mechanisms, and coolants with high heat transfer capability to enhance the heat removal rate in order to maintain their normal operating temperature. Unless they are cooled properly, their normal performance and longevity can deteriorate faster than expected. In addition, the failure rate of electronic equipment increases with increasing operating temperature. Reviews and analyses on research and advancement of conventional and emerging cooling technologies reveal that microchannel-based forced convection and phase-change cooling (liquid) are among the most promising techniques that are capable of achieving very high heat removal rates [2–6].

On the other hand, most of the cooling techniques cannot achieve the required performance due to the limitations in heat transfer capabilities of traditional coolants such as air, oil, water, and water/ethylene glycol/methanol mixtures, which inherently possess poor heat transfer characteristics, particularly thermal conductivity and convective heat transfer coefficient (HTC). For instance, in order to accommodate a heat flux of 100 W/cm^2 at a temperature difference of 50 K, it requires an effective HTC (including a possible area enlarging factor) of 20,000 W/m^2K, which is usually not possible through free and forced convections of these coolants [7]. Thus, there is always a desperate need to find cooling fluids with superior heat transfer performance. Consequently, there are several recently emerged fluids, which can potentially be used as advanced coolants. One such fluid is nanofluid—a new class of heat transfer fluids, which are suspensions of nanometer-sized particles in conventional heat transfer fluids such as water (W), ethylene glycol (EG), oils, and W/EG. Nanofluids were found to possess considerably higher thermal properties, particularly thermal conductivity and convective as well as boiling heat transfer compared to their base conventional fluids [8–12]. With highly desirable enhanced thermal properties, this new class of fluids can offer immense benefits and potentials in wide range of applications including cooling of electronics and other high-tech industries [12–14]. Recently, another novel class of fluids—termed "ionanofluids" was proposed by our group [15–16]. Ionanofluids, which are suspensions of nanoparticles in only ionic liquids, were also found to have superior thermal properties compared to their base ionic liquids [15–17]. In addition to their unique features like green fluids and designable for specific tasks, ionanofluids show great potential as advanced heat transfer fluids in cooling electronics.

In this chapter, an overview of various cooling methods and traditional coolants for electronic devices is presented first. Then, heat transfer properties and performances of new coolants are summarised, followed by their potential in electronics cooling.

2. Cooling methods

Despite impressive progress made on electronic cooling systems in recent years, the required high heat flux removal from the high-tech electronic devices remains inadequate and very challenging. There are a number of cooling methods widely used in electronic industries. Based on heat transfer effectiveness, the existing cooling modes can be classified into four general categories which are [18]:

- Natural convection,
- Forced convection air cooling,
- Forced convection liquid cooling,
- Liquid evaporation.

Based on the approximate range of heat flux removal rate of these methods, it is known that liquid evaporation is the best technique followed by the forced convections of liquids and then air [18]. However, forced air convection, which is widely used in cooling electronics such as CPU of computing devices, has very low heat removal rate (though higher than radiation and natural convection). As well known, besides heat removal mode, cooling fluids also play a major role in overall cooling performance.

High-performance electronic devices and chips need innovative techniques and systems design to enhance the heat removal rate in order to minimize their operating temperature and maximize longevity. Traditional cooling approaches, consisting typically of air-cooled heat sinks, are increasingly falling short in meeting the cooling demands of modern electronic devices with high-powered densities. Thus, in recent years, various techniques for cooling such electronics have been studied extensively and employed in various thermal management systems. These include thermosyphons [19], heat pipes [20], electro-osmotic pumping [21], microchannels [4, 5], impinging jets [22], thermoelectric coolers [23], and absorption refrigeration systems [24]. These cooling techniques can be categorized into passive and active systems. Passive cooling systems utilize capillary or gravitational buoyancy forces to circulate the working fluid, while active cooling systems are driven by a pump or compressor for higher cooling capacity and improved performance. As a passive cooling and given high latent heat of fusion, high specific heat, and controllable temperature stability of phase change materials (PCMs), PCMs-based heat sinks are relatively new techniques that can be used for transient electronic cooling applications [25].

Microscale cooling systems can sufficiently cool those high heat-generating electronic devices or appliances. For example, the heat transfer performances of microchannel based heat-sinks and micro-heat pipes are much higher compared to traditional heat exchangers. Because of the very compact, lightweight, suitable for small electronic devices, and superior cooling performance, microchannel-based cooling systems have received great attention from researchers and industries. The forced convective liquid cooling through microchannel heat sink is one of the promising and high-performance cooling technologies for small-sized high heat-generating electronic devices. Besides significantly minimizing the package size, this emerging cooling technology is also amenable to on-chip integration [4, 5].

Heat pipes-based electronics cooling is very popular and is recently receiving great attention from the researchers as well as industries and are already used in various electronic devices. Thus, a couple of chapters have particularly been devoted on this topic and it is not discussed here further.

On the other hand, direct liquid immersion cooling offers a very high HTC, which reduces the temperature rise of the chip surface. **Figure 1** compares the relative magnitudes (approximate) of HTCs of various commonly used coolants and cooling modes. The relative magnitude of HTC is directly affected by both the coolant and the mode of heat transfer (**Figure 1**). While water (deionized) is the most effective coolant, the boiling and condensation offer the highest HTCs.

Whatever methods are used to cool the devices or chips, transferring the heat to a fluid with or without phase transitions, it is necessary to dissipate the heat to the environment. This is mostly done with the forced convection of air, which is not sufficient particularly for high heat removal situations. Thus, it is also of tremendous importance to efficiently take away the heat from the coolants.

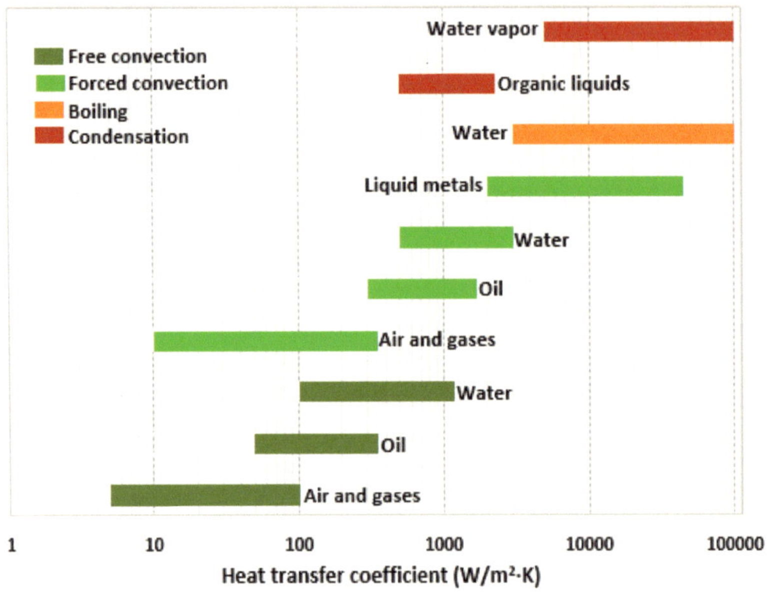

Figure 1. Range of overall heat transfer coefficients for different fluids and cooling modes.

3. Cooling fluids

3.1. Conventional coolants

There are a number of aqueous and non-aqueous conventional coolants which are used in various electronics cooling systems. As water possesses higher thermal conductivity and specific heat and lower viscosity compared to other coolants, it is the most widely used coolant for electronics. But water is not used in closed loop systems due to its high freezing point and the expansion upon freezing.

Nonetheless, it is important to select the best coolant for any specific device or cooling system. There are some general requirements for coolants and they may vary depending on the type of cooling systems and electronic devices. As well discussed in the literature [26], the liquid coolants for electronics cooling must be non-flammable, non-toxic, and inexpensive with excellent thermophysical properties and features, which include high thermal conductivity, specific heat and HTC, and low viscosity. Besides good chemical and thermal stability, coolants must also be compatible (e.g., non-corrosive) with the materials of the components of the cooling systems and devices. However, selection of a coolant for direct immersion cooling cannot be made only based on the heat transfer features. Chemical compatibility of the coolant with the chips and other packaging materials must be considered as well. The commonly used coolants for electronics cooling are mainly classified into two groups: dielectric and non-dielectric coolants.

There are several types of dielectric coolants, which are aromatics, aliphatics, silicones, and fluorocarbons-based fluids. Aromatics coolants such as diethylbenzene (DEB), toluene, and benzenes are the most commonly used coolants. Aliphatic hydrocarbons of paraffinic and isoparaffinic types (including mineral oils) and aliphatic polyalphaolefins (PAO) are used in a variety of direct cooling of electronics. Silicones-based coolant is another popular type of coolant widely known as silicone oils, e.g., Syltherm XLT. The fluorocarbons series of coolants such as FC-40, FC-72, FC-77 and FC-87 are widely accepted in the electronics industries.

Non-dielectric liquids are also used for electronics cooling because of their better thermal properties compared to their dielectric counterparts. They are normally aqueous solutions and thus exhibit high heat capacity and thermal conductivity. Water, EG, and mixture of these two (W/EG) are very popular and widely used as electronics coolants. Other popular non-dielectric coolants include propylene glycol (PG), water/methanol, W/ethanol, NaCl solution, potassium formate (KFO) solution, and liquid metals (e.g., Ga-In-Sn). Mohapatra and Loikits [26] evaluated that among the various coolants, KFO solution possesses highest overall efficiency. Comparisons of various properties and characteristics of all types of available coolants can help selecting the right coolants.

3.2. Potential new coolants

As mentioned before, the cooling demands of modern electronics devices or systems cannot be met by those conventional coolants due to their inherently poor thermal properties which greatly limit the cooling performance. Here, the newly emerged heat transfer fluids like nanofluids and ionanofluids, which have highly desirable superior thermal properties and are suitable for even microsystems, can be the cooling solutions. These new fluids can also offer immense benefits and potential applications in a wide range of industrial, electronics, and energy fields [12–14, 17]. Results of key heat transfer features including thermal conductivity, convective and boiling of these new coolants are briefly summarized in the following subsection.

3.2.1. *Summary of thermal properties and performance*

Extensive research has been performed on the thermal conductivity of nanofluids and studies showed that nanofluids possess considerably higher thermal conductivity compared to their base fluids [8, 12, 27–28]. However, results from different research groups are not very consistent and sometimes also controversial particularly regarding the heat transfer mechanisms [29]. Nanofluids also exhibit superior other thermophysical properties than those of base fluids [8, 27, 30–32]. With significantly high thermal properties, nanofluids can meet the cooling demand of high-tech electronics devices.

Evaluating the convective heat transfer performance of nanofluids is very important in order for their application as coolants in electronics. There have been large number of studies on convective heat transfer of nanofluids and nanofluids are found to exhibit enhanced HTC compared to their base fluids at any flow conditions. The enhanced HTC (*h* or *Nu*) further increases considerably with increasing concentration of nanoparticles as well as Reynolds number (*Re*) or flow rate [9, 33–34]. The enhancement of HTC is even more significant at turbulent regime. Based on the findings of convective heat transfer, it is considered that nanofluids can perform better cooling compared to conventional fluids in electronics cooling systems.

Another very important and efficient mode of cooling is boiling or phase change of fluids in various heat exchange systems. There is an increasing research focus on this key-cooling feature of nanofluids. Studies on boiling heat transfer of nanofluids revealed an undisputed substantial increase (up to few times of base fluids) in the boiling critical heat flux of nanofluids [9, 35–36]. Research also demonstrated that the boiling performance of nanofluids can be enhanced further with nanoparticle concentration and various other factors such as deposition of nanoparticles on heater wall, roughness of wall surface, and addition of surfactant [35–38]. Given the superior convective and boiling heat transfer performances, these new fluids can considerably increase the HTC and can act as better coolants than water or other conventional coolants.

Like nanofluids, ionanofluids also exhibit superior thermal properties, particularly thermal conductivity and heat capacity compared to their base ionic liquids [15–17]. Besides good thermal stability, thermophysical properties of ionanofluids can be adjusted by changing the ionic composition and structure of base ionic liquids. Early research revealed that these new nanofluids showed great potential to be used as advanced coolants for electronics cooling [16–17].

3.2.2. Potential of new fluids in electronics cooling

In recent years, extensive research works have been performed on the application of microchannel cooling systems (e.g., heat sinks) for electronics cooling [4, 5, 39]. Since the convective HTC is inversely proportional to the hydraulic diameter of the channel, very high heat transfer performance can be achieved by using microchannel at any flow regime. The forced convective heat transfer of cooling fluids through microchannel heat sinks is among the more promising technologies, which can offer very high heat removal rates [4, 5, 21, 39]. Nevertheless, the main limitation of cooling performance actually raised from the low heat transfer capability of the coolants used. In this regards, nanofluids with superior heat transfer performance can potentially boost the heat removal performance of microchannel cooling systems even further and be able to remove high heat flux of high-tech electronics devices.

Nanofluids have directly been employed in cooling systems of electronic or computing devices to evaluate the performance of these new fluids [40–42]. Results were very promising as the application of nanofluids in those cooling systems resulted in better cooling performance compared to traditional base fluids [39–43]. Thus, applications of nanofluids in conventional and emerging techniques such as microchannels and heat pipes can be the next-generation electronics cooling systems. A detailed discussion and analysis on the potential benefits and applications of nanofluids in cooling electronics can also be found in an ongoing study by the author [44].

4. Conclusions

Advances in electronics and semiconductor technologies have led to a dramatic increase in heat flux density for high-performance chips and components, whereas conventional cooling techniques and coolants are increasingly falling short in meeting the ever-increasing cooling need of such high heat-generating electronic devices or microprocessors. Despite good progress been made during the past decades, there remain some serious technical challenges in thermal management and cooling of these electronics. High-performance chips and devices need innovative mechanisms, techniques, and coolants with high heat transfer capability to enhance the cooling rate for their normal performance and longevity. With superior thermal properties and cooling features, nanofluids offer great promises to be used as coolants for high-tech electronic devices and industries. The emerging techniques like microchannels with these new fluids can be the next-generation cooling technologies.

Author details

S M Sohel Murshed

Address all correspondence to: smmurshed@ciencias.ulisboa.pt

Faculty of Sciences, University of Lisbon, Lisbon, Portugal

References

[1] Pfahl RC and McElroy J. The 2004 international electronics manufacturing initiative (iNEMI) technology roadmaps. Proceedings of the IEEE. 2005; 2005:1-7.

[2] Agostini B, Fabbri M, Park JE, Wojtan L, Thome JR and Michel B. State of the art of high heat flux cooling technologies. Heat Transfer Engineering. 2007; 28:258-281.

[3] Ebadian MA and Lin CX. A review of high-heat-flux heat removal technologies. Journal of Heat Transfer. 2011; 133(11):110801.

[4] Wei Y and Joshi YK. Stacked microchannel heat sinks for liquid cooling of microelectronic components. Journal of Electronic Packaging. 2004; 126:60-66.

[5] Garimella SV, Singhal V and Liu D. on-chip thermal management with microchannel heat sinks and integrated micropumps. Proceedings of the IEEE. 2006; 94(8):1534-1548.

[6] Chang YW, Cheng CH, Wang JC and Chen SL. Heat pipe for cooling of electronic equipment. Energy Conversion and Management. 2008; 49(11):3398-3404.

[7] Lasance C and Simons R. Advances in high performance cooling for electronics. Electronics Cooling. 2005; 11(4):22-39

[8] Murshed SMS, Leong KC, Yang C. Thermophysical and electrokinetic properties of nanofluids: a critical review. Applied Thermal Engineering. 2008; 28:2109-2125.

[9] Murshed SMS, Nieto de Castro CA, Lourenço MJV, Lopes MLM and Santos FJV. A review of boiling and convective heat transfer with nanofluids. Renewable and Sustainable Energy Reviews. 2011; 15:2342-2354.

[10] Murshed SMS and Nieto de Castro CA. Boiling heat transfer and droplet spreading of nanofluids. Recent Patents on Nanotechnology. 2013; 7:216-223.

[11] Murshed SMS and Nieto de Castro CA. Nanofluids: Synthesis, Properties and Applications. New York: Nova Science Publishers. 2014.

[12] Murshed SMS and Nieto de Castro CA. Superior thermal features of carbon nanotubes based nanofluids: a review. Renewable and Sustainable Energy Reviews. 2014; 37:155-167.

[13] Wong KV and De Leon O. Applications of nanofluids: current and future. Advances in Mechanical Engineering. 2010; 2010: (ID 519659) 11.

[14] Murshed SMS and Nieto de Castro CA. Nanofluids as advanced coolants. In: Green Solvents I: Properties and Applications in Chemistry, Ed., Mohammad A and Inamuddin, 397-415. London: Springer. 2012.

[15] Nieto de Castro CA, Lourenço MJV, Ribeiro APC, Langa E, Vieira SIC, Goodrich P, Hardacre C. Thermal properties of ionic liquids and ionanofluids of imidazolium and pyrrolidinium liquids. Journal of Chemical Engineering Data 2010; 55(2):653-661.

[16] Nieto de Castro CA, Murshed SMS, Lourenço MJV, Santos FJV, Lopes MLM and França JMP, Enhanced thermal conductivity and heat capacity of carbon nanotubes-ionanofluids. International Journal of Thermal Sciences. 2012; 62:34-39.

[17] Nieto de Castro CA, Ribeiro APC, Vieira SIC, Lourenço MJV, Santos FJV, Murshed SMS, Goodrich P and Hardacre C. Synthesis, properties and physical applications of ionanofluids. In: Ionic Liquids New Aspects for the Future, Ed., Kadokawa J, 165-193. Rijeka: INTECH. 2013.

[18] Scott WA. Cooling of Electronic Equipment. New York: John Wiley and Sons. 1974.

[19] Pal A, Joshi YK, Beitelmal MH, Patel CD and Wenger TM. Design and performance evaluation of a compact thermosyphon. IEEE Transactions on Components and Packaging Technologies. 2002; 25(4): 601-607.

[20] Maydanik YF, Vershinin SV, Korukov MA and Ochterbeck JM. Miniature loop heat pipes-a promising means for electronics cooling. IEEE Transactions on Components and Packaging Technologies. 2005; 28(2):290-296.

[21] Jiang L, Mikkelsen J, Koo JM, Huber D, Yao S, Zhang L, et al. Closed-loop electroosmotic microchannel cooling system for VLSI circuits. IEEE Transactions on Components and Packaging Technologies. 2002; 25(3):347-355.

[22] Bintoro JS, Akbarzadeh A and Mochizuki M. A closed-loop electronics cooling by implementing single phase impinging jet and mini channels heat exchanger. Applied Thermal Engineering. 2005; 25:2740-2753.

[23] Simons RE. Application of thermoelectric coolers for module cooling enhancement. Electronics Cooling. 2000; 6(2):18-24.

[24] Kim YJ, Joshi YK and Fedorov AG. An absorption miniature heat pump system for electronics cooling. International Journal of Refrigeration. 2008; 31(1):23-33.

[25] Kandasamy R, Wang XQ and Mujumdar AS. Transient cooling of electronics using phase change material (PCM)-based heat sinks. Applied Thermal Engineering. 2008; 28:1047-1057.

[26] Mohapatra S and Loikits D. Advances in liquid coolant technologies for electronics cooling. Proceedings of the 21st IEEE Semiconductor Thermal Measurement and Management Symposium. 2005.

[27] Murshed SMS, Leong KC and Yang C. Investigations of thermal conductivity and viscosity of nanofluids. International Journal of Thermal Sciences. 2008; 47:560-568.

[28] Murshed SMS, Leong KC and Yang C. Enhanced thermal conductivity of TiO_2-water based nanofluids. International Journal of Thermal Sciences. 2005; 44:367-373.

[29] Murshed SMS. Correction and comment on "Thermal conductance of nanofluids: is the controversy over?" Journal of Nanoparticle Research. 2009; 11:511-512.

[30] Murshed SMS, Leong KC and Yang C. Determination of the effective thermal diffusivity of nanofluids by the double hot-wire technique. Journal of Physics D: Applied Physics. 2006; 39:5316-5322.

[31] Murshed SMS. Determination of effective specific heat of nanofluids. Journal of Experimental Nanoscience. 2011; 6:539-546.

[32] Murshed SMS. Simultaneous measurement of thermal conductivity, thermal diffusivity, and specific heat of nanofluids. Heat Transfer Engineering. 2012; 33(8):722-731.

[33] Murshed SMS and Nieto de Castro CA. Forced convective heat transfer of nanofluids in minichannel. In: Two Phase Flow, Phase Change and Numerical Modeling, Ed., Ahsan A, 419-434. Rijeka: INTECH, 2011.

[34] Murshed SMS, Leong KC, Yang C and Nguyen NT. Convective heat transfer characteristics of aqueous TiO_2 nanofluids under laminar flow conditions. International Journal of Nanoscience. 2008; 7:325-331.

[35] Barber J, Brutin D and Tadrist L. A review on boiling heat transfer enhancement with nanofluids. Nanoscale Research Letters. 2011; 6:280.

[36] Murshed SMS and Nieto de Castro CA. Boiling heat transfer and droplet spreading of nanofluids. Recent Patents on Nanotechnology. 2013; 7:216-223.

[37] Kim HD, Kim J and Kim MH. Experimental studies on CHF characteristics of nanofluids at pool boiling, International Journal of Multiphase Flow. 2007; 33:691-706.

[38] Murshed SMS, Milanova D and Kumar R. An experimental study of surface tension-dependent pool boiling characteristics of carbon nanotubes-nanofluids. Proceedings of 7th International ASME Conference on Nanochannels, Microchannels and Minichannels. 2009; pp.75-80 (doi:10.1115/ICNMM2009-82204).

[39] Khan M G and Fartaj A. A review on microchannel heat exchangers and potential applications. International Journal of Energy Research. 2011; 35(7):553-582.

[40] Roberts NA and Walker DG. Convective performance of nanofluids in commercial electronics cooling systems. Applied Thermal Engineering. 2010; 30(16):2499-2504.

[41] Yousefi T, Mousavi SA, Farahbakhsh B, Saghir MZ. Experimental investigation on the performance of CPU coolers: effect of heat pipe inclination angle and the use of nanofluids. Microelectronics Reliability. 2013; 53:1954-1961.

[42] Nazari M, Karami M and Ashouri M. Comparing the thermal performance of water, ethylene glycol, alumina and CNT nanofluids in CPU cooling: experimental study. Experimental Thermal and Fluid Science. 2014; 57:371-377.

[43] Liu ZH and Li YY. A new frontier of nanofluid research: application of nanofluids in heat pipes. International Journal of Heat and Mass Transfer. 2012; 55:6786-6797.

[44] Murshed SMS and Nieto de Castro CA. A critical review of traditional and emerging cooling techniques and fluids for electronics cooling. Renewable and Sustainable Energy Review. 2016 (submitted).

Chapter 2

Boiling of Immiscible Mixtures for Cooling of Electronics

Haruhiko Ohta, Yasuhisa Shinmoto,
Daisuke Yamamoto and Keisuke Iwata

Additional information is available at the end of the chapter

http://dx.doi.org/10.5772/62341

Abstract

To satisfy the requirements for the cooling of small and large semiconductors operated at high heat flux density, an innovative cooling method using boiling heat transfer to immiscible liquid mixtures is proposed. Immiscible liquid mixtures discussed here are composed of more-volatile liquid with higher density and less-volatile liquid with lower density, and appropriate volumetric ratios become a key to realize high-performance cooling. The chapter reviews the experimental results obtained by the present authors, where critical heat flux accompanied by the catastrophic surface temperature excursion is increased up to 300 W/cm^2 for FC72/water by using a flat heating surface of 40 mm in diameter facing upwards under the pressure 0.1 MPa.

To apply the superior heat transfer characteristics in boiling of immiscible mixtures to flow boiling system, preliminary experiments using a horizontal heated tube are performed and the classification of flow pattern with liquid-liquid interface and corresponding heat transfer performance are discussed.

Keywords: cooling of electronics, immiscible mixture, insoluble mixture, pool boiling, flow boiling

1. Introduction

1.1. Possibility of non-azeotropic mixtures

For the systems of air conditioning and refrigeration, non-azeotropic miscible mixtures are often used as the working fluids alternative to the discontinued ones. However, these fluids have a well-known unavoidable disadvantage of heat transfer deterioration resulting from the increased interfacial temperature due to the existence of mass diffusion resistance. At the same time, for the non-azeotropic miscible mixtures, there is an unknown effect of Marangoni force exerted mainly by the concentration difference along the liquid-vapor interface as a result of the preferential evaporation of more-volatile component. In aqueous solutions of alcohol with a large carbon number, the surface tension is increased with increasing temperature depending on the range of concentration and the level of temperature. In such a condition, Marangoni force due to the concentration gradient is enhanced by also the temperature gradient along the interface, especially near the three-phase interline extended at the base of bubbles. The enhancement of critical heat flux (CHF) was shown by Vochten-Petre [1] and Van Stralen [2] based on the experiments using a wire heater. Abe [3] verified the drastic increase of maximum heat transportation for heat pipes using "self-rewetting mixtures". Sakai et al. [4] confirmed the small enhancement of heat transfer in the ranges of very low alcohol concentration in water, while no appreciable increase in CHF for a flat heating surface facing upwards. As a consequence, non-azeotropic mixtures have no advantage from the view point of the improvement of heat transfer.

1.2. Expected performance of immiscible mixtures

Innovative cooling systems which meet the requirement for the increased heat generation density from electronic devices are urgently required. To enhance the values of CHF for the cooling of a large area at high heat flux larger than 200 W/cm^2 as shown in **Figure 1**, the present authors confirmed the validity of the devised structure which reduces the effective heating length by the liquid supply directly to the downstream of the heating duct from the transverse direction. An example of the structure is illustrated in **Figure 2** [5,6]. However, such structure is rather complicated. On the other hand, to ensure the high reliability for a long-term operation, microstructures on the "enhanced surface" cannot be accepted depending on their application. The present authors noticed the superior heat transfer characteristics in nucleate boiling of immiscible mixtures even on a smooth surface (Kobayashi et al. [7], Ohnishi et al. [8], Kita et al. [9]), which are summarized as follows.

1. The value of critical heat flux is increased by the self-sustained subcooling of less-volatile liquid as a result of the excessive compression by the high partial vapor pressure of more-volatile component.

2. The operation at a pressure higher than the atmospheric is possible keeping low liquid temperature to prevent the mixing of incondensable air which seriously deteriorates the heat transfer in the condensation process, i.e., a final heat dissipation process, due to the existence of mass diffusion resistance.

3. The surface temperature is decreased during the free convection or nucleate boiling of less-volatile liquid, which is caused by the substantial heat transfer enhancement by the existence of vapor bubbles generated form the more-volatile component.

4. The excessive overshooting of the surface temperature at the initiation of boiling can be reduced by the selection of more-volatile component and the optimization of its distribution on the heating surface, which is required, e.g., for the cooling of automobile power controllers with a large fluctuation of thermal load.

http://dx.doi.org/10.5772/62341

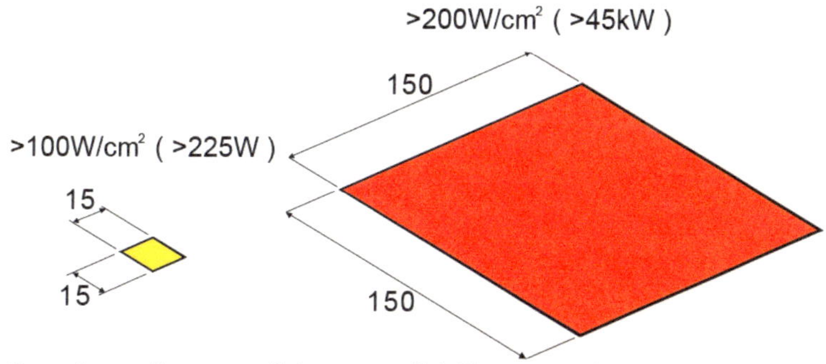

(a) Semiconductor chip (b) Power electronics

Figure 1. Difference in the size and heat flux level of semiconductors as a target of cooling.

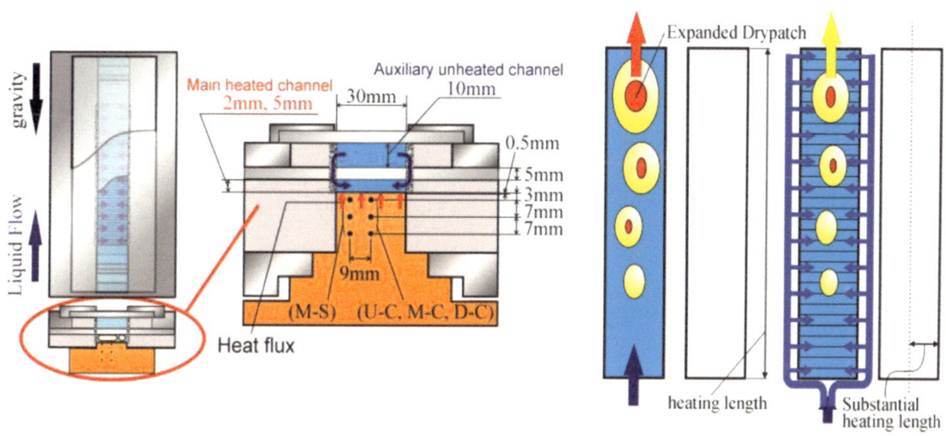

(a) Structure of narrow heated channel with an auxiliary unheated channel and grooves on the heating surface.

(b) Decrease in substantial heating length by the change in the direction of liquid supply.

Figure 2. Devised structure of cold plate for the cooling by flow boiling in a narrow channel [5,6].

1.3. Existing researches on boiling of immiscible mixtures

A large number of reports on nucleate boiling of oil mixtures exist. Filipczak et al. [10] used emulsions of oil and water, where the distribution of two liquids and vapor was investigated at different levels of heat flux. The heat transfer coefficients for high oil concentration were quite smaller than those for pure water, because the free convection of oil dominates the heat transfer to water-oil mixture. At the initial stage of nucleate boiling, foaming was observed before the formation of emulsion. Roesle and Kulacki [11] studied nucleate boiling of FC72/water and pentane/water on a horizontal wire. The discontinuous phase of more-volatile components FC72 and pentane were dispersed in a continuous phase of water, where the concentrations of more-volatile component were varied as 0.2–1.0% and 0.5–2.0%, respectively.

Nucleate boiling of dispersed component or of dispersed and continuous components was observed depending on the level of heat flux. The heat transfer was enhanced by nucleate boiling of dispersed liquid if its volume fraction was larger than 1%. Bulanov and Gasanov [12] studied the heat transfer to four emulsions, n-pentane/glycerin, diethyl ether/water, R113/water and water/oil, where more-volatile liquids were dispersed in the continuous phase of less-volatile liquids. The reduction of surface superheat at the boiling initiation was observed compared to that for pure less-volatile liquids.

On the other hand, the number of investigations on immiscible mixtures which form stratified layers of component liquids before the heating is quite limited. There are old studies by Bonilla and Eisenbuerg [13], Bragg and Westwater [14], Sump and Westwater [15]. Bragg and Westwater [14] classified heat transfer modes for individual layers of liquids. The interpretation of data, however, was not described in detail. Gorenflo et al. [16] studied boiling of water/1-butanol on a horizontal tube, where the liquid mixture becomes soluble or partially soluble depending on its concentration, and levels of temperature and pressure. From the experiments performed under various combinations of concentration and pressure, they reported that the nucleate boiling heat transfer is not largely depending on the solubility.

2. Immiscible mixtures

2.1. Phase equilibrium

Immiscible mixtures employed here consist of insoluble component liquids and their phenomena during nucleate boiling have a unique feature characterized by self-sustaining subcooling of liquids. An example of phase equilibrium diagrams for FC72/water at the total pressure of 0.1 MPa is shown in **Figure 3**. The concentration where the two curves merge, which is corresponding to the azeotropic point frequently observed in miscible mixtures, is the concentration of vapor phase independent of the liquid composition for immiscible mixtures. The concentrations Y_1 and $1-Y_1$ (=Y_2) on the dew point curves for lower and higher concentrations of more-volatile component in liquid phase are calculated by the following equations, respectively (e.g., Prigogine and Defay [17]).

$$\ln Y_1 = -\frac{h_{fg,1}}{R_1}\left(\frac{1}{T}-\frac{1}{T_{sat,1}}\right) \tag{1}$$

$$\ln(1-Y_1) = -\frac{h_{fg,2}}{R_2}\left(\frac{1}{T}-\frac{1}{T_{sat,2}}\right) \tag{2}$$

where Y_1: mole fraction of more-volatile component in vapor on dew point curve [−], T: dew point temperature [K], T_{sat}: saturation temperature [K] for a given total pressure, h_{fg}: latent heat of vaporization [kJ/kg] and R: gas constant [kJ/kg·K]. The equations are easily derived from the Clausius-Clapeyron equation and the ideal gas relation applied approximately to vapor phase.

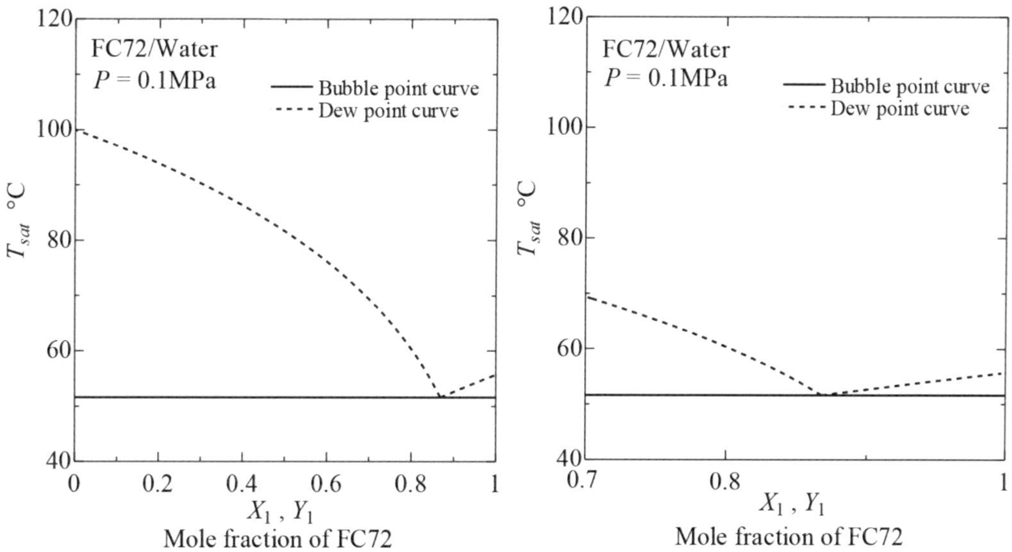

Figure 3. Phase equilibrium diagram of FC72/water mixture.

2.2. Conditions of component liquids

The conditions of liquid phase are represented in **Figure 4**, where two saturated vapor pressure curves with a red line for a more-volatile component and a blue line for a less-volatile one are drawn. Since immiscible mixtures have the total pressure P_{total} as the sum of saturated vapor pressures corresponding to the equilibrium temperature T_e, the equilibrium state of the mixture is represented by a black point in the figure and the relation $P_{sat,1}(T_e) + P_{sat,2}(T_e) = P_{total}$ holds true. Immiscible liquids are separated because of the difference in their densities, and one component liquid contacts or tends to contact the surface located at the bottom. The equilibrium temperature of immiscible mixtures is realized by the evaporation of both components. The degree of subcooling becomes the difference between the saturation temperature of each component corresponding to the total pressure and the equilibrium temperature of the mixture. If either of two components is not evaporated enough or not satisfy the saturation state corresponding to the equilibrium temperature but the vapor of one component is superheated, the liquid state of the other component is deviated from the equilibrium state represented in the figure. The equilibrium temperature of mixtures tested here and the degree of subcooling for each component liquid are shown in **Tables 1** and **2**, respectively. The subcooling of less-volatile liquid excessively compressed by the high vapor pressure of more-volatile component becomes very high, while the subcooling of more-volatile liquid is very low.

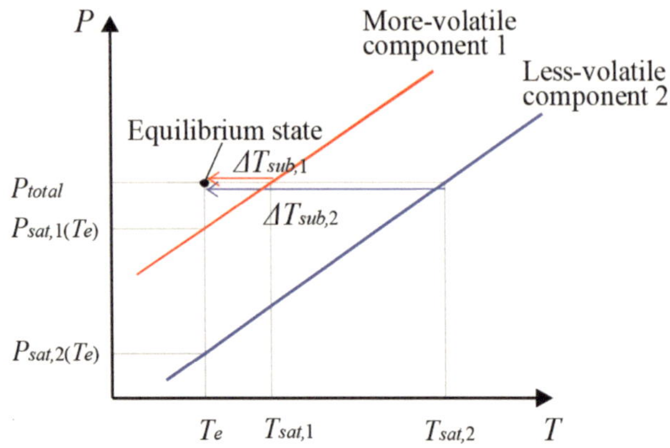

Figure 4. Vapor pressure curves of components for immiscible mixtures.

More-volatile component ($T_{sat,1}$)	Less-volatile component ($T_{sat,2}$)	Mixtures T_e
FC72 (55.9°C)	Water (100°C)	51.6°C
Novec7200 (78.4°C)	Water (100°C)	66.4°C

Table 1. Saturation temperature of each component and equilibrium temperature of immiscible mixtures at 0.1 MPa

Mixtures	Subcooling	
	More-volatile component $\Delta T_{sub,1}$	Less-volatile component $\Delta T_{sub,2}$
FC72/Water	4.3 K	48.4 K
Novec7200/Water	12.0 K	33.6 K

Table 2 Degree of subcooling for component liquids at 0.1 MPa

3. Pool Boiling

3.1. Experimental apparatus for pool boiling

The outline of the apparatus is shown in **Figure 5**. A flat heating surface of 40 mm in diameter made of copper is located horizontally facing upwards. The upper surface of cylindrical copper heating block is operated as the heating surface surrounded by a thin fin cut out in one unit body to prevent the preferential nucleation at the periphery. Nineteen cartridge heaters are inserted in the heating block and the maximum amount of heat generation is 5700 W. Eight thermocouples are inserted in the center and side of copper heating block at four different depths of 1, 7, 13 and 19 mm below the heating surface to estimate the heat flux and heating surface temperature. Fluid temperatures are measured by three thermocouples at 2, 80 and

160 mm above the heating surface in the boiling vessel, where the liquid level is located between the second and third thermocouples.

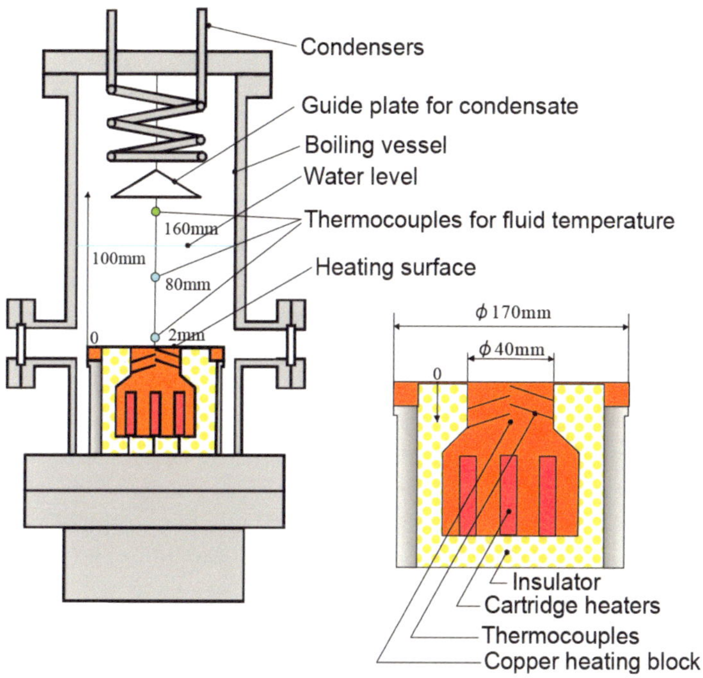

Figure 5. Outline of pool boiling experimental apparatus.

The experiments are performed at 0.1 MPa changing volume ratio of the components. Immiscible mixtures of FC72/water and Novec7200/water are used as test fluids, where FC72 and Novec7200 are more-volatile components with higher density and water is less-volatile one with lower density. The conditions for the volume ratio of component liquids are represented by **Figure 6** [9], where H_1 is the height of the more-volatile liquid from the heating surface and H_2 is for the less-volatile liquid. The total height is kept at 100 mm, i.e., $H_1 + H_2 =$ 100mm, and tested compositions are listed in **Table 3**.

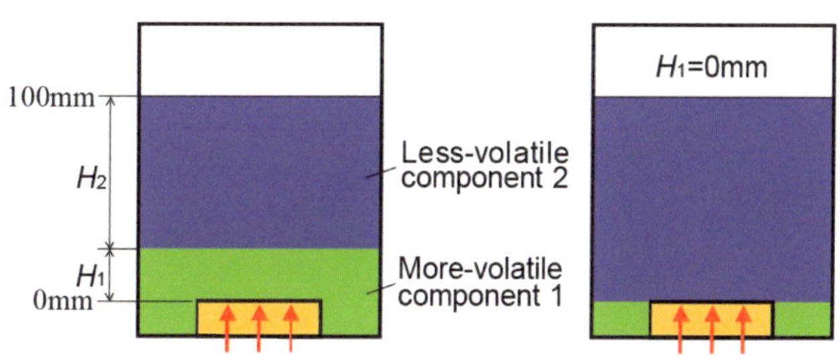

Figure 6. Condition representing volume ratio of immiscible liquids [9].

1. More-volatile c. / 2. Less-volatile c.	Height of liquid [H_1 mm /H_2 mm]
FC72/Water	[0/100], [5/95], [10/90], [50/50]
Novec7200/Water	[0/100], [5/95], [10/90]

Table 3. Tested composition of liquids

3.2. Experimental results for pool boiling

Experimental results are shown in **Figures 7** and **8** for FC72/water and Novec7200/water, respectively. **Figure 7** represents the relation between heat flux q and heating surface temperature T_w for FC72/water, where representative heat transfer characteristics of immiscible liquids are known. Independent of volume ratios, the heating surface temperatures for mixtures are located between those for pure liquids. The curve for [50 mm/50 mm] almost coincides with that for the saturated boiling of FC72. For [10 mm/90 mm], a temperature jump similar to burnout phenomena occurs, which is referred to as the "intermediate heat flux burnout" by the present authors. For [5 mm/95 mm] and [0 mm/100 mm], the surface temperature increases with heat flux, where the heat transfer mode changes from natural convection to nucleate boiling of water under high subcooled conditions. For [5 mm/95 mm], the reduction of surface temperature from that of saturated nucleate boiling of water is clearly observed at high heat flux due to the heat transfer enhancement resulting from the generation of bubbles composed mainly by FC72 vapor. For [0 mm/100 mm], the value of CHF increases from 1.35 MW/m^2 of saturated water to 3.04 MW/m^2 of FC72/water mixtures at 0.1 MPa. The marked increase of CHF resulted from the high subcooling of water as much as 48.4 K due to the excessive compression by FC72 vapor. Similar results are obtained also for Novec7200/water despite of the quantitative difference in the effect of liquid height between the two mixtures tested here. In **Figure 9**, the values of CHF are compared with those of subcooled boiling of

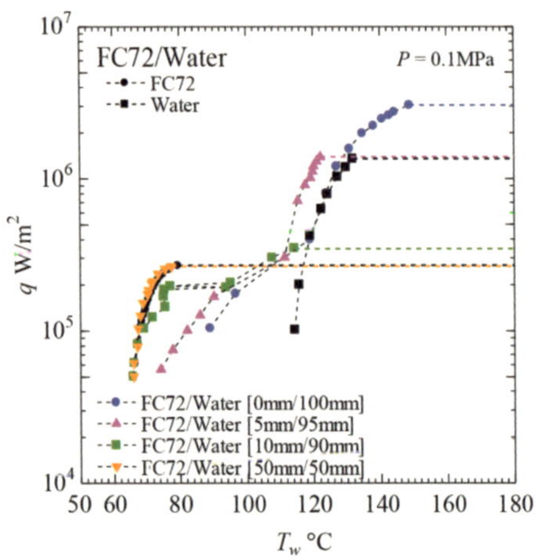

Figure 7. Heat flux versus heating surface temperature for FC72/water.

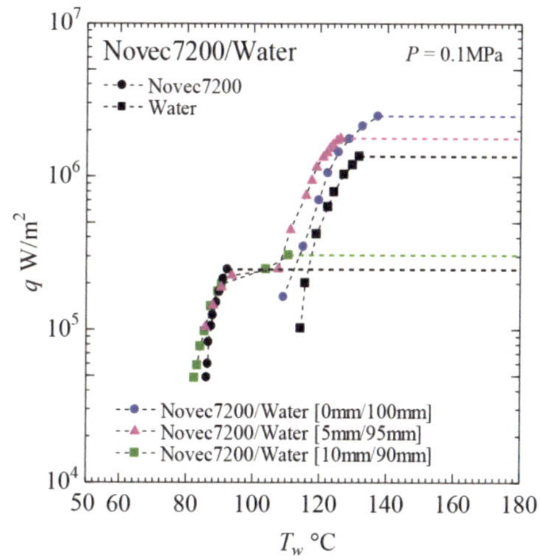

Figure 8. Heat flux versus heating surface temperature for Novec7200/water.

pure water estimated by Ivey-Morris correlation [18]. For [0 mm/100 mm], the experimental CHF values are close to the predicted ones, while the discrepancy is increased as the liquid height of more-volatile component increases. This is because boiling of the more-volatile component promotes the coalescence of bubbles and the dryout occurs at lower heat fluxes.

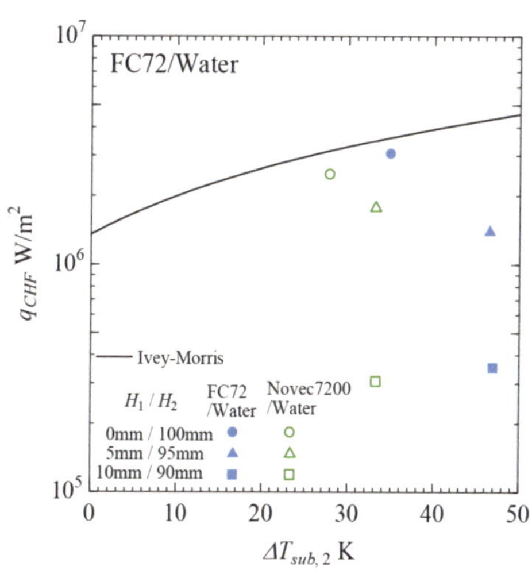

Figure 9. The comparison of CHF data with predicted values for subcooled boiling of less-volatile liquid.

3.3. Consideration on the mechanisms of intermediate heat flux burnout

The phenomena of limited jump of heating surface temperature referred here to as the intermediate heat flux burnout occurs if the thickness of the more-volatile liquid with higher density attached to the horizontal heating surface is small as observed for FC72/water [10 mm/90 mm] at $q = 2.0 \times 10^5$ W/m^2 in **Figure 7** and Novec7200/water [5 mm/95 mm] at $q = 2.3 \times 10^5$ W/m^2 in **Figure 8**.

After the jump of the surface temperature, the heat transfer mode is changed from the nucleate boiling of more-volatile liquid to the natural convection or nucleate boiling of less-volatile liquid at higher heat fluxes. It is very important that the generation of bubbles or vapor slugs of more-volatile component continues also in this region enhancing the heat transfer to the less-volatile liquid. The intermediate heat flux burnout is observed when Taylor instability occurs by the growth of a coalesced bubble with more-volatile component after its lateral coalescence below the bulk of less-volatile liquid with lower density.

The value of minimum bubble diameter d_{min} penetrating across the liquid-liquid interface is evaluated from the minimum volume of a bubble V_{min}, assuming the sphere bubble shape (Greene et al. [19], Onishi et al. [20]).

$$V_{\min} = \left[\frac{3.9\sigma}{g(\rho_{L2} - \rho_{V1})} \right]^{\frac{3}{2}} \quad (3)$$

where σ: interfacial tension [m/s], g: gravitational acceleration [m/s^2], ρ_{L2} : density of upper liquid, i.e., less-volatile liquid with lower density [kg/m^3], ρ_{V1}: density of lower vapor, i.e., vapor mainly of more-volatile component [kg/m^3]. The correlation implies that the penetration criteria is determined by two conflicting forces of the buoyancy acting upwards on a bubble and of the interfacial tension to suppress the bubble penetration. **Table 4** listed the most dangerous wavelength of Taylor instability λ_d, minimum bubble penetration diameter d_{min} and bubble departure diameter d_b under pool boiling conditions evaluated at 0.1 MPa.

More-volatile component	**FC72**	**Novec7200**
Less-volatile component	**Water**	**Water**
Most dangerous wavelength λ_d [mm]	28.9	28.4
Minimum penetration diameter d_{min} [mm]	4.2	3.9
Bubble departure diameter d_b[mm]	0.36	0.43

Table 4. Wavelength for Taylor instability and minimum bubble diameter for more-volatile component to penetrate into upper less-volatile liquid at 0.1 MPa

Bubbles of more-volatile component grow by the evaporation or lateral coalescence in the vicinity of liquid-liquid interface and become sizes beyond d_{min}. The enlarged bubbles penetrate into the less-volatile liquid layer accompanying the entrainment of more-volatile liquid as shown in **Figure 10**. Under this condition, bubbles of more-volatile component do not grow to the size of the wavelength λ_d, and no mixing of liquids occurs in the vicinity of heating surface. The penetration of generated bubbles thorough the liquid-liquid interface delays their coalescence. However, at a certain value of heat flux, the rate of bubble generation exceeds the elimination of bubbles by the penetration, and the lateral bubble coalescence occurs under the liquid-liquid interface. The diameter of flattened bubble radius exceeds the wave length of Taylor instability λ_d, and the less-volatile liquid descends and starts to contact the heating surface. The large subcooling of less-volatile liquid is enough to suppress the excessive jump of heating surface temperature.

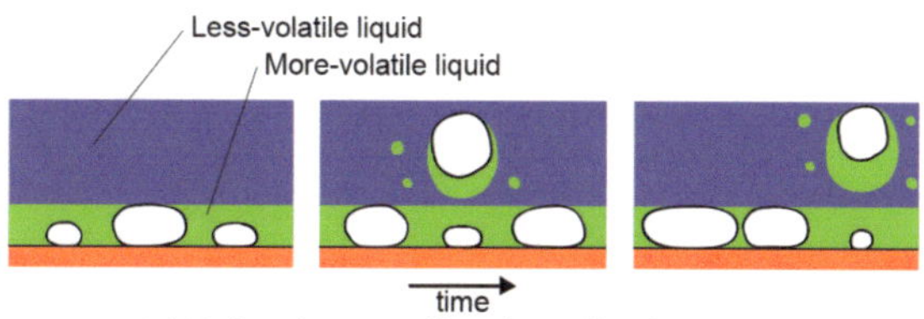

(a) Before intermediate heat flux burnout.

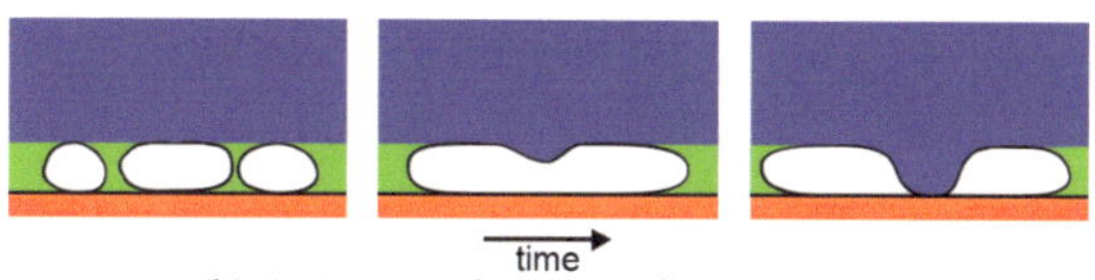

(b) At intermediate heat flux burnout.

Figure 10. Expected behaviors of bubble in the vicinity of liquid-liquid interface.

There is another type of intermediate heat flux burnout confirmed by the present authors, where the heating surface temperature gradually deviates from that for nucleate boiling of pure more-volatile liquid [9]. In such a case, bubbles can coalesce easily below the liquid-liquid interface because of thicker thickness of its layer and exceed the value of most dangerous wave length at lower heat flux. As a consequence, the less-volatile liquid starts to contact partially the heating surface, and the contribution of the heat transfer to the less-volatile liquid gradually increased as the increase of heat flux keeping the steady-state conditions at each heat flux level. Similar phenomenon occurs in the cases of smaller wavelength of Taylor instability or of partially soluble combination of liquids depending on the selection of component liquids. It is clear that the physical and/or chemical mixing of component liquids is a key factor to determine the heat transfer characteristics at low heat flux.

4. Flow boiling

4.1. Experimental apparatus for flow boiling

Figures 11 and **12** show the outline of test section and test loop [21]. Test loop is composed of test section, condenser, liquid-vapor separation tank, circulating pump, pre-heater. Immiscible liquids are stratified in liquid-vapor separation tank, and both flow rates are controlled by valves. The test section is composed of a heated section of stainless tube spirally coiled by sheath heaters on the outer surface and a transparent unheated section of Pyrex glass for the observation of liquid-liquid and liquid-vapor interfaces. The inner diameter of both tubes is 7 mm and heated length is 310 mm. Six thermocouples are inserted in the top and bottom tube walls at the upstream, midstream and downstream locations. The experiments are conducted for the combination of FC72 and water, i.e. more-volatile component with higher density and less-volatile one with lower density whose saturation temperatures as pure components are 55.7 and 100°C, respectively, at 0.1 MPa.

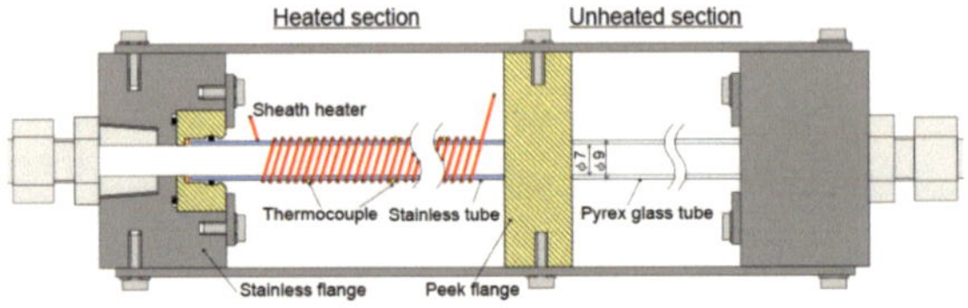

Figure 11. Outline of test section [21].

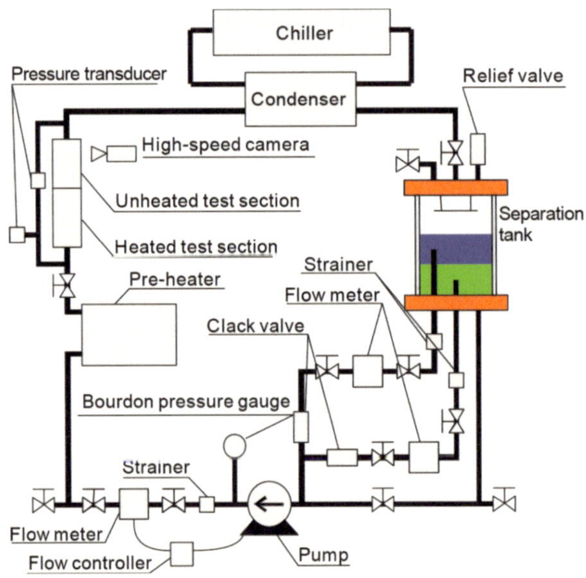

Figure 12. Test loop [21].

4.2. Experimental results for flow boiling

Various flow patterns such as stratified flow, FC72 slug flow, emulsion-like flow, "wavy stratified + FC72 droplet flow", "FC72 churn + FC72 droplet flow" and "FC72 slug + FC72 droplet flow" are observed depending on the combinations of flow rates for both components under unheated conditions, and they are summarized as a liquid-liquid flow pattern map in **Figures 13** and **14** [21].It is known by the preliminary experiments that the heat transfer characteristics at low heat fluxes are strongly influenced by the liquid-liquid behaviors under unheated conditions.

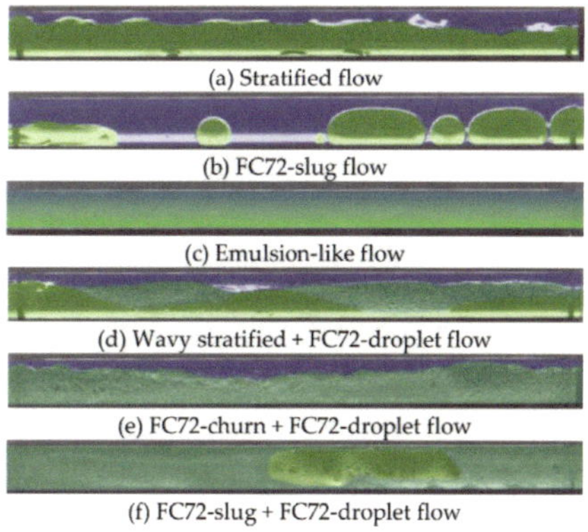

Figure 13. Typical flow patterns of FC72/water [21].

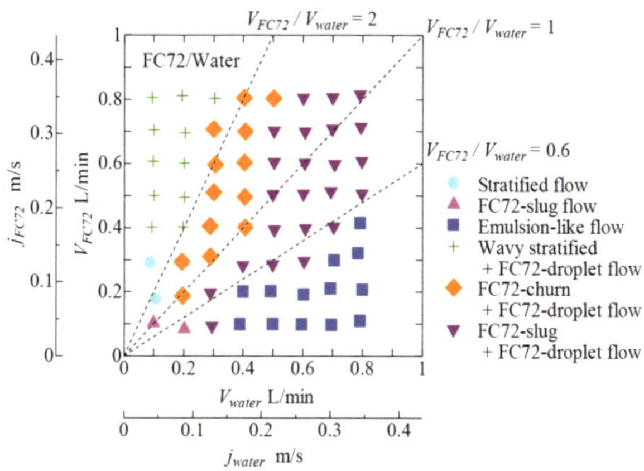

Figure 14. Flow pattern map for FC72/water. [21]

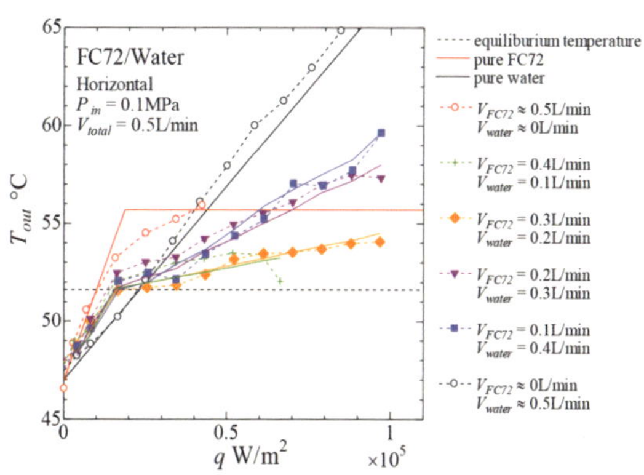

Figure 15. Outlet fluid temperature versus heat flux.

■ : Water, ■ : FC72, ■ : Emulsion

	Stratified flow	FC72 slug flow	Emulsion flow
Very low heat flux	Top: Forced convection of water 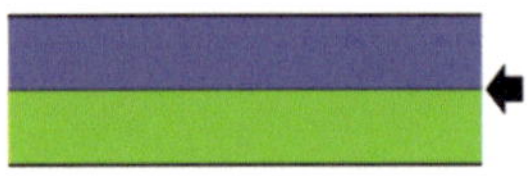 Bottom: Forced convection of FC72	Top: Forced convection of water 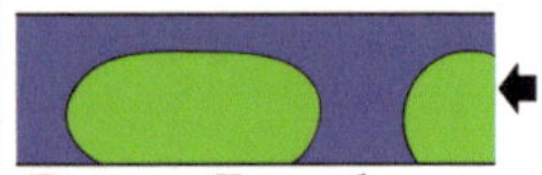 Bottom: Forced convection of FC72 and water	Top: Forced convection of water and FC72 emulsion 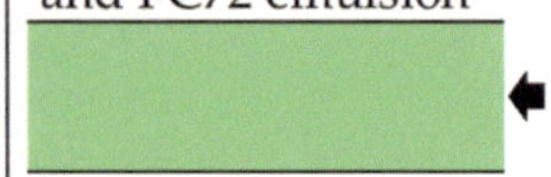 Bottom: Forced convection of water and FC72 emulsion
Low heat flux	Top: Forced convection of water with increased velocity by generation of FC72 bubbles 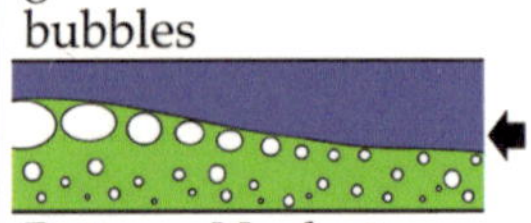 Bottom: Nucleate boiling of FC72	Top: Forced convection of water with increase velocity by generation of FC72 bubbles 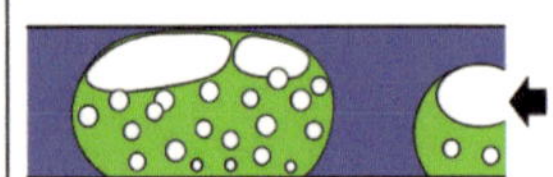 Bottom: Nucleate boiling of FC72	Top: Two-phase forced convection due to boiling of FC72 and convection of water and FC72 emulsion 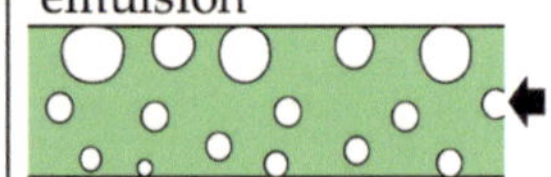 Bottom: Two-phase forced convection due to boiling of FC72 and convection of water and FC72 emulsion
Moderate heat flux	Top: Forced convection by FC72 vapor 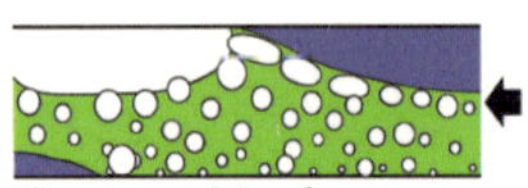 Bottom: Nucleate boiling of FC72	Top: Forced convection by FC72 vapor + Water liquid phase flow boiling 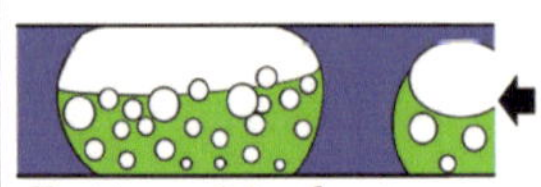 Bottom: Nucleate boiling of FC72	Top: Two-phase forced convection due to boiling of FC72 and convection of water and FC72 emulsion  Bottom: Two-phase forced convection due to boiling of FC72 and convection of water and FC72 emulsion

Table 5. Liquid-vapor behaviors for flow boiling of FC72/Water

To evaluate the local heat transfer coefficients, the distribution of mixture temperature along the tube axis is needed. Outlet mixture temperature can be reproduced by the heat balance equations which introduce a parameter ξ representing the ratio of heat supplied to more-volatile component FC72 to the total. **Figure 15** shows the outlet mixture temperature versus heat flux. The solid lines and broken lines are calculated and experimental outlet temperatures, respectively. The parameter ξ depends only on the flow rate ratio and not on the heat flux. This could be possible if the liquid-liquid flow pattern is not strongly dependent on the bubble generation at low heat flux as shown in **Table 5**. The error of the prediction is less than ±1.0K.

Figures 16 and **17** show heat transfer coefficient and wall temperature versus heat flux at midstream averaged by the top and the bottom values. Heat transfer coefficient is higher and wall temperature is lower than pure water for immiscible liquid because the convection of water is enhanced by the generation of FC72 bubbles.

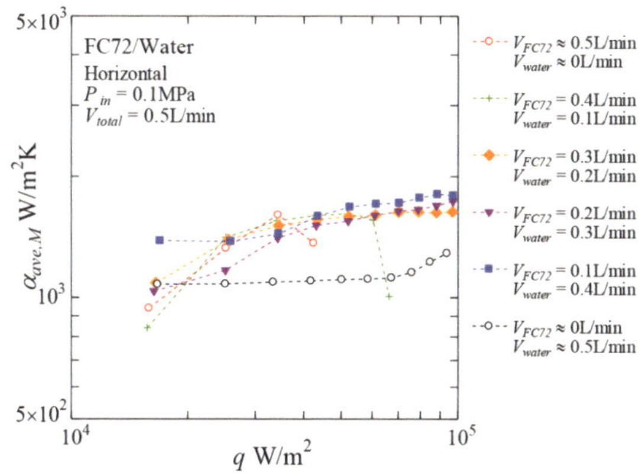

Figure 16. Heat transfer coefficient versus heat flux at midstream.

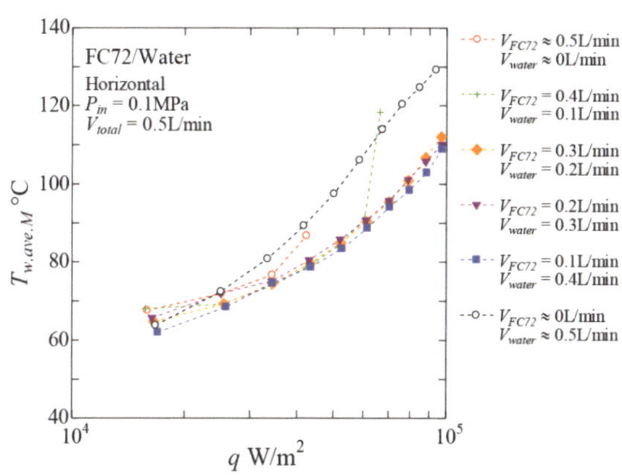

Figure 17. Wall temperature versus heat flux at midstream.

5. Conclusions

To clarify the boiling heat transfer characteristics of immiscible mixtures, experiments of pool boiling and flow boiling in a tube were conducted, and the following results were obtained.

1. By optimizing the volume ratio of immiscible mixtures in pool boiling using a flat heating surface facing upwards, the drastic increase of CHF and/or the decrease of heating surface temperature from those of pure less-volatile component become possible.

2. The above characteristics resulted from the self-sustaining high subcooling of less-volatile liquid and the substantial heat transfer enhancement caused by the preferential evaporation of more-volatile liquid.

3. In flow boiling, outlet fluid temperature is well reproduced by heat balance equations, which introduced a parameter representing the ratio of heat supplied to more-volatile component to the total.

4. In flow boiling, at low and moderate heat fluxes, the convection of less-volatile liquid is enhanced by boiling of more-volatile liquid, and the enhancement is largest corresponding to the flow pattern of emulsion-like flow at low flow rate of more-volatile component classified under the unheated conditions.

For the cooling systems in an enclosure, the distribution of liquid layers for both immiscible components becomes a key to determine the heat transfer characteristics due to nucleate boiling. For a vertical heating surface or a heating surface operated under the reduced gravity conditions, some methods to transfer the heat to the more-volatile liquid with larger density are needed to obtain the superior cooling characteristics.

6. Nomenclature

h_{fg} latent heat of vaporization, J/kg

H height of liquid, mm

j superficial velocity, m/s

P pressure, N/m^2

P_{total} total pressure, N/m^2

q heat flux, W/m^2

R bubble radius or gas constant, m or J/kg·K

T temperature, °C or K

T_e equilibrium temperature, °C

T_{sat} saturation temperature, K

T_w surface temperature, °C

V volumetric flow rate, L/min

X mole fraction in liquid, -

x vapor quality, -

Y mole fraction in vapor, -

Greek symbols

α heat transfer coefficient, $W/m^2 \cdot K$

ΔT_{sub} degree of subcooling, K

ξ ratio of heat supplied to more-volatile component to the total, -

Subscripts

1 more-volatile component

2 less-volatile component

ave average

M midstream

out outlet

sat saturated

Author details

Haruhiko Ohta*, Yasuhisa Shinmoto, Daisuke Yamamoto and Keisuke Iwata

*Address all correspondence to: ohta@aero.kyushu-u.ac.jp

Department of Aeronautics and Astronautics, Kyushu University, Fukuoka, Japan

References

[1] Vochten R. and Petre G. Study of the heat of reversible adsorption at the air-solution interface. J. Colloid Interface Sci. 2005; 42: 320-327.

[2] Van Stralen SJD Heat transfer to boiling binary liquid mixtures at atmospheric and subatmospheric pressures. Chem. Eng. Sci. 1956; 5: 290-296.

[3] Abe Y. Thermal management with phase change of self-rewetting fluids. Proc. IMECE2005. 2005.

[4] Sakai T., Yoshii S., Kajimoto K, Kobayashi H., Shinmoto Y. and Ohta H. Heat transfer enhancement observed in nucleate boiling of alcohol aqueous solutions at very low concentration. Proc. 14th Int. Heat Transfer Conf. 2010; IHTC14-22737.

[5] Ohta H., Shinmoto Y., Ishikawa Y. and Ariki K. High Heat Flux Cooling of large areas by improved liquid supply for flow boiling in narrow channels. Proc. 13th Int. Heat Transfer Conf. (IHTC-13). 2006; CD-ROM 12 pages.

[6] Miura S., Inada Y., Shinmoto Y. and Ohta H. Development of cooling system for a large area at high heat flux by using flow boiling in narrow channels. Proc. ASME 7th International Conference on Nanochannels, Microchannels and Minichannels (ICNMM2009). 2009; CD-ROM 8 pages.

[7] Kobayashi H., Ohtani N. and Ohta H. Boiling heat transfer characteristics of immiscible liquid mixtures. Proc. 9th Int. Conf. on Heat Transfer, Fluid Mechanics and Thermodynamics, HEFAT2012. 2012; 771-776.

[8] Ohnishi S., Ohta H., Ohtani N., Fukuyama Y. and Kobayashi H. Boiling heat transfer by nucleate boiling of immiscible liquids. Interfac. Pheno. Heat Transfer. 2013; 1(1): 63-83.

[9] Kita S., Ohnishi S., Fukuyama Y. and Ohta H. Improvement of Nucleate boiling heat transfer characteristics by using immiscible mixtures. Proc. 15th Int. Heat Transfer Conf., Kyoto, Japan. 2014; IHTC15-8941.

[10] Filipczak G., Troniewski L. and Witczak S. Pool boiling of liquid-liquid multiphase systems, evaporation, condensation and heat transfer, Ed. Ahsan A., INTECH. 2011; Chap.6: 123-150.

[11] Roesle ML and Kulacki FA An experimental study of boiling in dilute emulsions. Part A: Heat Transfer. Int. J. Heat Mass Transfer. 2012; 55(7-8): 2160-2165.

[12] Bulanov NV and Gasanov BM Peculiarities of boiling of emulsions with a low-boiling disperse phase. High Temp. 2006; 44(2): 267-282.

[13] Bonilla CF and Eisenbuerg AA Heat transmission to boiling binary mixtures. Indus. Eng. Chem. 1948; 40: 1113-1122.

[14] Bragg JR and Westwater JW Film boiling of immiscible liquid mixture on a horizontal plate. Heat Transfer 1970. Proc. 4th Int. Heat Trans. Conf. 1970; 6: B7.1.

[15] Sump GD and Westwater JW Boiling heat transfer from a tube to immiscible liquid-liquid mixtures. Int. J. Heat Mass Transfer. 1971; 14: 767-779.

[16] Gorenflo D., Gremer F., Danger E. and Luke A. Pool boiling heat transfer to binary mixtures with miscibility gap: experimental results for a horizontal copper tube with 4.35 mm O.D. Experiment. Thermal. Fluid Sci. 2001; 25(5): 243-254.

[17] Prigogine I. and Defay R. Chemical thermodynamics. Longmans Green and Co. 1954.

[18] Ivey H. J. and Morris D. J. Critical heat flux of saturation and subcooled pool boiling in water at atmospheric pressure. Proc. Third Int. Heat Transfer Conf. 1966; 3: 129-142.

[19] Green G A, Chen JC and Conlin MT Onset of entrainment between immiscible liquid layers due to rising gas bubbles. Int. J. Heat Mass Transfer. 1988; 31(6): 1309-1317.

[20] Onishi S., Ohtani N., Kanazawa S. and Ohta H. Improvement nucleate boiling heat transfer characteristics by using immiscible mixtures. Proc. 8th World Conf. Experiment. Heat Transfer Fluid Mechanics Thermodynamics (ExHFT-8). 2013; UFD 6 pages.

[21] Yamasaki Y., Kita S., Iwata K., Shinmoto Y. and Ohta H. Heat transfer in boiling of immiscible mixtures. Interfac. Pheno. Heat Transfer. 2015; 3(1): 19-39.

Chapter 3

Heat Pipe and Phase Change Heat Transfer Technologies for Electronics Cooling

Chan Byon

Additional information is available at the end of the chapter

http://dx.doi.org/10.5772/62328

Abstract

The heat pipe is a well-known cooling module for advanced electronic devices. The heat pipe has many applications, particularly in electronics and related area such as PC, laptop, display, artificial satellite, and telecommunication modules. The heat pipe utilizes phase change heat transfer inside enveloped structures, where the working fluid evaporates in heated zone, and vapor moves to the condenser, and the condensed liquid is pumped back through microporous structure call wick. The performance of applicability in electronics of heat pipe is strongly dependent on the geometry, working fluid, and microstructure of wick. Therefore, it is worth considering the theory and technologies related to heat pipes for advanced electronics cooling. According to the purpose of this chapter mentioned above, the author considers fundamental aspects regarding heat pipe and phase change phenomena. First, the working principle of heat pipe is introduced. Important parameters in heat pipe are considered, and theoretical model for predicting the thermal performance of the heat pipe is introduced. In addition, design method for heat pipe is presented. Finally, applications of heat pipe to electronics cooling are presented. This chapter covers knowledge and state-of-art technologies in regard to heat pipe and phase change heat transfer. For a reliable operation of future electronics that have ultra-high heat flux amounts to 1000 W/m^2, heat pipe and phase change heat transfer are essential. This chapter provides the most valuable opportunity for all readers from industry and academia to share the professional knowledge and to promote their ability in practical applications.

Keywords: Heat pipe, phase change, wick, design, analysis

1. Introduction

Effective cooling technology is a crucial requirement for a reliable operation of electronic components. The electronics cooling methods can be hierarchically classified as chip level cooling, package level cooling, and system level cooling, depending on the geometrical scale. In the package or system level cooling, the cooling modules such as heat sinks and heat pipes are widely employed for an efficient dissipation of heat as well as uniform temperature distribution. Especially, the use of heat pipes for electronics cooling has recently been increasing abruptly because the heat pipe is an attractive passive cooling scheme, which can offer high effective thermal conductivity and large heat transport capability. As shown in **Figure 1**, the heat pipes have been conventionally used for PCs, laptops, telecommunication units, solar collectors, small energy systems such as geothermal pipes, and satellites. Recently, the application of heat pipe even includes smart phones, vehicle headlight, gas burner, LED products, and agricultural systems, as shown in **Figure 2**.

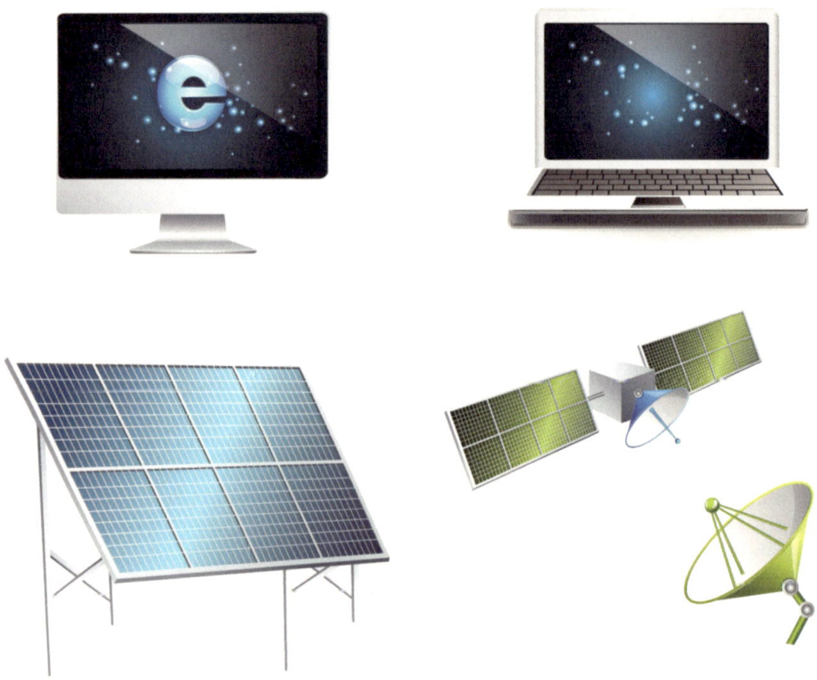

Figure 1. Heat pipe applications.

The heat pipe is a thermal superconductor of which thermal conductivity amounts to several thousands of Watts per meter-Kelvin. Due to the extremely high effective thermal conductivity, the heat pipe can handle a large amount of heat transfer with a negligible temperature drop. In addition, the heat pipe is a passive cooling module, which accompanies no power consumption or moving parts. Literally, the heat pipe is apparently just a pipe without any accessories for operating it. Furthermore, the shape of the heat pipe does not necessarily have to be cylindrical, but it can be formed into various shapes such as disks, flat plates, and airfoils. Attributable to these characteristics, the heat pipe is regarded as an ultimate candidate for addressing the thermal problem of concurrent high-power-density semiconductor industry, which encompasses solar cell, LEDs, power amplifiers, lasers, as well as electronic devices.

Figure 2. Recent applications.

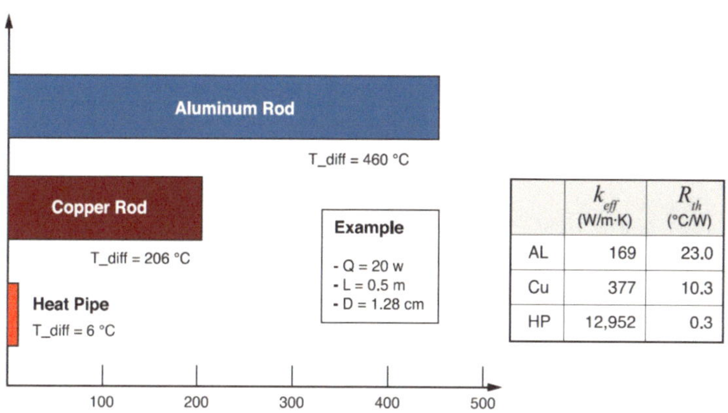

Figure 3. The superiority of heat pipe over other thermally conducting materials.

Figure 3 clearly illustrates the superiority of the heat pipe. The goodness of the heat transfer module is characterized by the effective thermal conductivity (k_{eff}) or thermal resistance (R_{th}) of the module. As an example, a typical value of effective thermal conductivity of a copper–water heat pipe with 0.5-m length and 1/2 inch diameter is around 10,000 W/mK, which is much larger than those of thermally conductive metals such as copper (~377 W/mK) or aluminum (~169 W/mK). This results in very low thermal resistance (~0.3 K/W), indicating low temperature drop with respect to the given thermal load. When 20 W heat is applied, this heat pipe would yield 6°C temperature difference between heat source and sink, whereas metal rods with same geometry have 206°C and 460°C for copper and aluminum, respectively. Provided that the ambient air is at 20°C, the chip temperature is only 26°C, which enables designers to easily come up with plausible and fascinating thermal solution.

In this chapter, general aspects of heat pipes for electronics cooling are introduced. The contents cover the working principle of heat pipes, design and analyzation methods, components and structure of heat pipes, implementation in electronics cooling, characterization and theories, and design and manufacturing process.

2. Working principle

2.1. Introduction to working principle

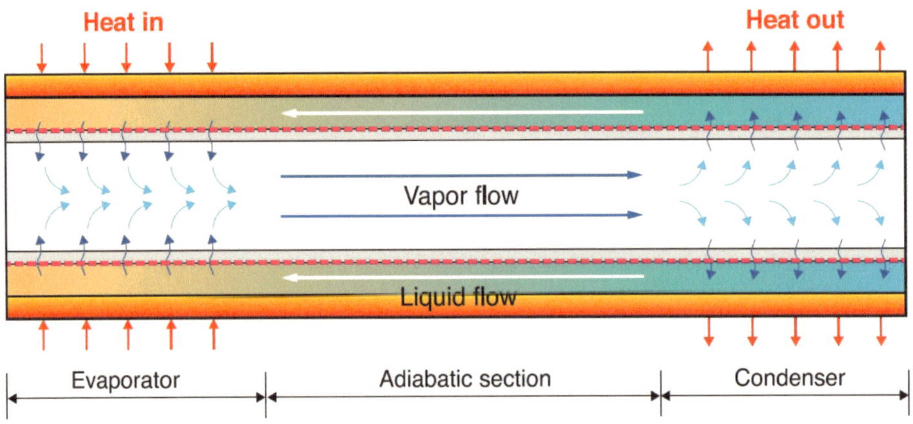

Figure 4. Working principle of heat pipe.

The working principle of the heat pipe is summarized in **Figure 4**. The heat pipe consists of metal envelope, wick, and working fluid. The wick is a microporous structure made of metal and is attached to the inner surface of the envelope. The working fluid is located in the void space inside the wick. When the heat is applied at the evaporator by an external heat source, the applied heat vaporizes the working fluid in the heat pipe. The generated vapor of working fluid elevates the pressure and results in pressure difference along the axial direction. The pressure difference drives the vapor from evaporator to the condenser, where it condenses releasing the latent heat of vaporization to the heat sink. In the meantime, depletion of liquid by evaporation at the evaporator causes the liquid–vapor interface to enter into the wick surface, and thus a capillary pressure is developed there. This capillary pressure pumps the condensed liquid back to the evaporator for re-evaporation of working fluid. Likewise, the working fluid circulates in a closed loop inside the envelope, while evaporation and condensation simultaneously take place for heat absorption and dissipation, respectively. The high thermal performance of the heat pipe is originated from the latent heat of vaporization, which typically amounts to millions of Joules per 1 kg of fluid.

2.2. Wick for heat pipe

The flow in the wick is attributable to the same mechanism with the suction of water by a sponge. The microsized pores in the sponge (or wick) can properly generate the meniscus at the liquid–vapor interfaces, and this yields the capillary pressure gradient and resulting liquid movement. It should be noted that the wick provides the capillary pumping of working fluid, which must be steadily supplied for the operation of heat pipe as well as the flow passage of the working fluid. In addition, the wick also acts as a thermal flow path because the applied heat is transferred to the working fluid through the envelope and wick. Therefore, the thermal performance of the heat pipe is strongly dependent on the wick structure.

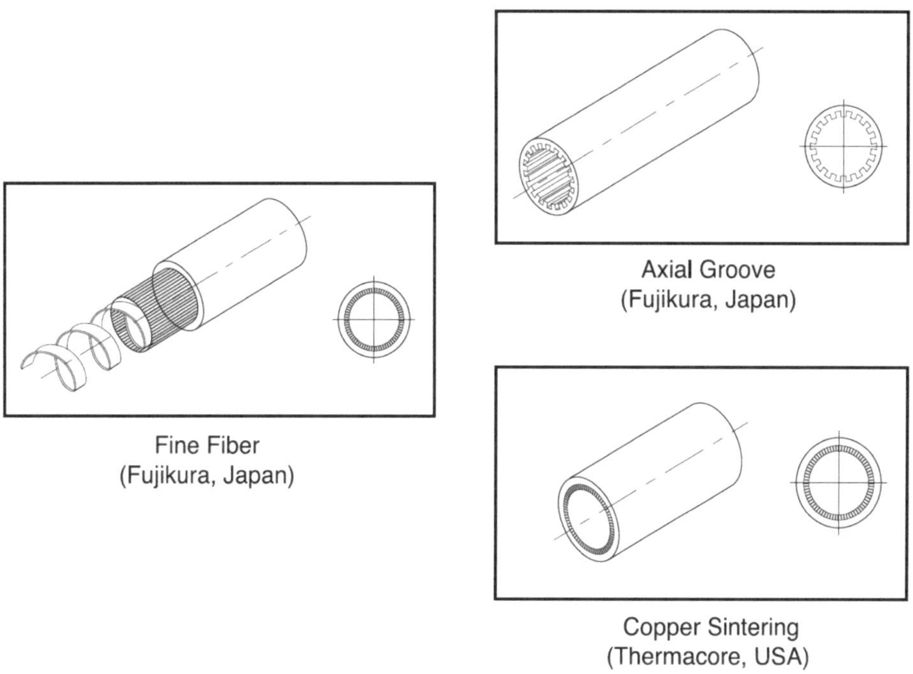

Figure 5. Typical wick structures.

In this regard, various types of wick structures have been used for enhancing the thermal performance of heat pipes. **Figure 5** shows three representative types of wick structures: mesh screen wick (it is also often termed as fiber mesh or wrapped screen), grooved wick, and sintered particle (or sintered powder) wick. The mesh screen wick is the most common wick structure, which made of wrapped textiles of metal wires. The grooved wick utilizes axial grooves directly sculptured on the envelope inner surface as the flow channel. The sintered particle wick is made of slightly fusing microsized metal particles together in the sintering process. The major characteristics of aforementioned wick types are shown in **Figure 6**. The mesh screen wick can have high capillary pressure and moderate permeability because numerous pores per unit length and the tightness of the structure can be controlled, where the permeability is a measure of the ability of a porous medium to transmit fluids through itself under a given pressure drop as follows:

$$U = -\frac{K}{\mu}\frac{dP}{dx} \tag{1}$$

Wick structure	Capillary force	Permeability	Thermal conductivity
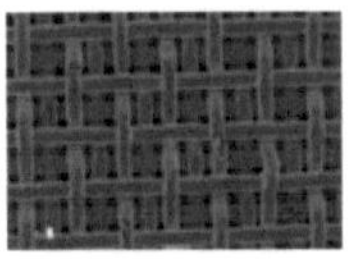 Mesh screen	High	Low-average	Low
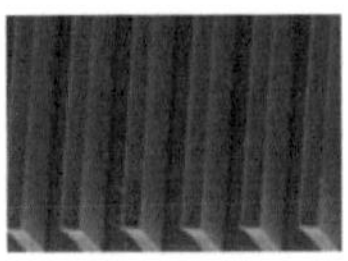 Groove	Low	Average-high	High
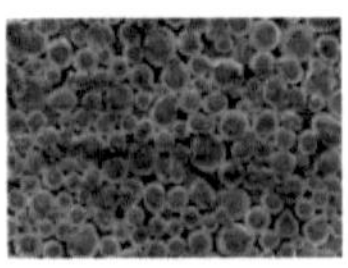 Sintered particle	High	Low-average	Average-high

Figure 6. Characteristics of wick structures.

where K is the permeability, U is the mean velocity of flow inside porous media, μ is the viscosity, and dP/dx is the applied pressure gradient.

However, the effective thermal conductivity is low because the screens are not thermally connected to each other. In case of grooved wick, the effective thermal conductivity is high due to the sturdy thermal path. It has an additional advantage in which the wide and straight (not tortuous) flow path can bring about high permeability. However, the capillary pressure is strongly limited, due to the fact that the scale of the grooves, which are machined through extrusion process, cannot be reduced beyond several tens of micrometers. It should be noted that the maximum developable capillary pressure is inversely proportional to the characteristic length of the pore structure. On the other hand, the sintered particle wick has high capillary pressure as well as moderate-to-high effective thermal conductivity, due to the tailorable particle size and fused contact between particles. However, the permeability of the sintered particle wick is relatively low, due to the narrow and tortuous flow path. As shown, the type of wick has its pros and cons. Therefore, the designers choose the wick type in accordance with the corresponding suitable applications.

http://dx.doi.org/10.5772/62328

3. Thermal performance

3.1. Various mechanisms

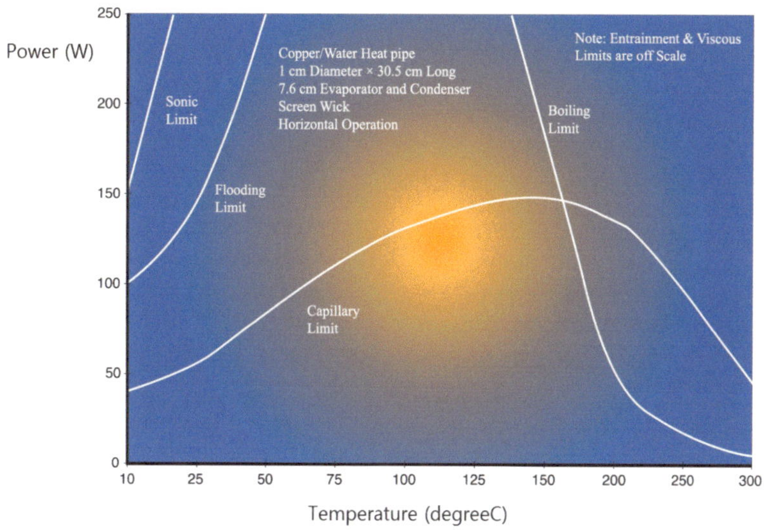

Figure 7. Performance limitations with respect to the temperature.

In case of other cooling modules, there is no heat transfer 'limitation,' implying that increasing heat transfer rate just keeps increasing the temperature drop and worsening the situation. On the contrary, there is a definite limitation of thermal performance for heat pipe, beyond which the heat transfer rate cannot be increased for a reliable operation. The thermal performance of the heat pipe is limited by one of various mechanisms depending on the working temperature range and geometry of the heat pipe. The viscous limit typically occurs during unsteady start-up at low temperature, when the internal pressure drop is not large enough to move the vapor along the heat pipe. The sonic limit also typically takes place during unsteady start-up at low temperature, when the chocked flow regime is reached at the sonic speed of the vapor. The capillary limit is related to the ability of the wick to move the liquid through the required pressure drop. It happens when the circulation rate of working fluid increases so that the pressure drop along the entire flow path reaches the developed capillary pressure. When the capillary limit happens, dry out occurs in the evaporator, while more fluid is vaporized than that can be supplied by the capillary action of the wick. The entrainment limit is related to the liquid–vapor interface where counterflows of two phases are met. In some circumstances, the drag imposed by the vapor on the returning liquid can be large enough to entrain the flow of condensate in the wick structures, resulting in dry out. The boiling limit is known to occur when the bubble nucleation is initiated in the evaporator section. The bubble generally cannot easily escape the wick with microsized pores and effectively prevent the liquid to wet the heated surface, which in turn results in burnout. The burnout heat flux is known to typically range from 20 to 30 W/cm^2 for sintered particle wicks.

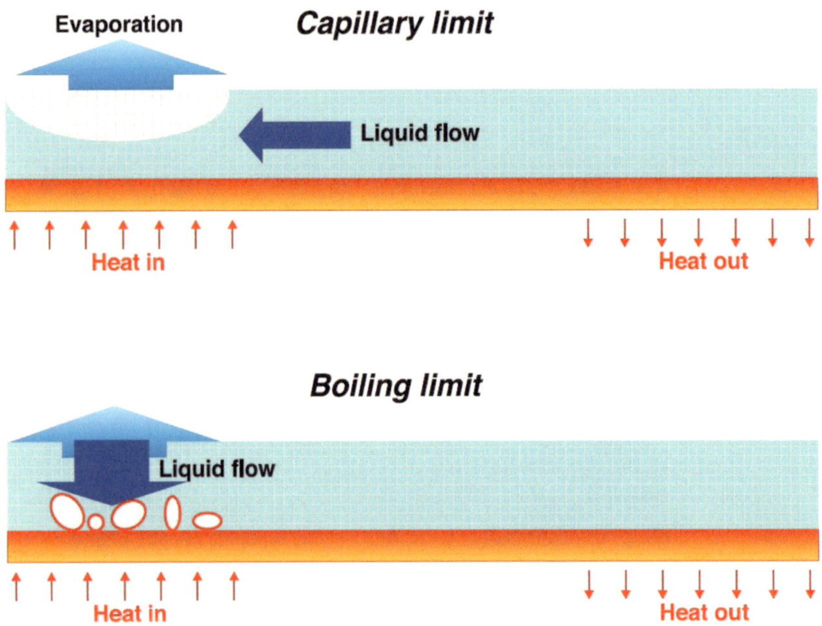

Figure 8. Capillary limit and boiling limit.

Figure 7 shows the thermal capacity of a heat pipe (copper–water, 1 cm diameter, 30 cm long) determined by various limiting mechanisms with respect to temperature. As shown in this figure, the viscous limit, the sonic limit, and the entrainment limit do not play an important role in determining the thermal capacity of the heat pipe, unless the temperature is very low (< −20°C). The heat pipes operating above atmospheric temperature are practically only governed by the capillary limit or the boiling limit, as shown in **Figure 7**. There is a good method for distinguishing those two limitations (see **Figure 8**). The capillary limit occurs when the liquid flow along the axial direction cannot afford the evaporation rate due to the limited capillary pressure. The boiling limit occurs when the bubble barricades the liquid flow onto the heated surface. In other words, the capillary limit is represented by the axial (or lateral) fluid transportation limit while the boiling limit is represented by the radial (or vertical) fluid transportation limit. It should be noted that, in the heat pipe, the limitation on the fluid transport represents the heat transfer limit because the heat transfer rate is given as the multiplication of latent heat coefficient and mass flow rate of working fluid. In this regard, the boiling limit becomes dominant when the effective heat pipe length is relatively small, and vice versa. The boiling limit also becomes important when the operating temperature is high because bubble nucleation is more likely to happen in high superheat. The next two subsections will be devoted to the models for capillary limit and boiling limit, respectively.

3.2. Capillary limit

The capillary limit is also called the wicking limit. As mentioned, the capillary limit occurs when the liquid flow along the axial direction cannot afford the evaporation rate. This situation happens under the condition where the pressure drop along the entire flow path is equal to the developed capillary pressure. The pressure drop of working fluid consists of that of liquid flow path (ΔP_l), that of vapor flow path (ΔP_v), additional pressure drop imposed by counter-flow at the phase interface (ΔP_{l-v}), and the gravitational pressure drop (ΔP_g). Thus, the condition for the capillary limit is described by the following equation:

$$\Delta P_c = \Delta P_l + \Delta P_{l-v} + \Delta P_v + \Delta P_g \tag{2}$$

where ΔP_c is the capillary pressure difference between evaporator and condenser sections. Generally, the vapor pressure drop (ΔP_v) and interfacial pressure drop (ΔP_{l-v}) are negligible when compared with others; thus, the equation reduces to the following:

$$\frac{2\sigma}{R_{\text{eff}}} = \frac{\mu_l L_{\text{eff}}}{K A_{\text{w}} \rho_l}\dot{m} + \rho_l g L_{\text{eff}} \sin\phi \tag{3}$$

where the left-hand side represents ΔP_c, the first term on the right-hand side is ΔP_l, and the second term corresponds to ΔP_g. In this equation, σ is the surface tension coefficient, R_{eff} is the effective pore radius of the wick structure, μ_l is the liquid viscosity of working fluid, L_{eff} is the effective length of heat pipe, K is the permeability, A_w is the cross-sectional area of the wick, ρ_l is the liquid density of working fluid, $\dot{m}$ is the mass flow rate, g is the gravitational constant, and φ is the orientation angle with respect to the horizontal plane. The heat transport capacity of the heat pipe is directly proportional to the mass flow rate of the working fluid as follows:

$$Q_{\max} = h_{\text{fg}}\dot{m} \tag{4}$$

where h_{fg} is the latent heat coefficient of working fluid. Combining Equations (3) and (4) yields the following equation for the capillary limit:

$$Q_{\max} = \frac{K A_{\text{w}} h_{\text{fg}} \rho_l}{\mu_l L_{\text{eff}}}\left[\frac{2\sigma}{R_{\text{eff}}} - \rho g L_{\text{eff}} \sin\phi\right] \tag{5}$$

It should be underlined that the K and R_{eff} are related to the microstructure of the wick; h_{fg}, σ, μ_l, and ρ_l are the fluid properties; and L_{eff} and A_w represents the macroscopic geometry of the heat pipe. When the gravitational force can be neglected, the Equation (5) can be rewritten and each kind of parameters can be detached as independent term as follows:

$$Q_{\max} = \left(\frac{2\sigma h_{\text{fg}} \rho_l}{\mu_l}\right)\left(\frac{A_{\text{w}}}{L_{\text{eff}}}\right)\left(\frac{K}{R_{\text{eff}}}\right) \tag{6}$$

Wick type	K	R_{eff}	Typical value of K/R_{eff} (micron)
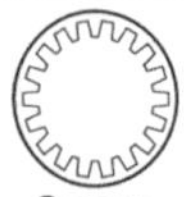 Groove	$\frac{2\varepsilon r_{h,l}^{2}}{f\mathrm{Re}}$	w	~1
 Sintered particle	$\frac{\varepsilon^3 d^2}{150(1-\varepsilon)^2}$	$\frac{d}{5}$	~ 0.3
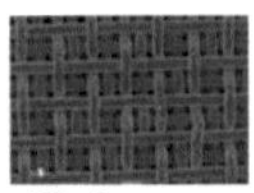 Mesh screen	$\frac{\varepsilon^3 d^2}{122(1-\varepsilon)^2}$	$\frac{w+d}{2}$	~ 0.3

Figure 9. K and R_{eff} values for typical wick structures.

The first paragraphed term is a combination of the fluid properties, suggesting that the capillary limit of heat pipe is proportional to this term. This term is called the figure of merit of working fluid. The second paragraphed term is about the macroscopic geometry of the heat pipe. The last term is related to the wick microstructure, thus, in regard to the wick design, we have to maximize this term. This term is often called the capillary performance of wick. The permeability K is proportional to the pore characteristic length, whereas R_{eff} is inversely proportional to the pore size. Therefore, the ratio between K and R_{eff} captures a trade off between those two competing effects. The K and R_{eff} values for representative wick structure are shown in **Figure 9**.

3.3. Boiling limit

Regarding the boiling limit, it has been postulated that the boiling limit occurs as soon as the bubble nucleation is initiated. Onset of nucleate boiling within the wick was considered as a mechanism of failure and was avoided. On the basis of that postulation, the following correlation for predicting boiling limit has been widely used [1]:

$$Q_{max} = \frac{2\pi L_e k_e T_v}{h_{fg}\rho_v \ln(r_i / r_v)}\left(\frac{2\sigma}{r_b} - P_c\right) \tag{7}$$

where L_e is the evaporator length, k_e is the effective thermal conductivity of wick, T_v is the vapor core temperature, h_{fg} is the latent heat, ρ_v is the vapor density, r_v is the vapor core radius, r_i is the radius of outer circle including the wick thickness, and σ is the surface tension coefficient. In Equation (7), important design parameters related to the wick microstructure are r_b and P_c, which are bubble radius and capillary pressure, respectively. Even though Equation (7) is simple and in a closed form, it is difficult to implement this equation in which these parameters

http://dx.doi.org/10.5772/62328

are quite arbitrary, and thus, it is difficult to exactly predict those values. To accurately determine r_b and P_c, additional experiment should be performed [1]. Another fundamental problem also exists in which the nucleate boiling within the wick does not necessarily represent a heat transfer limit unless bubbles cannot escape from the wick, as indicated by several researchers [2]. Indeed, nucleate boiling may not stop or retard the capillary-driven flow in porous media according to the literatures. Some researchers even insisted that the nucleate boiling in the moderate temperature heat pipe wicks is not only tolerable but could also produce performance enhancement by significantly increasing the heat transfer coefficient over the conduction model and consequently reducing the wick temperature drop [3]. Therefore, new light should be shed on the model for the boiling limit. As illustrated in Equation (6), key parameters for capillary limit are K and R_{eff}. Equation (7) shows that key parameter for boiling limit is k_e, excluding the effect of permeability. Recently, it has been shown that the boiling limit does not occur with the nucleate boiling if the vapor bubble can escape the wick efficiently [4]. This suggests that the K is also an important parameter for the boiling limit.

4. Heat pipe designs

4.1. Heat pipe design procedure

The design procedure of the heat pipe is as follows:

1. working fluid selection,
2. wick type selection,
3. container material selection,
4. determining diameter,
5. determining thickness,
6. wick design, and
7. heat sink and source interface design.

The followed subsections will be devoted to each procedure.

4.2. Working fluid selection

The first step for designing the heat pipe is to select the working fluid according to the operating temperature of the heat pipe. Each fluid has its vapor pressure profile with respect to the temperature. The vapor pressure increases as the temperature increases, and when the vapor pressure reaches the pressure of environment, boiling occurs. The heat pipe is designed to operate nearly at the boiling temperature for facilitating the heat transfer rate associated with the latent heat. Therefore, the working fluid should be selected under the consideration of the operating temperature of heat pipe. Various kinds of working fluids and their operating temperature ranges and corresponding inner pressures are shown in **Figure 10**. In case of water-based heat pipe that operates at the room temperature, the inner pressure of heat pipe is typically set to be approximately 0.03 bar for maximizing the thermal performance. When the operating temperature is 200°C, the inner pressure of the heat pipe should be set at roughly 16 bar. For cryogenic applications, helium or nitrogen gas is used. For medium or high temperature applications, liquid metals such as sodium and mercury are typically used. The inner pressure of heat pipe should be properly adjusted according to its operating temperature.

Range	Name	Temp(°C)	Pressure(bar)
Cryogenic	Helium	-271:-268	0.06:2.29
	Nitrogen	-203:-150	0.48:28.8
Low	Ammonia	-60:120	0.27:90.44
	Water	-20:200	0.02:16.19
	Ethanol	-30:130	0.01:4.30
	Acetone	-40:140	0.01:10.49
Medium	Naphthalene	100:400	0.02:17.5
	Mercury	150:750	0.01:63
High	Sodium	500:1300	0.01:15.91
	Caesium	375:825	0.02:3.41
	Lithium	1030:1730	0.07:8.90

Figure 10. Operating temperature of working fluids.

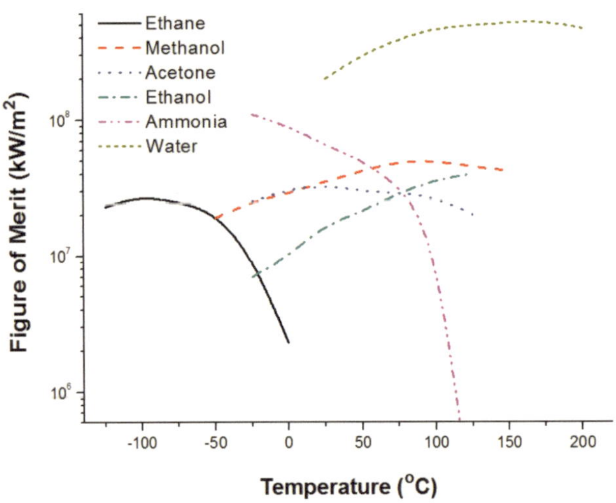

Figure 11. Figure of merit numbers of working fluids.

The working fluid selection is also important in terms of the thermal performance. Equation (6) shows that the thermal performance of heat pipe is directly proportional to a fluid property, $\rho_l \sigma h_{fg}/\mu_l$. This is often called the figure of merit of working fluid. **Figure 11** shows the figure of merit with respect to the temperature for various working fluids. As shown in this figure, occurring in low to moderate temperatures, water is the liquid with the highest figure of merit number. This is why the water is the most commonly used for heat pipe. Another common fluid is ammonia, which is used for low-temperature applications.

	Water	Acetone	Ammonia	Methanol
Copper	R	R	I	R
Aluminum	N	R	R	I
Stainless steel	N	I	R	N
Nickel	I	I	R	R
R	Recommended			
I	Indefinite			
N	Not compatible			

Figure 12. Material compatibility.

4.3. Wick type selection

The second step is to select the wick type. Typically, five selections can be considered: no wick (for thermosiphon), mesh screen wick, grooved wick, sintered particle wick, and heterogeneous type wick. The reason we select the wick type prior to choosing the material is that the manufacturable microstructure is dependent on the material.

4.4. Container and wick material selection

After choosing the wick type, the material for container and wick is selected. Here, the major consideration is the compatibility between the working fluid and the material. Water–copper combination is known to have a good compatibility. On the other hand, the water is not compatible with aluminum due to unpreferred gas generation. The material compatibility with working fluid is shown in **Figure 12**. Copper is shown to be compatible with water, acetone, and methanol. The aluminum has good compatibility with acetone and ammonia, but not with water.

4.5. Determination of diameter

The next step is to determine the diameter of the heat pipe. The diameter becomes a major geometric parameter upon consideration of the vapor velocity. When the diameter of heat pipe is too small, the vapor velocity increases much, and compressibility effect appears, which in turn aggravates the performance of heat pipe significantly. Typically, it is known that the compressibility effect is negligible when the Mach number is less than 0.2. To fulfill this criterion, the following equation should be satisfied.

$$d_v > \sqrt{\frac{20Q_{\max}}{\pi\rho_v h_{fg}\sqrt{\gamma_v R_v T_v}}} \tag{8}$$

where d_v is the vapor core diameter, Q_{max} is the maximum axial heat flux, ρ_v is the vapor density, γ_v is the vapor-specific heat ratio, h_{fg} is the latent heat of vaporization, R_v is the gas constant for vapor, and T_v is the vapor temperature.

4.6. Determination of thickness

As the heat pipe is like a pressure vessel, it must satisfy the ASME vessel codes. Typically, the maximum allowable stress at any given temperature can only be one-fourth of the material's maximum tensile strength. The maximum hoop stress in the heat pipe wall is given as follows [1]:

$$f_{max} = \frac{Pd_o}{2t} \tag{9}$$

where f_{max} is the maximum stress in the heat pipe wall; P is the pressure differential across the wall, which causes the stress; d_o is the heat pipe outer wall; and t is the wall thickness. The safety criterion is given as follows:

$$f_{max} < \frac{\sigma_Y}{4} \tag{10}$$

where σ_Y is the yielding stress of the container material. Combining Equations (9) and (10) yields:

$$\frac{2Pd_o}{\sigma_Y} < t \tag{11}$$

4.7. Wick design

The maximum thermal performance of heat pipe is given in Equation (6). Let us retrieve Equation (6) as Equation (12).

$$Q_{max} = \left(\frac{2\sigma h_{fg}\rho_l}{\mu_l}\right)\left(\frac{A_w}{L_{eff}}\right)\left(\frac{K}{R_{eff}}\right) \tag{12}$$

In Equation (12), design parameters related to the wick are K and R_{eff}. The K is known to proportional to the square of the characteristic pore size, whereas R_{eff} is inversely proportional to the characteristic pore size. Therefore, the capillary performance, K/R_{eff}, is directly proportional to the characteristic pore size. However, when the pore size is too large, the capillary pressure becomes too small so that the gravity effect cannot be overcome, which in turn makes the heat pipe useless. In addition, large pore size represents significant effect of inertia force.

http://dx.doi.org/10.5772/62328

It should be noted that Equation (12) is derived under the postulation that the flow rate of working fluid is determined upon the balance between capillary force and viscous friction force where the inertia force is negligible in microscale flow. When the inertia force becomes significant, the thermal performance is significantly deviated from the prediction by Equation (12), in other words, is degraded much. For these reasons, the particle size of the sintered particle wick typically ranges from 40 μm to 300 μm. In case of looped heat pipe (LHP) where extremely high capillary pressure is required, nickel particles with 1–5 μm diameter are used.

4.8. Heat sink–source interface design

Besides design of heat pipe itself, the interfaces of heat pipe with heat sink–source are also of significant interest because the interfacial contact thermal resistance is much larger than that of heat pipe itself. The contact thermal resistance between the evaporator and the heat source and that between the condenser and the heat sink is relatively large. Therefore, they have to be carefully considered and minimized.

4.9. Thermal resistance considerations

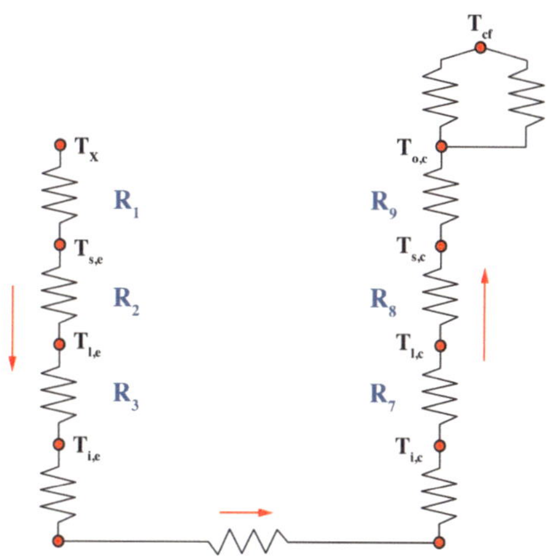

Figure 13. Thermal resistance network.

Through Sections 4.1–4.7, only the maximum heat transport capability has been regarded as the performance index of the heat pipe. However, sometimes another performance index, the thermal resistance, is more important when the heat transfer rate is not of an important consideration while the temperature uniformization is more important. The thermal resistance of the heat pipe can be estimated based on the thermal resistance network, as shown in **Figure 13**. T_x is the heat source temperature, and T_{cf} is the heat sink temperature. The subscripts *e* and *c* represent the evaporator and condenser, respectively. The subscripts *s*, *l*, and *i* represent the shell, liquid, and interface, respectively. The various thermal resistance components and correlations for predicting them are shown in **Figure 14**.

Location	Heat flow	Thermal resistance (R)
Evaporator B.C. to shell	$q_1 = \frac{1}{R_1}(T_X - T_{s,e})$	$\frac{1}{2\pi r_o L_e}[\frac{1}{h_{xs}} + \frac{\Delta r_s}{2k_s}]$
Evaporator shell to liquid	$q_2 = \frac{1}{R_2}(T_{s,e} - T_{l,e})$	$\frac{1}{2\pi r_i L_e}[\frac{\Delta r_s}{2k_s} + \frac{\Delta r_l}{2k_l}]$
Evaporator liquid to evaporator interface	$q_3 = \frac{1}{R_3}(T_{l,e} - T_{i,e})$	$\frac{1}{2\pi r_w L_e}[\frac{\Delta r_l}{2k_l}]$
Liquid-vapor interface in the evaporator	$q_4 = m'_w h_{fg} = f(T_{i,e}, T_v)$	
Vapor region	$q_5 = q_4$	
Liquid-vapor interface in the condenser	$q_6 = m'_w h_{fg} = f(T_{i,c}, T_v)$	
Liquid-vapor interface to liquid,condenser	$q_7 = \frac{1}{R_7}(T_{i,e} - T_{l,c})$	$\frac{1}{2\pi r_w L_c}[\frac{\Delta r_l}{2k_l}]$
Liquid to shell, condenser	$q_8 = \frac{1}{R_8}(T_{l,c} - T_{s,c})$	$\frac{1}{2\pi r_i L_c}[\frac{\Delta r_s}{2k_s} + \frac{\Delta r_l}{2k_l}]$
Shell to B.C., condenser	$q_9 = \frac{1}{R_9}(T_{s,c} - T_{c,f})$	$\frac{1}{2\pi r_o L_c}[\frac{1}{h_{cf}} + \frac{\Delta r_s}{2k_s}]$

Figure 14. Thermal resistance correlations.

5. Application to electronics cooling

The types of heat pipe applications to electronics cooling are as follows: use of flat-plate heat pipe, heat pipe–embedded heat spreader, block to fin, block to block, and fin to fin. The tubular heat pipe cannot solely used because its interface cannot be fully attached to the electronic devices having flat interface. For heat pipe to be adapted to the electronics cooling, the heat pipe itself should be formed into flat-plate type, or the tubular heat pipe should be fitted to rectangular-shaped based block, as shown in **Figure 15**. The heat pipe–embedded heat spreader is shown in **Figure 16**.

The block-to-fin applications are shown in **Figure 17**. The heat pipe has to be anyhow connected to the heat sink for the final heat dissipation to the air. The heat pipe–embedded block can be directly connected to the fin, as shown in this figure. In some applications such as sever computer and telecommunication unit handle a large amount of data, block-to-block module is employed, as shown in **Figure 18**. In some applications, the fin-to-fin module is also used.

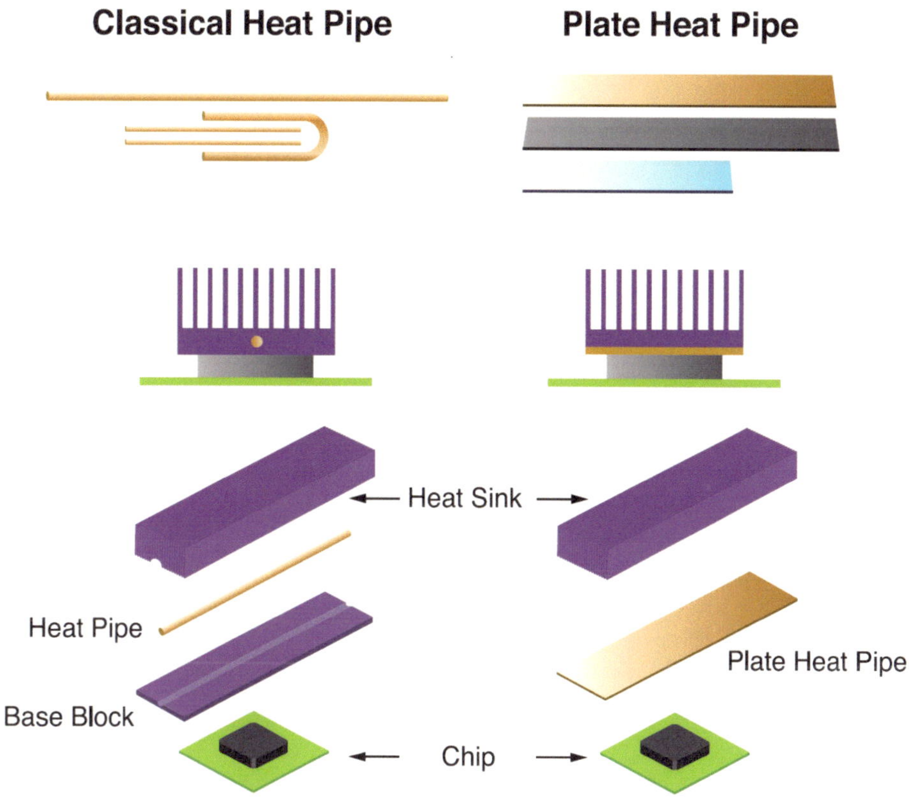

Figure 15. Use of tubular heat pipe and flat-plate heat pipe.

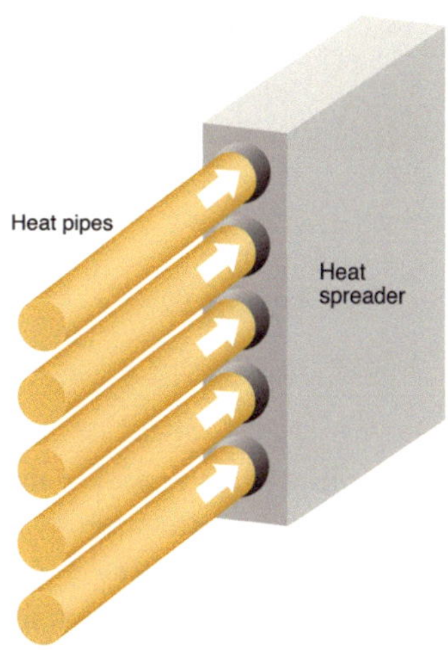

Figure 16. Heat pipe–embedded heat spreaders.

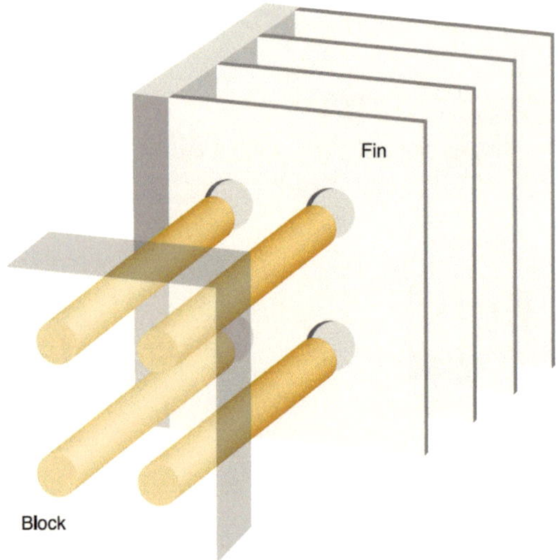

Figure 17. Block-to-fin applications.

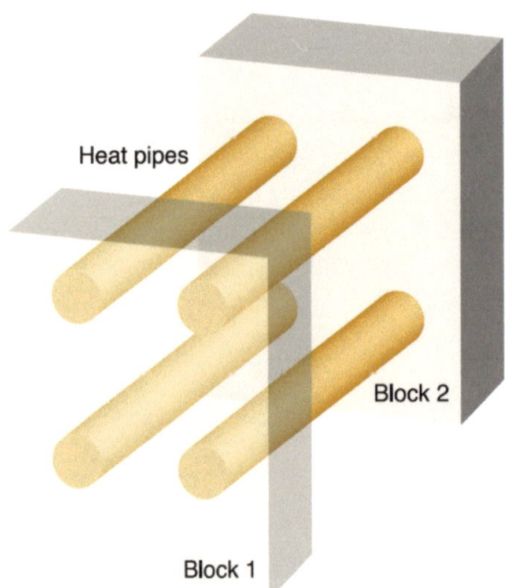

Figure 18. Block-to-block applications.

The use of heat pipe to electronics cooling is diversified into portable devices, VGA, mobile PC, LED projector and related devices, telecommunication repeater, and so on. The heat pipe is also widely employed in solar heat collection, snow melting, heat exchanger and related energy applications, and pure science applications demanding ultra-precise temperature control. Especially for the semiconductor devices whose performance and lifetime are sensitive to the temperature, heat pipe is an ultimate thermal solution. The use of heat pipe will surely expand, and it will gradually have more ripple effect in various industrial areas.

http://dx.doi.org/10.5772/62328

6. Summary

In this chapter, the general aspects of heat pipes are introduced. The working principle of the heat pipe is based on two phase flows pumped by capillary pressure formed at the wick. The wick plays an important role in determining the thermal performance of the heat pipe. In this regard, various types of wick structures have been developed, such as mesh screen wick, grooved wick, and sintered particle wick. The thermal performance of heat pipe is generally determined by capillary limit, which can be readily predicted based on simple analytic method represented by Equation (6). Boiling limit is also important in high operation temperature. However, a definite model for the boiling limit is still not available. The heat pipe design starts with working fluid selection, followed by wick type and container material selections, determining diameter and thickness, wick design, and heat sink–source interface design. The application of heat pipe to electronics cooling can be classified by the configuration: heat pipe–embedded spreader, block-to-block, block-to-fin, and fin-to-fin applications.

Author details

Chan Byon

Address all correspondence to: cbyon@ynu.ac.kr

School of Mechanical Engineering, Yeungnam University, Gyeongsan, South Korea

References

[1] ChiSW, Heat Pipe Theory and Practice. Washington, DC: Hemisphere Publishing Corporation, 1976.

[2] FaghriA, Heat Pipe Science and Technology. New York: Taylor & Francis Ltd., 1995.

[3] GontarevYK, NavruzovYV, PrisnyakovVF, and SerebryanskiiVN. Mechanism for boiling of a liquid in heat pipe wicks. Journal of Engineering Physics. 1984;47(3):1056–1060.

[4] ByonC and KimSJ. Effects of geometrical parameters on the boiling limit of bi-porous wicks. International Journal of Heat and Mass Transfer. 2013;55(25–26):7884–7891.

[5] IncroperaFP, TLBergman, and ASLavine, Foundations of Heat Transfer. Washington. Wiley. 2013

Chapter 4

Heat Pipes for Computer Cooling Applications

Mohamed H.A. Elnaggar and Ezzaldeen Edwan

Additional information is available at the end of the chapter

http://dx.doi.org/10.5772/62279

Abstract

There is an increasing demand for efficient cooling techniques in computer industry to dissipate the associated heat from the newly designed and developed computer processors to accommodate for their enhanced processing power and faster operations. Such a demand necessitates researchers to explore efficient approaches for central processing unit (CPU) cooling. Consequently, heat pipes can be a viable and promising solution for this challenge. In this chapter, a CPU thermal design power (TDP), cooling methods of electronic equipments, heat pipe theory and operation, heat pipes components, such as the wall material, the wick structure, and the working fluid, are presented. Moreover, we review experimentally, analytically and numerically the types of heat pipes with their applications for electronic cooling in general and the computer cooling in particular. Summary tables that compare the content, methodology, and types of heat pipes are presented. Due to the numerous advantages of the heat pipe in electronic cooling, this chapter definitely leads to further research in computer cooling applications.

Keywords: Heat pipes, Electronic cooling, Wick structure, Working fluids, Computer cooling applications

1. Introduction

Effective cooling of electronic components is an important issue for successful functionality and high reliability of the electronic devices. The rapid developments in microprocessors necessitate an enhanced processing power to ensure faster operations. The electronic devices have highly integrated circuits that produce a high heat flux, which leads to increase in the operating temperature of devices, and this results in the shortening of life time of the electronic devices [1]. Consequently, the need for cooling techniques to dissipate the associated heat is quiet obvious. Thus, heat pipes have been identified and proved as one of the viable and promising options to achieve this purpose prior to its simple structure, flexibility and high efficiency, in particularly. Heat pipes utilize the phase changes in the working fluid inside in order to facilitate the heat transport. Heat pipes are the best choice for cooling electronic devices, because depending on the length, the effective thermal conductivity of heat pipes can be up to several thousand times higher than that of a copper rod. The main perception of a heat pipe involves passive two-phase heat transfer device that can transfer large quantity of heat with minimum temperature drop. This method offers the possibility of high local heat removal rates with the ability to dissipate heat uniformly.

Heat pipes are used in a wide range of products such as air conditioners, refrigerators, heat exchangers, transistors, and capacitors. Heat pipes are also used in desktops and laptops to decrease the operating temperature for a better performance. Heat pipes are commercially presented since the mid-1960s. Electronic cooling has just embraced heat pipe as a dependable and cost-effective solution for sophisticated cooling applications.

2. Thermal design power

The thermal design power (TDP) has attracted the topmost interest of thermal solution designers, and it refers to the maximum power dissipated by a processor across a variety of applications [2]. The purpose of TDP is to introduce thermal solutions, which can inform manufacturers of how much heat their solution should dissipate. Typically, TDP is estimated as 20–30% lower than the CPU maximum power dissipation. Maximum power dissipation is the maximum power a CPU can dissipate under the worst conditions, such as the maximum temperature, maximum core voltage, and maximum signal loading conditions, whereas the minimum power dissipation refers to the power dissipated by the processor when it is switched into one of the low power modes. The maximum TDP ranges from 35 to 77 W for modern processors such as Intel® Core™ i5-3400 Desktop Processor Series [3], whereas the maximum TDP for modern notebook computers ranges from 17 to 35 W [4].

3. Cooling methods of electronic equipments

The air cooling is the most important technology that contributes to the cooling of electronic devices [5]. In the past, there were three main ways to cool the electronic equipment: (1) passive air cooling that dissipates heat using the airflow generated by differences in temperature, (2) forced air cooling that dissipates heat by forcing air to flow using fans, and (3) forced liquid cooling that dissipates heat by forcing coolants like water to pass [6]. The conventional way to dissipate heat from desktop computers was forced convection, using a fan with a heat sink directly. The advantages, such as simple machining, simple structure, and lower cost, have made heat sinks with plate fins very useful in cooling of electronic devices [7]. However, with the smaller CPU size and increased power as encountered in modern computers, the heat flux at the CPU has been significantly increased [8]. At the same time, restrictions have been imposed on the size of heat sinks and fans and on the noise level associated with the increased fan speed. Consequently, there has been a growing concern for improved cooling techniques

http://dx.doi.org/10.5772/62279

that suit the modern CPU requirements. As alternatives to the conventional heat sinks, two-phase cooling devices, such as heat pipe and thermosyphon, have emerged as promising heat transfer devices with effective thermal conductivity over 200 times higher than that of copper [9].

4. Heat pipe theory and operation

In order for heat pipe to operate, the maximum capillary pressure must be greater than the sum of all pressure drops inside the heat pipe to overcome them; thus, the prime criterion for the operation of a heat pipe is as follows

$$\Delta P_c \geq \Delta P_l + \Delta P_v + \Delta P_g \quad (1)$$

where, ΔP_c is the maximum capillary force inside the wick structure; ΔP_l is pressure drop required to return the liquid from the condenser to the evaporation section; ΔP_v is the pressure drop to move the vapor flow from the evaporation to the condenser section; and ΔP_g is the pressure drop caused due to the difference in gravitational potential energy (may be positive, negative, or zero, depends on the heat pipe orientation and a direction).

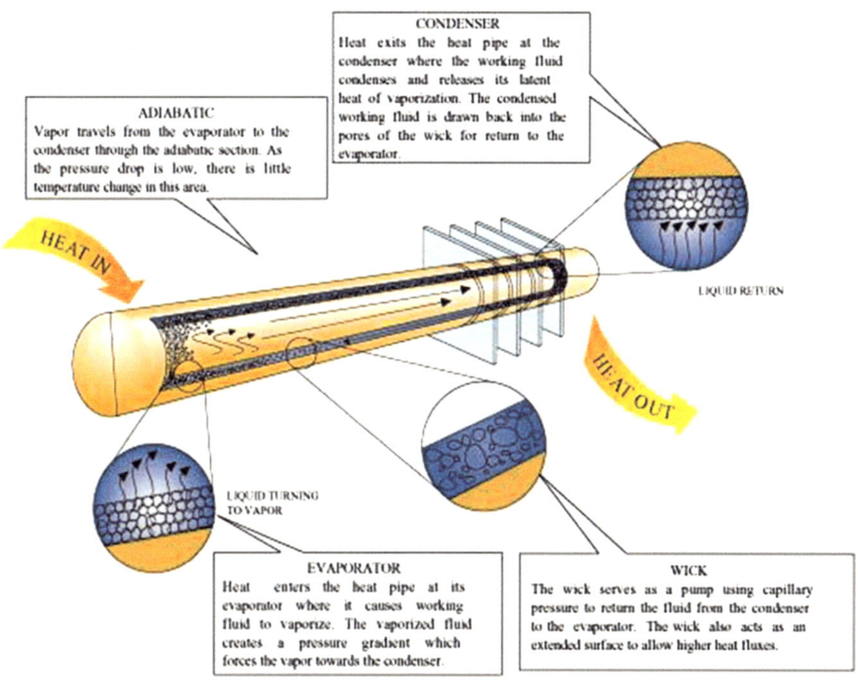

Figure 1. Heat pipe operation [10].

The basic steps of heat pipe operation are summarized as follows, with reference to **Figure 1** [10]:

1. The heat added at the evaporator section by conduction through the wall of heat pipe enables the evaporation of working fluid.

2. The vapor moves from the evaporator section to the condenser section under the influence of vapor pressure drop resulted by evaporation of the working fluid.

3. The vapor condenses in the condenser section releasing its latent heat of evaporation.

4. The liquid returns from the condenser section to the evaporator section through the wick under the influence of capillary force and the liquid pressure drop.

The liquid pressure drop can be calculated from the empirical relation [11]:

$$\Delta P_l = \frac{\mu_l L_{eff} Q}{\rho_l K A_w h_{fg}} \tag{2}$$

where μ_l=liquid viscosity, L_{eff}=effective length of the heat pipe, ρ_l=liquid density, K=wick permeability, A_w=wick cross-sectional area, and h_{fg}=heat of vaporization of liquid. The vapor pressure drop can be calculated from the following equation [12]:

$$\Delta P_v = \frac{16\mu_v L_{eff} Q}{2\left(\frac{D_v}{2}\right)^2 A_v \rho_v h_{fg}} \tag{3}$$

where μ_v=vapor viscosity, ρ_v=vapor density, D_v=vapor space distance, and A_v=vapor core cross-sectional area.

The maximum capillary pressure ΔP_c generated inside the wick region is given by the Laplace–Young equation [13].

$$\Delta P_c = \frac{2\sigma_l}{r_{eff}} \tag{4}$$

where σ_l is surface tension and r_{eff} is the effective radius of the pores of the wick.

The maximum achievable heat transfer by the heat pipe can be obtained from the equation [11]:

$$Q_{max} = \left(\frac{\rho_l \sigma_l h_{fg}}{\mu_l}\right)\left(\frac{A_w K}{L_{eff}}\right)\left(\frac{2}{r_{eff}} - \frac{\rho_l g L_{eff} sin\phi}{\sigma_l}\right) \tag{5}$$

where φ is the angle between the axis of the heat pipe and horizontal (positive when the evaporator is above the condenser and it is negative if vice versa).

At horizontal orientation φ=0, equation (5) will become

$$Q_{max} = \left(\frac{\rho_l \sigma_l h_{fg}}{\mu_l} \right) \left(\frac{A_w K}{L_{eff}} \right) \left(\frac{2}{r_{eff}} \right) \qquad (6)$$

5. Advantages of heat pipe

The heat pipe has many advantages compared with other cooling devices such as the following:

- The effective thermal conductivity is very high since the heat pipe operates on a closed two-phase cycle. Therefore, it can transport large quantity of heat with very small temperature difference between evaporator and condenser sections.
- It can transfer the heat without any moving parts so that the heat pipe is calm, noise-free, maintenance-free, and highly dependable.
- Due to its small size and weight, it can be used in cooling electronic devices.
- It is a simple device that works in any orientation and transfers heat from a place where there is no opportunity and possibility to accommodate a conventional fan; for instance, in notebooks.
- Heat pipes demonstrate precise isothermal control because of which the input heat fluxes can be varied without having to make significant changes in the operating temperature [14].
- The evaporator and condenser work independently, and it needs only common liquid and vapor so that the size and shape of the region of heat addition are different from the region of heat dissipation, provided that the rate of evaporation of the fluid does not exceed the rate of condensation of the vapor. Thus, the heat fluxes generated over smaller areas can be dissipated over larger areas with lower heat fluxes.

6. Heat pipes components

To obtain sufficient information on a heat pipe, researchers should study its basic components, which play an important role in the efficiency of the pipe. Many researchers focused their research on the most important aspects of these components, such as the heat pipe container, the wick structure, and the working fluid. The studies of these components were through experimental and numerical analysis.

6.1. The container or the wall of a heat pipe

A container is a metal seal, which is capable of transferring heat through it to the working fluid. This metal has a good heat conductivity. Many factors affect the selection of the material of the container, e.g., wettability, strength to weight ratio, machinability and ductility, compatibility with external environment and working fluid, thermal conductivity, weldability, and porosity. The container material must possess high strength to weight ratio, it must be nonporous to avoid any diffusion of vapor particles and, at the same time, should ensure minimum temperature difference between the wick and the heat source owing to its higher thermal conductivity.

6.2. Wick or capillary structure

The wick structure is the most important component of a heat pipe. It is responsible for the return of liquid from the condenser section to the evaporator section by the capillary property, even against the direction of gravity. Thus, the presence of wick makes the heat pipes operate in all orientations. The grooved wick, sintered wick, and screen mesh wick are the most important types of wick studied abundantly. These wick types are used widely in the electronics industry and are detailed next.

6.2.1. Metal sintered powder wick

As shown in the **Figure 2**, this type of the wick has a small pore size, resulting in low wick permeability, leading to the generation of high capillary forces for antigravity applications. The heat pipe that carries this type of wick gives small differences in temperature between evaporator and condenser section. This reduces the thermal resistance and increases the effective thermal conductivity of the heat pipe.

Figure 2. Metal sintered powder wick [15].

Leong et al. [16] investigated the heat pipe with sintered copper wicks. Flat plate heat pipes with rectangular porous wicks were fabricated using copper powder (63 μm) sintered at 800 and 1000 °C. They used mercury intrusion porosimetry and scanning electron microscopy (SEM) techniques to investigate the porosity and pore size distribution in these wicks. Results indicated a unimodal pore size distribution with most pore sizes distributed within 30–40 μm.

Moreover, the cylindrical wicks fabricated by injection molding technique with the same binder and sintering temperature were also compared. The calculated permeability values of the rectangular wicks were as good as those of the commercially produced cylindrical wicks. Compared with the wire mesh, the sintered wicks had smaller pores and had the controllability of porosity and pore size to get the best performance.

6.2.2. Grooved wick

The grooved wick is shown in **Figure 3**; this type of wick generates a small capillary driving force, but is appropriate or sufficient for low power heat pipes, which operates horizontally or with the direction of gravity.

Figure 3. Grooved wick [15].

Zhang and Faghri [17] simulated the condensation on a capillary grooved structure. They investigated the impacts of surface tension, contact angle, temperature drop, and fin thickness using the volume of fluid (VOF) model. Results indicated that the contact angels and heat transfer coefficients decreased when temperature difference increased. Significant increase in the liquid film thickness was also observed upon the increase of the fin thickness. Ahamed et al. [18] investigated thin flat heat pipe with the characteristic thickness of 1.0 mm, experimentally. A special fiber wick structure, which consisted of the combination of copper fiber and axial grooves as a capillary wick along the inner wall of the heat pipe, was used. The thin flat heat pipe was a straight one with rectangular cross section of 1.0 mm×5.84 mm. The heat pipe was made from copper pipe of 4 mm diameter, and the working fluid was pure deionized water. Their observation showed that the maximum heat that could be transported by the thin flat heat pipe of 1.0 mm thickness was 7 W. The thermal resistance of the heat pipe was 0.44 °C/W. The new fiber wick structure was also found to provide an optimum vapor space and capillary head for better heat transfer capabilities with less thermal resistance.

6.2.3. Screen mesh wick

Figure 4 shows the screen mesh wick, which is used in many of the products, and they have demonstrated useful characteristics with respect to power transport and orientation sensitivity.

Figure 4. Screen mesh wick [15].

Wong and Kao [19] presented visualization of the evaporation/boiling process and thermal measurements of horizontal transparent heat pipes. The heat pipes had two-layered copper mesh wick consisting of 100 and/or 200 mesh screens, glass tube, and water as the working fluid. Under lower heat load conditions, the thickness of the water film was less than 100 μm, and the nucleate boiling was observed at Q=40 W and Q=45 W, respectively. Optimal thermal characteristics were determined for the wick/charge combination, which provided the smallest thermal resistance across the evaporator with lowest overall temperature distribution. In contrast to lower load conditions, the higher heat loads with small charge led to partial dry out in the evaporator. However, under a larger charge, there was limited liquid recession with increasing heat load, and the bubble growth was found to be unsustainable and bursting violently. Liou et al. [20] presented the visualization and thermal resistance measurement for the sintered mesh–wick evaporator in flat plate heat pipes. The wick thickness was between 0.26 and 0.80 mm with different combinations of 100 and 200 mesh screens. Results showed that the increasing heat load tend to decrease the resistance of the evaporation until partial dry out occurred. Following this, the resistance of the evaporation started to increase slowly. Low permeability of the wick limited the reduction of evaporation resistance and prompted dry out.

The studies of wick types have the following main conclusions:

- Metal sintered powder wick has a small pore size, resulting in low wick permeability. This leads to generation of high capillary forces for antigravity applications. The heat pipe that carries this type of wick produces small temperature differences between evaporator and condenser section. Therefore, the thermal resistance is reduced, and the effective thermal conductivity of the heat pipe is increased.

- Grooved wick generates a small capillary driving force, which is appropriate or sufficient for low power heat pipes, that operates horizontally or with the direction of gravity.
- The efficiency of heat pipe with screen mesh wick depends on the number of layers and mesh counts used because it presents facilely variable characteristics whence heat transport and orientation sensitivity.

6.3. Working fluids

Selection of the working fluid depends primarily on the operating vapor temperature range. This is because the basis in the operation of the heat pipe is the process of evaporation and condensation of the working fluid. The selection of appropriate working fluid must be done carefully, taking into account the following factors [21]:

- must have very high surface tension;
- should demonstrate good thermal stability;
- wettability of wall materials and wick;
- should have high latent heat;
- should possess high thermal conductivity;
- should have low liquid and vapor viscosities; and
- it must be compatible with both wall materials and wick.

The most important property of the working fluid is high surface tension so that the heat pipe works against gravity as it generates high force of the capillarity characteristic. **Table 1** summarizes the properties of some working fluids with their useful ranges of temperature [21].

Medium	Melting point (°C)	Boiling point (°C)	Useful range (°C)
Helium	−271	−261	−271 to −269
Nitrogen	−210	−196	−203 to −160
Ammonia	−78	−33	−60 to 100
Acetone	−95	57	0 to 120
Methanol	−98	64	10 to 130
Flutec PP2	−50	76	10 to 160
Ethanol	−112	78	0 to 130
Water	0	100	30 to 200
Toluene	−95	110	50 to 200
Mercury	−39	361	250 to 650

Table 1. Heat pipe working fluid properties.

Distilled water is the most appropriate fluid for the heat pipes used for electronic equipment cooling. However, few researchers attempted to improve the thermal performance of the heat pipes by adding metal nanoparticles, which have good thermal conductors, such as silver, iron oxide, and titanium, to the distilled water in which the fluid is known as nanofluids. Some researchers looked into various ways to improve the performance of heat pipe through using different working fluids. Uddin and Feroz [22] experimentally investigated the effect of acetone and ethanol as working fluids on the miniature heat pipe performance. The experiments aimed to draw the heat from the CPU into one end of miniature heat pipes while providing the other end with extended copper fins to dissipate the heat into the air. The results illustrate that acetone had better cooling effect than ethanol. Fadhil and Saleh [23] reported an experimental study of the effect of ethanol and water as working fluids on the thermal performance of the heat pipe. The heat pipe was at the horizontal orientation during the experiments. The range of the heat flux changed within 2.8–13.13 kW/m^2, whereas all other conditions were constant. The results show that the thermal performance of the heat pipe with water as a working fluid was better than that with ethanol.

7. Types of heat pipes

7.1. Cylindrical heat pipe

Cylindrical heat pipe with closed ends is a common and conventional type of heat pipe. It involves circulation of working fluid and a wick to return the liquid. Basically, it consists of three sections, namely evaporator, adiabatic, and condenser, as shown in **Figure 5**.

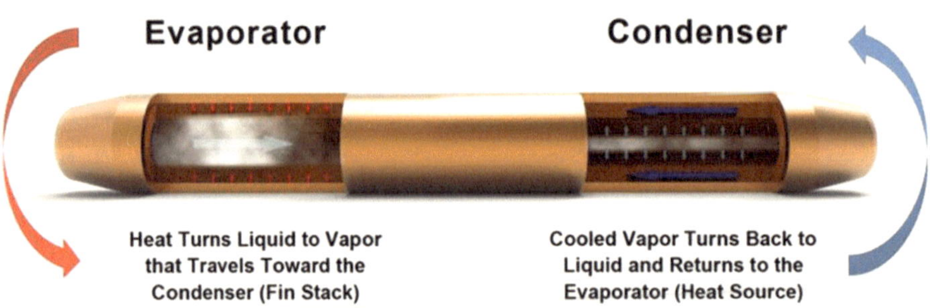

Figure 5. Cylindrical heat pipe [24].

El-Genk and Lianmin [25] reported on the experimental investigation of the transient response of cylindrical copper heat pipe with water as working fluid. The copper heat pipe with copper screen wick consisted of two layers of 150 meshes. Results showed that the temperature of the vapor was uniform along the heat pipe whereas the wall temperature drop was very small (maximum variation less than 5 K) between the evaporator section and the condenser section. The steady-state value of the vapor temperature was increased when the heat input was increased or the cooling water flow rate was decreased. Said and Akash [26] experimentally studied the performance of cylindrical heat pipe using two types of heat pipes with and without wick, and water as the working fluid. They also studied the impact of different inclined angles, such as 30°, 60°, and 90°, with the horizontal on the performance of heat pipe. Results showed that the performance of heat pipe with wick was better than the heat pipe without wick. The overall heat transfer coefficient was the best at the angle of 90°.

7.2. Flat heat pipes

Wang and Vafai [27] presented an experimental investigation on the thermal performance of asymmetric flat plate heat pipe. As shown in **Figure 6**, the flat heat pipe consists of four sections with one evaporation section in the middle and three condenser sections. The heat transfer coefficient and the temperature distribution were obtained. The results indicated that the temperature was uniform along the wall surfaces of the heat pipe, and the porous wick of the evaporator section had significant effect on the thermal resistance. The heat transfer coefficient was also found to be 12.4 W/m^2 °C at the range of input heat flux 425–1780 W/m^2.

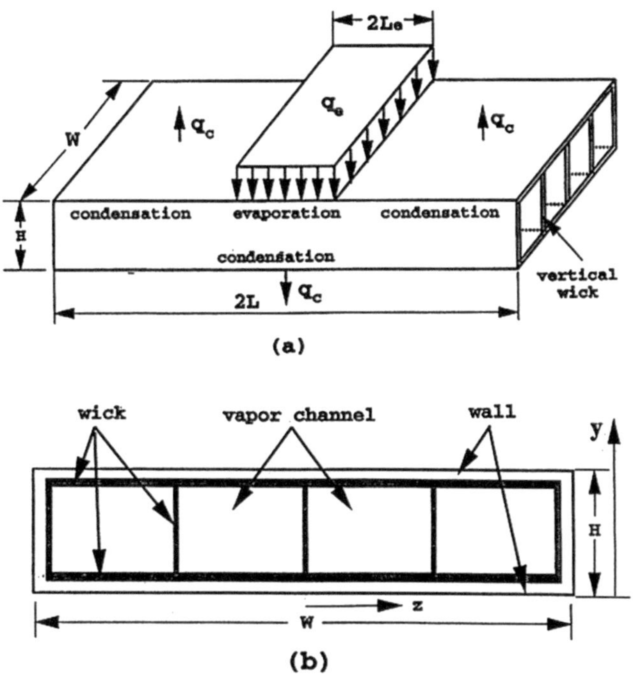

Figure 6. Schematic of the flat plate heat pipe: (a) geometry of the heat pipe and (b) cross-sectional view of the heat pipe [27].

Thermal performance of a flat heat pipe thermal spreader was investigated by Carbajal et al. [28]. They carried out quasi-three-dimensional numerical analysis in order to determine the field variable distributions and the effects of parametric variations in the flat heat pipe system. Investigations showed that flat heat pipe operating as a thermal spreader resulted in more uniform temperature distribution at the condenser side when compared to a solid aluminum plate having similar boundary conditions and heat input.

7.3. Micro-heat pipes

Micro-heat pipes differ from conventional heat pipes in the way that they replace wick structure with the sharp-angled corners, which play an important role in providing capillary pressure for driving the liquid phase. Hung and Seng [29] studied the effects of geometric design on thermal performance of star-groove micro-heat pipes. As shown in **Figure 7**, three different types of cross-sectional shapes of micro-heat pipes such as square star (4 corners), hexagonal star (6 corners), and octagonal star (8 corners) grooves with corner width w, were considered. Accordingly, the corner apex angle 2θ was varied from 20° to 60°. At steady-state mode, one-dimensional mathematical model was developed to yield the heat and fluid flow characteristics of the micro-heat pipe. Results indicated that the geometrical design of the star-groove micro-heat pipes provides a better insight on the effects of various geometrical parameters, such as cross-sectional area, total length, cross-sectional shape, number of corners, and acuteness of the corner apex angle.

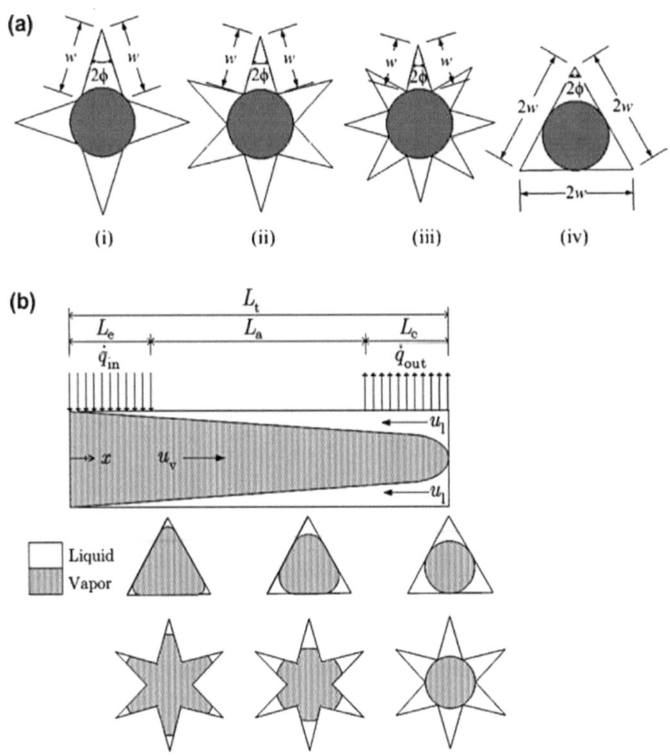

Figure 7. (a) Geometry of different cross-sectional shapes of micro-heat pipe: (i) square star groove, (ii) hexagonal star groove, (iii) octagonal star groove, and (iv) equilateral triangle. (b) Schematic diagram of optimally charged equilateral triangular and star-groove micro-heat pipes [29].

7.4. Oscillating (pulsating) heat pipe

Oscillating (pulsating) heat pipe (OHP) is one of the promising cooling devices in modern application that can transport heat in quick response in any orientation, where the oscillating phenomena offer an enhanced heat transfer mechanism as shown in **Figure 8**. The unique feature of OHPs, compared with conventional heat pipes, is that there is no wick structure to return the condensate to the heating section; thus, there is no countercurrent flow between the liquid and vapor [30]. The fluctuation of pressure waves drives the self-exciting oscillation inside the heat pipe, and the oscillator accelerates end-to-end heat transfer [31]. The pressure change in volume expansion and contraction during phase change initiates and sustains the thermally excited oscillating motion of liquid plugs and vapor bubbles between evaporator and condenser [32], this is because both phases of liquid and vapor flow has the same direction. The thermally driven oscillating flow inside the capillary tube effectively produces some free surfaces that significantly enhance the evaporating and the condensing heat transfer.

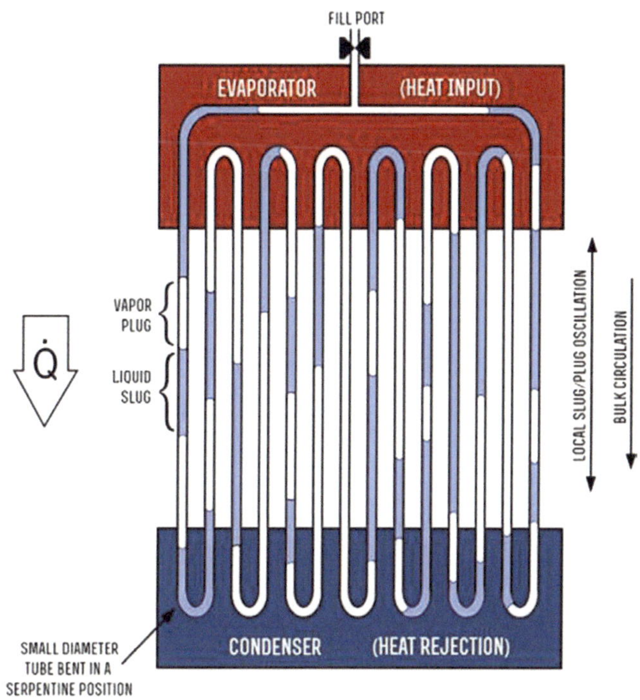

Figure 8. Schematic of an oscillating heat pipe [33].

Although many of researchers have considered the effect of OHP parameters on thermal performance, such as internal diameter, number of turns, filling ratio, and nanofluids, the development of comprehensive design tools for the prediction of OHP performance is still lacking [30]. Moreover, according to Zhang and Faghri [34], the previous theoretical models of OHPs were mainly lumped, one-dimensional, or quasi-one-dimensional, and many unrealistic assumptions were predominantly presented.

8. Mathematical modelling and numerical simulations

Mathematical models of heat pipes are categorized into analytical method and numerical simulations. The analytical method validates the experimental and simulation results, which cannot be measured experimentally, such as pressure and velocity of working fluid inside the heat pipe. Numerical simulation is vital for investigating the thermal behavior of the working fluid inside the heat pipes and predicting the temperature of heat pipe wall, from which the thermal resistance and the amount of heat transmitted by the heat pipes can be calculated. Moreover, characterization of the liquid inside the wick, and predictions of the pressures and velocities of vapor and liquid, enables designing a highly efficient heat pipe for cooling electronic devices.

8.1. Assumptions of the mathematical model

The following assumptions were made for the mathematical formulation:

i. Vapor and liquid flows are assumed to be steady state, two-dimensional, laminar, and incompressible.

ii. The vapor is treated as ideal gas.

iii. There is no heat generation due to phase change and chemical reaction in the system.

iv. At the liquid–vapor interface, the liquid and vapor phases are coupled, and the vapor injection and suction are uniform [34].

v. The physical properties are constant.

8.2. Governing equations

Based on the above assumptions, the continuity, the momentum, and energy equations are listed as follows:

8.2.1. Vapor region

Continuity:

$$\frac{u_v}{x} + \frac{v_v}{y} = 0 \tag{7}$$

where, u and v are components of velocity in x and y directions, respectively.

Momentum:

$$\rho_v\left(u_v\frac{u_v}{x}+v_v\frac{u_v}{y}\right)=\frac{-p}{x}+\mu_v\left(\frac{u_v^2}{x^2}+\frac{u_v^2}{y^2}\right) \tag{8}$$

$$\rho_v\left(u_v\frac{v_v}{x}+v_v\frac{v_v}{y}\right)=\frac{-p}{y}+\rho g+\mu_v\left(\frac{v_v^2}{x^2}+\frac{v_v^2}{y^2}\right) \tag{9}$$

Energy:

$$\rho_v c_p\left(u_v\frac{T}{x}+v_v\frac{T}{y}\right)=k_v\left(\frac{T^2}{x^2}+\frac{T^2}{y^2}\right) \tag{10}$$

where, g is the acceleration of gravity, ρ_v vapor density, μ_v is the effective viscosity of vapor for laminar case is merely the dynamic viscosity, c_p specific heat, and k_v is thermal conductivity of vapor.

8.2.2. Liquid wick region

Continuity:

$$\frac{u_1}{x}+\frac{v_1}{y}=0 \tag{11}$$

where, u and v are components of velocity in x and y directions, respectively.

Momentum:

$$\rho_l\left(u_l\frac{u_l}{x}+v_l\frac{u_l}{y}\right)=\frac{-P_l}{x}+\mu_l\left(\frac{u_1^2}{x^2}+\frac{u_1^2}{y^2}\right)+R_x \tag{12}$$

$$\rho_l\left(u_l\frac{v_l}{x}+v_l\frac{v_l}{y}\right)=\frac{-P_l}{y}+\rho_l g+\mu_l\left(\frac{v_1^2}{x^2}+\frac{v_1^2}{y^2}\right)+R_y \tag{13}$$

R_x and R_y are distributed resistance components in x and y directions, respectively. A distributed resistance is a proper method to estimate the effect of porous media.

Energy:

$$\rho_l c_{p,l}\left(u_l \frac{T_l}{x} + v_l \frac{T_l}{y}\right) = k_e\left(\frac{T_l^2}{x^2} + \frac{T_l^2}{y^2}\right) + Q_v \tag{14}$$

where, g, ρ, μ, C_p, k_e, and Q_v are gravitational acceleration, density, dynamic viscosity, specific heat, effective thermal conductivity for liquid wick structure, and volumetric heat flux, respectively. Subscripts v and l refers to vapor and liquid regions, respectively. k_e is the effective thermal conductivity of the liquid wick structure for sintered powder wick, as expressed by [12]:

$$k_e = \frac{k_l\left[(2k_l + k_w) - 2(1-\varphi)(k_l - k_w)\right]}{(2k_l + k_w) + (1-\varphi)(k_l - k_w)} \tag{15}$$

For screen mesh wick, k_e is calculated from [12]:

$$k_e = \frac{k_l\left[(k_l + k_w) - (1-\varphi)(k_l - k_w)\right]}{(k_l + k_w) + (1-\varphi)(k_l - k_w)} \tag{16}$$

where, φ is porosity and k_l and k_w are thermal conductivity of liquid and wick material, respectively.

The steady-state thermal conductivity equation to predict the wall temperature is as follows:

$$k_s\left(\frac{T_s^2}{x^2} + \frac{T_s^2}{y^2}\right) = 0 \tag{17}$$

where, k_s is solid thermal conductivity and T_s is wall (surface) temperature.

8.3. Boundary conditions

At both ends of the heat pipe, u_v=v_v=u_l =v_l=0, and P_v=P_l.

At the centerline of evaporator section, v_v= 0, $\frac{u_v}{y}$=0, and $\frac{T}{y}$=0.

At the centerline of condenser section, u_v=0, $\frac{v_v}{y}$=0, and $\frac{T}{x}$=0.

At r=R_w, u_l=v_l=0.

At the adiabatic section, $\rho_v v_v$=$\rho_l v_l$=0.

The continuity of mass fluxes in y direction at the vapor–liquid interface yields

$\rho_v v_v$=$\rho_l v_l$=$-\rho_v v_1$

where, v_1 is the vapor injection velocity expressed as [35]:

$$v_1 = \frac{Q_{hp}}{2\rho_v \pi R_v L_e h_{fg}} \tag{18}$$

Similarly, the continuity of mass fluxes in x direction at the vapor–liquid interface yields

$\rho_v u_v = \rho_l u_l = \rho_v u_1$

where, u_1 is the vapor suction velocity as given in the study by Kaya and Goldak [35]:

$$u_1 = \frac{Q_{hp}}{2\rho_v \pi R_v L_c h_{fg}} \tag{19}$$

The interface temperature ($\int_T$) is calculated by the Clausius–Clapeyron equation, assuming the saturation temperature (T_0) and vapor pressure (P_0) at the liquid–vapor interface [36]:

$$\int = \frac{1}{\frac{1}{T_0} - \frac{R}{h_{fg}} ln\left(\frac{P_v}{P_0}\right)} \tag{20}$$

T

For the solid–liquid interface:

At the evaporator part, $K_e \frac{T_l}{y} = k_s \frac{T_s}{y}$

At the condenser part, $K_e \frac{T_l}{x} = k_s \frac{T_s}{x}$

where K_e is the effective thermal conductivity of the liquid wick region, and K_{eff} is the effective thermal conductivity of the whole heat pipe.

$$\text{At the external heat pipe wall} = \left\{ \begin{array}{c} \text{Evaporator}\, k_s \frac{T}{y} = q_e \\ \text{Adiabatic}\, \frac{T}{y} = \frac{0 \wedge T}{x} = 0 \\ \text{Condenser} - k_s \frac{T}{x} = h\left(T_s - T_a\right) \end{array} \right\}$$

where, h is convection heat transfer coefficient, and T_w and T_a are wall surface and ambient temperatures, respectively.

Mistry et al. [37] carried out two-dimensional transient and steady-state numerical analysis to study the characteristics of a cylindrical copper-water wicked (80 mesh SS-304 screen) heat pipe with water as a coolant at a constant heat input. Finite difference and Euler's explicit method (marching scheme) was used to solve the governing equations. As shown in **Figure 9**, a two-dimensional computational study using the concept of a growing thermal layer in the wall and the wick region was carried out. The transient axial temperature distributions were measured, and all the three sections of the heat pipe were compared with the numerical solution of the developed two-dimensional model. The time required to reach steady state was obtained. The transient and steady-state predictions of temperatures from the two-dimensional model were in close agreement with the experimentally obtained temperature profiles.

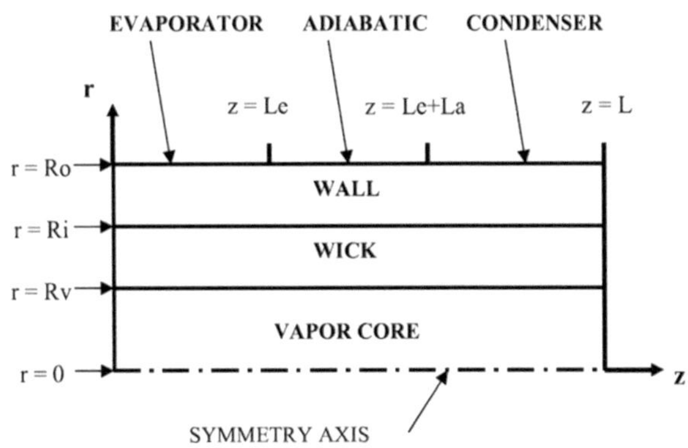

Figure 9. Coordinate system of the heat pipe [38].

Table 2 summarizes and compares some mathematical studies on heat pipes in terms of model, methodology, wick structure, orientation, and types of heat pipes.

Author	Model	Method	Type	Wick structure	Orientation*	Regime**
Mistry et al. [37]	2D	Numerical, finite difference	Micro	Screen mesh	H	T, SS
Maziuk et al. [38]	1D, 2D	Analytical, software development	Flat miniature	Copper sintered powder	I	SS
Suman et al. [39]	1D	Analytical	Micro	Grooved	H	T
Zhu and Vafai [34]	2D	Analytical	Cylindrical	Porous media	H	SS
Noh and Song [40]	2D	Numerical, finite volume	Cylindrical	Screen mesh	H	T
Mahjoub and Mahtabroshan [41]	2D	Numerical, finite volume	Cylindrical	Porous media	H	SS
Kaya and Goldak [36]	3D	Numerical, finite element method	Cylindrical	Screen mesh	H	SS
Ranjan et al. [42]	3D	Numerical, macro model**	Flat	Sintered, screen mesh	H	T

*H, horizontal orientation; I, inclined orientation; **SS, steady state; and T, transient.

Table 2. An overview of some mathematical studies on heat pipes.

http://dx.doi.org/10.5772/62279

As shown in **Table 2**, the three-dimensional model received a little attention compared to the two-dimensional model. Additionally, most of the studies addressed horizontal heat pipes that cover both transient and steady-state cases.

9. Heat pipe for computer cooling applications (desktop and notebook)

Due to the high effective thermal conductivity of heat pipes compared to that of traditional heat sinks, heat pipes have been proposed and selected for electronic cooling. Therefore, the heat pipe transfers and dissipates the heat very fast. Many researchers focused their studies on using the heat pipe for cooling of electronic devices, and all of them proved that the heat pipe is the best tool for cooling the electronic devices such as desktop and notebook computers. Cooling fins equipped with heat pipes for high power and high temperature electronic circuits and devices were simulated by Legierski and Wiecek [43], and the superiority of the proposed system over the traditional devices was demonstrated. Kim et al. [44] developed a cooling module in the form of remote heat exchanger using heat pipe for Pentium-IV CPU as a means to ensure enhanced cooling and reduced noise level compared to the fan-assisted ordinary heat sinks. Saengchandr and Afzulpurkar [45] proposed a system that combines the advantages of heat pipes and thermoelectric modules for desktop PCs. As shown in **Figure 10**, the usage of the heat pipes with heat sink could enhance the thermal performance [46].

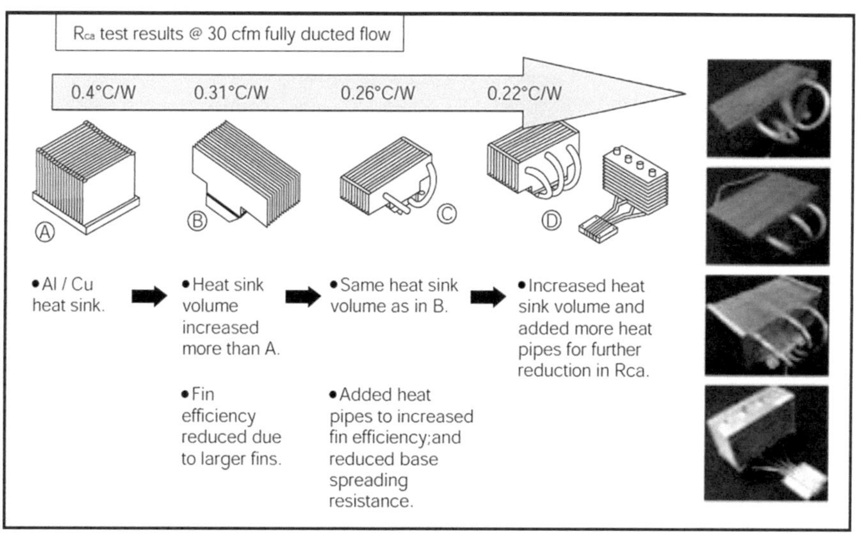

Figure 10. Heat pipe heat sink solution for cooling desktop PCs [47].

Yu and Harvey [47] designed a precision-engineered heat pipe for cooling Pentium II in Compact PCI. In this work, the design criteria, such as the maximum temperature, thermal transfer plate with a heat load, the maximum ambient air temperature, and the total thermal resistance of the solution, were considered for the processor module. It was observed that both thermal and mechanical management of the system was improved using the heat pipe. Kim et al. [44] presented the heat pipe cooling technology for CPU of desktop PC. They had developed a cooler using heat pipe with heat sink to decrease the noise of the fan. Results showed that the usage of heat pipe for desktop PC CPU cooling would increase the dissipated heat without the need for high speed fan. Thus, the problem of the noise generated by the traditional heat sink cooling was solved. Additionally, Closed-end Oscillating Heat pipe (CEOHP) used for CPU cooling of desktop PC was presented by Rittidech and Boonyaem [48]. As shown in **Figure 11**, the CEOHP kit is divided into two parts, i.e., the evaporator is 0.05 m long and a condenser section is 0.16 m long with and a vertical orientation. They selected R134a as the working fluid with filling ratio of 50%. The CEOHP kit should transfer at least 70 W of heat power to work properly. The CPU chip with a power of 58 W was 70°C. The results indicate that the cooling performance increases when the fan speed increases, where the fan speed of 2000 and 4000 rpm were employed. The thermal performance using CEOHP cooling module was better than using conventional heat sink.

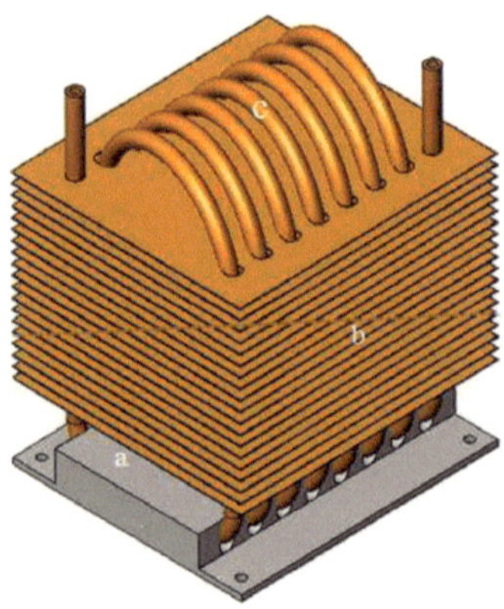

Figure 11. Prototype: (a) aluminum base plate, (b) copper fin, (c) CEOHP. [49].

Recently, heat sinks with finned U-shape heat pipes have been introduced for cooling the high-frequency microprocessors such as Intel Core 2 Duo, Intel Core 2 Quad, AMD Phenom series, and AMD Athlon 64 series, as reported by Wang et al. [49], Wang [50], and Liang and Hung [51]. Wang et al. [49] experimented on the horizontal twin heat pipe with heat sink. The heat input was transferred from CPU to the base plate and from the base plate to the heat pipes and heat sinks simultaneously. The heat was dissipated from fins to the surrounding by forced convection. As shown in **Figure 12**, experiments were conducted in two stages, in which the first stage measured the temperature for heat pipes only to calculate its thermal resistance. The second stage aimed to measure the temperature for heat sink without and with heat pipes in order to calculate their thermal resistances. It was observed that 64% of the total dissipated heat was transported from CPU to the base plate and then to fins, whereas 36% was transferred from heat pipes to fins. The lowest value of the total thermal resistance for the heat pipes with heat sink was 0.27°C/W.

http://dx.doi.org/10.5772/62279

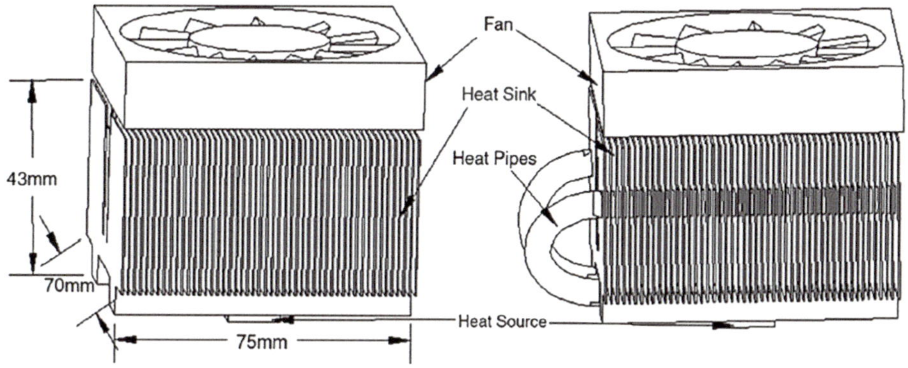

Figure 12. Heat sink without and with embedded heat pipes [50].

The investigations by Elnaggar et al. [52] on the experimental and finite element (FE) simulations of vertically oriented finned U-shape multi-heat pipes for desktop computer cooling are shown in **Figure 13a**. The total thermal resistance was found to decrease with the increase in heat input and coolant velocity. Moreover, the vertical mounting demonstrated enhanced thermal performance compared with the horizontal arrangement. The lowest total thermal resistance achieved was 0.181°C/W with heat load of 24 W and coolant velocity of 3 m/s. This study was further pursued by Elnaggar et al. [53] to determine the optimum heat input and the cooling air velocity for vertical twin U-shape heat pipe with the objective of maximizing the effective thermal conductivity as shown in **Figure 13b**.

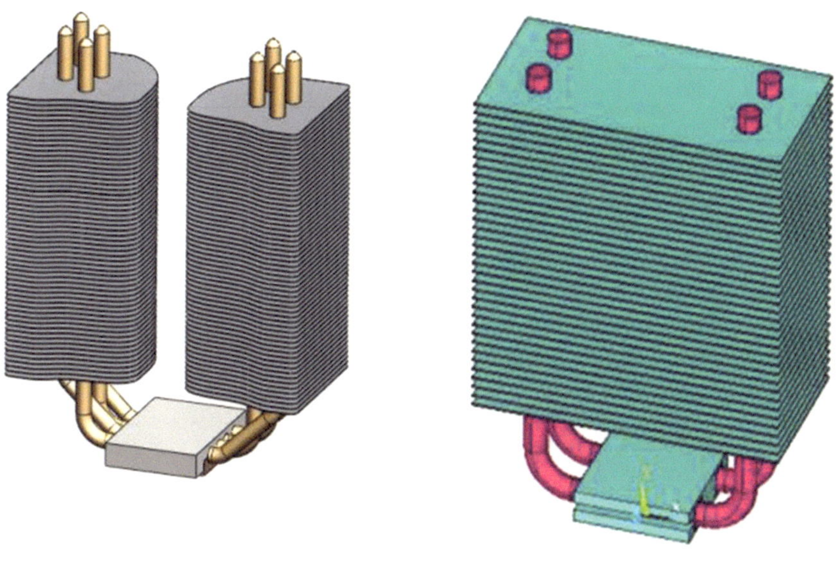

Figure 13. Finned U-shape heat pipe for desktop computer cooling [53, 54]. (a) Finned U-shape multi-heat pipe [53]. (b) Finned U-shape twin heat pipe [54].

A summary of studies on heat pipe with heat sink for CPU PC cooling are listed in **Table 3**.

Author	Orientation	Heat pipe shape	No. of heat pipe	Total thermal resistance
Kim et al. [44]	Horizontal	L-shape	3	0.475°C/W
Wang et al. [49]	Horizontal	U-shape	2	0.27°C/W
Wang [50]	Horizontal	U-shape	2 and 4	0.24°C /W
Liang and Hung [51]	Horizontal	U-shape	1	0.5°C/W
Wang [54]	Vertical	L-shape	6	0.22°C/W
Elnaggar et al. [52]	Vertical	U-shape	4	0.181°C/W
Elnaggar et al. [53]	Vertical	U-shape	2	0.2°C/W

Table 3. A summary of studies on heat pipe with heat sink for CPU PC cooling.

The following conclusions can be derived from the summary of heat pipe with heat sink used in CPU PC cooling:

- The performance of heat sink with heat pipes is much more efficient compared to heat sink without heat pipes.
- Orientation of heat pipe plays a vital role in which the vertical mounting could enhance the heat pipe performance compared to the horizontal arrangement.
- Multi heat pipe leads to a remarkable decrease in thermal resistance, the matter which improves heat pipe efficiency

Figure 14. Laptop's cooling using a heat pipe with heat sink [56].

The processor's surface in notebook or laptop computers, where most heat is generated, is usually small approximately 10 mm×10 mm. For useful cooling, the heat must spread over a larger surface area away from the processor, as the space available near the processor is limited as shown in **Figure 14**. Therefore, heat must be drawn from the processor and conveyed to a place from where it can be dissipated by conventional means. This task is successfully achieved by a heat pipe as it can be accommodated in a highly constrained space in such a way that its evaporator section communicates with the heat source while the finned condenser section is exposed to the sink [55].

10. Conclusion

In this chapter, we presented a TDP for cooling the CPU, cooling methods of electronic equipments, heat pipe theory and operation, heat pipes components, such as the wall material, the wick structure, and the working fluid. Moreover, we reviewed experimentally, analytically and numerically the types of heat pipes with their applications for electronic cooling in general and the computer cooling in particular. Clearly, the heat pipe can be regarded as a promising way for cooling electronic equipments. Due to its simplicity, it can work in any orientation and can transfer heat from a place where there is no opportunity and possibility to accommodate a conventional fan, such as notebooks or laptops. Finally, we believe this work would definitely open ways for further research in accordance with the growing attention for the use of heat pipes in electronic cooling.

Author details

Mohamed H.A. Elnaggar* and Ezzaldeen Edwan

*Address all correspondence to: mohdhn@yahoo.com

Palestine Technical College, Deir EL-Balah, Gaza Strip, Palestine

References

[1] Ma SP, Park KM, Joung W, Lee J. Operating Characteristics of a Loop Heat Pipe with a Novel Flat Evaporator. 10th International Heat Pipe Symposium. 2011.

[2] Mahajan R, Chia-pin C, Chrysler G. Cooling a microprocessor chip. Proceedings of the IEEE. 2006; 94(8): 1476–1486.

[3] Intel® Core™ i5-3400 Desktop Processor Series. [Available from: http://ark.intel.com/products/series/64902].

[4] Smith M. What Is Thermal Design Power? [Available from: http://www.makeuseof.com/tag/thermal-design-power-technology-explained/]. 2011.

[5] Ledezma G, Bejan A. Heat sinks with sloped plate fins in natural and forced convection. International Journal of Heat and Mass Transfer. 1996; 39(9): 1773–1783.

[6] Suzuki M, Hirano M. Fan-less Cooling Technology for Notebook Computers. Fujitsu Scientific & Technical Journal. 1998; 34(1): 87–95.

[7] Ismail MA, Abdullah MZ, Mujeebu MA. A CFD-based experimental analysis on the effect of free stream cooling on the performance of micro processor heat sinks. International Communications in Heat and Mass Transfer. 2008; 35(6): 771–778.

[8] Webb RL. Next Generation devices for electronic cooling with heat rejection to air. Journal of Heat Transfer. 2005; 127(1): 2–10.

[9] Chang Y-W, Cheng C-H, Wang J-C, Chen S-L. Heat pipe for cooling of electronic equipment. Energy Conversion and Management. 2008; 49(11): 3398–3404.

[10] Scott D, Garner PE. Heat Pipes for Electronics Cooling Applications. Electronics Cooling Magazine, Thermacore Inc. 1996.

[11] Kreith F, Bohn MS. Principles of Heat Transfer. Sixth edn. Pacific Grove, CA: Brooks/Cole. 2001.

[12] Peterson GP. An Introduction to Heat Pipes: Modeling, Testing, and Applications. New York: John Wiley & Sons, Inc. 1994.

[13] Nemec P, Čaja A, Malcho M. Mathematical model for heat transfer limitations of heat pipe. Mathematical and Computer Modelling. 2013 Jan 31;57(1):126-136.

[14] Yeh L-T, Chu RC. Thermal Management of Microelectronic Equipment: Heat Transfer Theory, Analysis Methods, and Design Practices. New York: ASME Press. 2002.

[15] Heat Pipe Wick Structures Exposed: Sintered, Groove and Mesh. [Available from: http://www.frostytech.com/articleview.cfm?articleID=2466] 2009.

[16] Leong KC, Liu CY, Lu GQ. Characterization of sintered copper wicks used in heat pipes. Journal of Porous Materials. 1997; 4(4): 303–308.

[17] Zhang Y, Faghri A. Numerical simulation of condensation on a capillary grooved structure. Numerical Heat Transfer, Part A: Applications. 2001; 39(3): 227–243.

[18] Ahamed MS, Mochizuki M, Mashiko K, Saito Y, Mabuchi T, Horiuchi Y. Experimental Study of Thin Flat Heat Pipe with a Special Fiber Wick Structure. 9th International Heat Pipe Symposium. 2008.

[19] Wong S-C, Kao Y-H. Visualization and performance measurement of operating mesh-wicked heat pipes. International Journal of Heat and Mass Transfer. 2008; 51(17–18): 4249–4259.

[20] Liou J-H, Chang C-W, Chao C, Wong S-C. Visualization and thermal resistance measurement for the sintered mesh-wick evaporator in operating flat-plate heat pipes. International Journal of Heat and Mass Transfer. 2010; 53(7–8): 1498–1506.

[21] Dunn PD, Reay DA. Heat Pipes. fourth Oxford, UK: Pergamon Press. 1982.

[22] Uddin A, Feroz C. Effect of working fluid on the performance of a miniature heat pipe system for cooling desktop processor. Heat and Mass Transfer. 2009; 46(1): 113–118.

[23] Fadhil OT, Saleh AM. Thermal performance of a heat pipe with sintered powder metal wick using ethanol and water as working fluids. Anbar Journal for Engineering Sciences. 2011; 4(1): 62–71.

[24] Blog C. Heat Pipes and Vapor Chambers – What's the Difference? [Available from:http://celsiainc.com/blog-heat-pipes-and-vapor-chambers-whats-the-difference/].

[25] El-Genk MS, Lianmin H. An experimental investigation of the transient response of a water heat pipe. International Journal of Heat and Mass Transfer. 1993; 36(15): 3823–3830.

[26] Said SA, Akash BA. Experimental performance of a heat pipe. International Communications in Heat and Mass Transfer. 1999; 26(5): 679–684.

[27] Wang Y, Vafai K. An experimental investigation of the thermal performance of an asymmetrical flat plate heat pipe. International Journal of Heat and Mass Transfer. 2000; 43(15): 2657–2668.

[28] Carbajal G, Sobhan CB, "Bud" Peterson GP, Queheillalt DT, Wadley HNG. A quasi-3D analysis of the thermal performance of a flat heat pipe. International Journal of Heat and Mass Transfer. 2007; 50(21–22): 4286–4296.

[29] Hung YM, Seng Qb. Effects of geometric design on thermal performance of star-groove micro-heat pipes. International Journal of Heat and Mass Transfer. 2011; 54(5–6): 1198–1209.

[30] Zhang Y, Faghri A. Advances and unsolved issues in pulsating heat pipes. Heat Transfer Engineering. 2008; 29(1): 20–44.

[31] Nine MJ, Tanshen MR, Munkhbayar B, Chung H, Jeong H. Analysis of pressure fluctuations to evaluate thermal performance of oscillating heat pipe. Energy. 2014; 70(0): 135–142.

[32] Charoensawan P, Khandekar S, Groll M, Terdtoon P. Closed loop pulsating heat pipes: Part A: parametric experimental investigations. Applied Thermal Engineering. 2003; 23(16): 2009–2020.

[33] Laun FF, Taft BS . Experimental investigation of in situ pressure measurement of an oscillating heat pipe. Frontiers in Heat Pipes. 2014; 5(8): 1–5.

[34] Zhu N, Vafai K. Analysis of cylindrical heat pipes incorporating the effects of liquid-vapor coupling and non-Darcian transport--a closed form solution. International Journal of Heat and Mass Transfer. 1999; 42(18): 3405–3418.

[35] Nouri-Borujerdi A, Layeghi M. A Numerical analysis of vapor flow in concentric annular heat pipes. Journal of Fluids Engineering. 2004; 126(3): 442–448.

[36] Kaya T, Goldak J. Three-dimensional numerical analysis of heat and mass transfer in heat pipes. Heat and Mass Transfer. 2007; 43(8): 775–785.

[37] Mistry PR, Thakkar FM, De S, DasGupta S. Experimental validation of a two-dimensional model of the transient and steady-state characteristics of a wicked heat pipe. Experimental Heat Transfer. 2010; 23(4): 333–348.

[38] Maziuk V, Kulakov A, Rabetsky M, Vasiliev L, Vukovic M. Miniature heat-pipe thermal performance prediction tool – software development. Applied Thermal Engineering. 2001; 21(5): 559–571.

[39] Suman B, De S, DasGupta S. Transient modeling of micro-grooved heat pipe. International Journal of Heat and Mass Transfer. 2005; 48(8): 1633-1646.

[40] Noh H-K, Song K-S. Temperature distribution of a low temperature heat pipe with multiple heaters for electronic cooling. ETRI Journal. 1998; 20(4): 380–394.

[41] Mahjoub S, Mahtabroshan A. Numerical Simiulation of a Conventional Heat Pipe. Proceedings of World Academy of Science, Engineering and Technology. 2008; 29: 117–122.

[42] Ranjan R, Murthy JY, Garimella SV, Vadakkan U. A numerical model for transport in flat heat pipes considering wick microstructure effects. International Journal of Heat and Mass Transfer. 2011; 54(1–3): 153–168.

[43] Legierski J, Wiecek B. Steady state analysis of cooling electronic circuits using heat pipes. IEEE Transactions on Components and Packaging Technologies. 2001; 24(4): 549–553.

[44] Kim K-S, Won M-H, Kim J-W, Back B-J. Heat pipe cooling technology for desktop PC CPU. Applied Thermal Engineering. 2003; 23(9): 1137–1144.

[45] Saengchandr B, Afzulpurkar NV. A novel approach for cooling electronics using a combined heat pipe and thermoelectric module. American Journal of Engineering and Applied Sciences. 2009; 2(4): 603–610.

[46] Mochizuki M, Saito Y, Kiyooka F, Nguyen T. The Way We Were and Are Going on Cooling High Power Processors in the Industries. 17th International Symposium on Transport Phenomena. 2006.

[47] Yu ZZ, Harvey T. The precision-engineered heat pipe for cooling Pentium II in CompactPCI design. Thermal and Thermomechanical Phenomena in Electronic

Systems, 2000. ITHERM 2000. The Seventh Intersociety Conference on. 2000; 2: 102–105 vol. 102.

[48] Rittidech S, Boonyaem A, P.Tipnet. CPU cooling of desktop PC by Closed-end Oscillating Heat-pipe (CEOHP). American Journal of Applied Sciences 2005; 2(12): 1574–1577.

[49] Wang JC, Huang H-S, Chen S-L. Experimental investigations of thermal resistance of a heat sink with horizontal embedded heat pipes. International Communications in Heat and Mass Transfer. 2007; 34(8): 958–970.

[50] Wang JC. Novel thermal resistance network analysis of heat sink with embedded heat pipes. Jordan Journal of Mechanical and Industrial Engineering. 2008; 2(1): 23–30.

[51] Liang TS, Hung YM. Experimental investigation on the thermal performance and optimization of heat sink with U-shape heat pipes. Energy Conversion and Management. 2010; 51(11): 2109–2116.

[52] Elnaggar MHA, Abdullah MZ, AbdulMujeebu M. Experimental analysis and FEM simulation of finned U-shape multi heat pipe for desktop PC cooling. Energy Conversion and Management. 2011; 52(8–9): 2937–2944.

[53] Elnaggar MHA, Abdullah MZ, Mujeebu MA. Experimental investigation and optimization of heat input and coolant velocity of finned twin U-shaped heat pipe for CPU cooling. Experimental Techniques. 2011: In press.

[54] Wang JC. L-type heat pipes application in electronic cooling system. International Journal of Thermal Sciences. 2011; 50(1): 97–105.

[55] Elnaggar MH, Abdullah MZ, Munusamy SR. Experimental and Numerical Studies of Finned L-Shape Heat Pipe for Notebook-PC Cooling. Components, Packaging and Manufacturing Technology, IEEE Transactions on. 2013 Jun;3(6):978-88.

[56] Wyatt G. Why eTray laptop trays don't have fans. [Available from: http://www.etray.co.uk/etraynews/index.php/why-etrays-dont-have-fans]. 2011.

Chapter 5

MEMS-Based Micro-heat Pipes

Qu Jian and Wang Qian

Additional information is available at the end of the chapter

http://dx.doi.org/10.5772/62786

Abstract

Micro-electro-mechanical systems (MEMS)-based micro-heat pipes, as a novel heat pipe technology, is considered as one of the most promising options for thermal control applications in microelectronic circuits packaging, concentrated solar cells, infrared detectors, micro-fuel cells, etc. The operating principles, heat transfer characteristics, and fabrication process of MEMS-based micro-grooved heat pipes are firstly introduced and the state-of-the-art of research both experimental and theoretical is thoroughly reviewed. Then, other emerging MEMS-based micro-heat pipes, such as micro-capillary pumped loop, micro-loop heat pipe, micro-oscillating heat pipe, and micro-vapor chamber are briefly reviewed as well. Finally, some promising and innovatory applications of the MEMS-based micro-heat pipes are reported. This chapter is expected to provide basic reference for future researches.

Keywords: micro-heat pipe, thermal control, capillary limitation, micro-cooler, MEMS

1. Introduction

Nowadays, the thermal management of electronics/optoelectronics remains to be a great challenge due to the continuous increasing heat flux to be dissipated with diminishing space associated with rapid advances in the microelectronic fabrication and packaging technology. Generally, the thermal control at the system level is not a serious problem since adequate conventional cooling schemes are available [1]. Cooling at the chip level that maintains both chip maximum temperature and temperature gradient at acceptable levels are in great demands. Many efforts have been made in the past two decades to develop novel micro-cooling technologies capable of removing larger amount of heat from chips [2–5], among which micro-heat pipes (MHPs) are considered as one of the most promising solutions.

MHPs, envisioned very small heat transfer components incorporated as an integral part of semiconductor devices as illustrated in **Figure 1**, have attracted considerable attention since they were first introduced by Cotter [6]. A MHP is also referred to micro-grooved heat pipe as depicted by Suman [7] and essentially has convex but cusped cross sections with dimension characteristics subject to the criterion given by Babin et al. [8]

$$\frac{r_c}{r_h} \geq 1 \tag{1}$$

where r_c and r_h are the capillary and hydraulic radius, respectively. Accordingly, the hydraulic radius of the total flow passage in a MHP is comparable in magnitude to the capillary radius of the vapor–liquid interface. This dimensionless expression better defines a MHP and helps to differentiate between small versions of conventional heat pipes and a veritable MHP. Typically, the cross-sectional dimensions of MHPs are in the range of 10–500 μm and lengths of up to several centimeters [9]. A MHP is so small that it does not necessitate additional wicking structures on the inner wall as used by conventional heat pipes to assist the return of condensate to the evaporator. Instead, the capillary forces are largely generated in the sharp edges of diverse small noncircular channel cross sections as illustrated in **Figure 2**, which serve as liquid arteries. The maximum heat flux dissipated using these micro-devices are reported to be as high as 60 W/cm^2 [11].

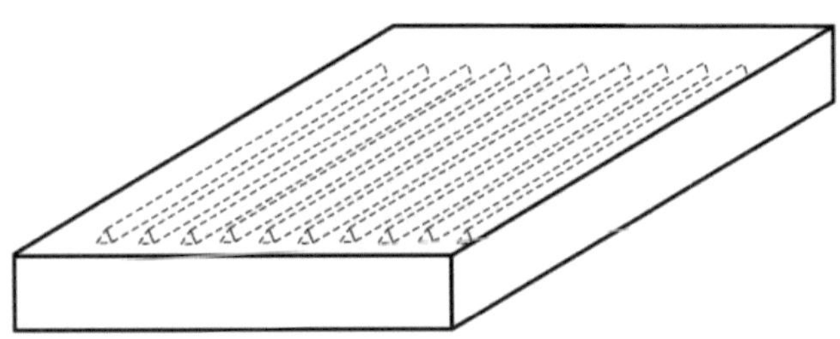

Figure 1. Micro-heat pipe array in silicon wafer.

Actually, MHPs are suitable for the direct heat removal from semiconductor devices because they could be fabricated and integrated into them, as envisioned by Cotter [6], on the basis of micro-electro-mechanical systems (MEMS) technology and work as thermal spreaders [12]. The advantages of MEMS-based MHPs mainly includes as follows: (1) It allows for precise temperature control at the chip level; (2) the overall cooling is more efficient because specific heat sources within the electronics package may be targeted and reduce the contact thermal resistance; (3) the overall size of the electronic system can be kept small and achieve material compatibility; and (4) easy to large scale replication and mass production. Due to the compact size, high local heat removal rates and can be used to effectively lower chip maximum temperature and attain temperature uniformity, MEMS-based MHPs could be considered as a promising option to meet future chip-level cooling demands.

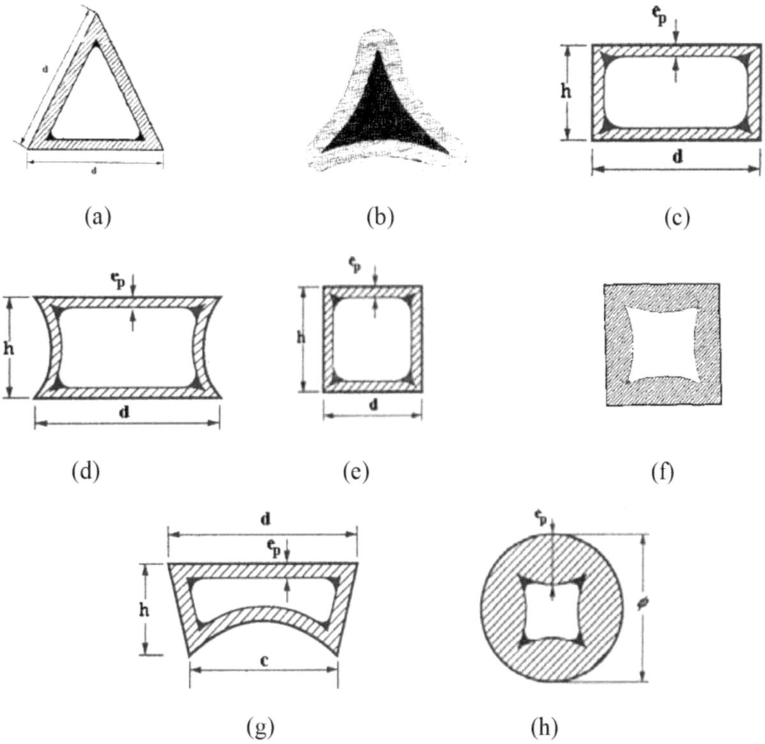

Figure 2. Cross-sections of individual micro-grooved heat pipes: (a, b) triangular section; (c, d) rectangular section; (e, f) square section; (g) trapezoidal section; (h) circular section [10].

For all practical situations, MHP is a general name for heat pipes with micro-wicks and mini-/micro-tubes in many references, and a heat pipe that satisfies the Bond number ($Bo = (\rho_l - \rho_g) g r_h^2 / \sigma$) to be on the order of 1 or less or capillary action dominates gravity can be termed as MHPs [7, 13]. The published reviews of MHPs were largely related to micro-grooved heat pipes [14–16], and there is no comprehensive introduction on MEMS-based MHPs. Moreover, the concept of MEMS-based MHPs, in this chapter, are not simply limited to micro-grooved heat pipes etched on silicon wafers but also other novel types that fabricated through MEMS technology. The overall size of a MEMS-based heat pipe device should be comparable to that of an electronic chip, regardless of having wicking structures or not.

In this chapter, we present a review on the MEMS-based MHPs that begin with a brief introduction of micro-grooved heat pipes, including working principles, heat transport limitations, and fabrication approach. The following section focuses on the state-of-the-art of research on MEMS-based micro-grooved heat pipes both experimentally and numerically, and then advances made in some other emerging MEMS-based MHPs. Meanwhile, some promising and potential applications of MEMS-based MHPs are also reported. It is expected to provide a basis for MEMS-based MHP design, performance improvement, and further expansion in its applications.

2. Micro-grooved heat pipe

2.1. Fundamental operating principles

The fundamental operating principles of micro-grooved heat pipes are essentially the same as those occurring in conventional heat pipes and can be easily understood by using a triangular cross section MHP as illustrated in **Figure 3**. Heat applied to one end of the MHP, called evaporator, vaporizes the liquid in that region and pushes the vapor toward the cold end, called condenser, where it condenses and gives up the latent heat of vaporization. In between the evaporator and the condenser is a heat transport section, called the adiabatic section, which may be omitted in some cases. MHPs do not contain any wicking structures, but consist of small non-circular channels and the role of wicks in conventional heat pipes gives way to the sharp-angled corner regions, serving as liquid arteries. The vaporization and condensation processes cause the curvature of liquid–vapor interface (see **Figure 3**) in the corner regions to change continually along the passage and result in a capillary pressure difference between the hot and cold ends. The capillary force generated from the corner regions pump the liquid back to the evaporator and the circulation of working fluid inside the MHP accompanied by phase change is then established [17, 18].

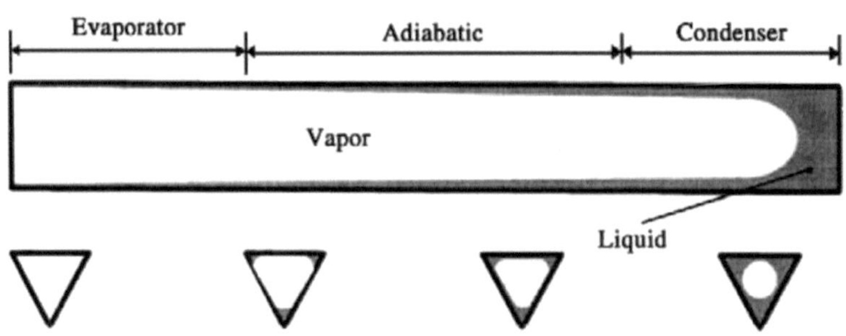

Figure 3. Schematic diagram of a micro-heat pipe with triangular cross-section.

2.2. Heat transport limitations

The operation and performance of heat pipes are dependent on many factors such as the tube size, shape, working fluid, and wicking structure. The maximum heat transport capability of a heat pipe operating at steady state is governed by a number of limiting factors, including the capillary, sonic, entrainment, and boiling limitations [18]. Theoretical and fundamental phenomena that cause each of these heat pipe limitations have been the subject of a number of investigations for conventional heat pipes. The representative work was given and discussed by many authors [19], while only a limited number concern the operating limitations in a MHP [20]. The experimental investigation by Kim and Peterson [21] revealed that the capillary limitation occurred before entrainment and boiling limitations. When the heat input is larger than a maximum allowable heat load, capillary limitation occurs and becomes the most commonly encountered limitation to the performance of a MHP [22, 23], which causes the dry-out of the evaporator and degrades the thermal performance significantly. As a result, the capillary limitation is the primary concern of MHP design and operation according to its working principles. It can be concluded from the operating principles that the primary mechanism by which MHPs operates result from the difference in the capillary pressure across the liquid–vapor interfaces in the evaporator and condenser sections. For proper operation, the capillary pressure difference should be greater than the sum of all the pressure losses throughout the liquid and vapor flow passages. The gravity force is usually not taken into account in two-phase micro-devices compared to surface tension, and thus, the hydrostatic pressure drop can be neglected [24]. Hence, the relationship can be expressed mathematically as follows

$$\Delta p_{\mathrm{c}} \geq \Delta p_{\mathrm{l}} + \Delta p_{\mathrm{v}} \tag{2}$$

where Δp_{c} is the net capillary difference, Δp_{l} and Δp_{v} are the viscous pressure drops in the liquid phase and vapor phase, respectively.

The left-hand side in Eq. (2) at a liquid–vapor interface can be estimated from Laplace-Young equation, and for most MHP applications it can be reduced to:

$$\Delta p_{\mathrm{c}} = \sigma\left(\frac{1}{r_{\mathrm{ce}}} - \frac{1}{r_{\mathrm{cc}}}\right) \tag{3}$$

where r_{ce} and r_{cc} represent the minimum meniscus radius appearing in the evaporator and maximum meniscus radius in the condenser, respectively. Both values depend on the shape of the corner region and the amount of liquid charged to the heat pipe.

For steady-state operation with constant heat addition and removal, the viscous pressure drop occurring in liquid phase is determined by

$$\Delta p_{\mathrm{l}} = \left(\frac{\mu_{\mathrm{l}}}{K A_{\mathrm{l}} h_{\mathrm{fg}} \rho_{\mathrm{l}}}\right) L_{\mathrm{eff}} q \tag{4}$$

where L_{eff} is the effective heat pipe length defined as:

$$L_{\mathrm{eff}} = 0.5(L_{\mathrm{e}} + L_{\mathrm{c}}) + L_{\mathrm{a}} \tag{5}$$

The viscous vapor pressure drop can be calculated similarly to the liquid vapor drop but is more complicated due to the mass addition and removal in the evaporator and condenser, respectively, as well as the compressibility of the vapor phase. Consequently, the dynamic pressure should be included for a more accurate computation and thus elaborately analyzed by several researchers [17]. The resulting expression, for practical values of Reynolds number and Mach number, is similar to the liquid pressure drop and can be expressed as follows:

$$\Delta p_{\mathrm{v}} = \left(\frac{C(f\,\mathrm{Re})_{\mathrm{v}}\,\mu_{\mathrm{v}}}{2r_{\mathrm{h,v}}^{2} A_{\mathrm{v}}\, h_{\mathrm{fg}}\, \rho_{\mathrm{v}}} \right) L_{\mathrm{eff}}\, q \tag{6}$$

where $r_{\mathrm{h,v}}$ is the hydraulic radius of the vapor space and C is a constant that depends on the Mach number [12, 25].

2.3. Fabrication process of MEMS-based micro-grooved heat pipes

In 1991, Peterson et al. [26] initialized the concept of using micro-grooved heat pipes as an integral part of the semiconductor devices. Normally, MEMS-based MHPs with hydraulic diameters on the order of 50–300 μm are directly etched into silicon wafers, and the directionally dependent wet etching or deep reactive ion etching (DRIE) processes are commercially available and widely utilized to create a series of parallel micro-grooves which shape the microdevices [27–30]. The wet chemical etching process could create trapezoidal or triangular grooves, allowing etching of silicon wafers in one particular direction at a higher rate as compared to other directions, while DRIE process that uses physical plasma tool generates rectangular grooves. Once the micro-grooves are etched into the silicon wafer, a Pyrex 7740 glass cover plate is often bonded to the surface to form the closed channels based on anodic bonding technique for the visualization of two-phase flow in MHPs.

The lithographic masking techniques, coupled with an orientation-dependent etching technique, are typically utilized and Peterson [17] has summarized this processes. **Figure 4** gives an example of six major fabrication process with respect to a MEMS-based MHP having trapezoidal cross sections, including photolithography, wet etching, and anodic bonding. After standard clean and drying, a two-side polished (100) silicon wafer is thermally dry oxidized to form a layer of SiO_2, which is used as a hard mask for anisotropic wet etching as illustrated below. Firstly, one side of the silicon wafer is spun coated with a photoresist (PR) (**Figure 4a**). The patterned transfer from a mask onto the wafer is established via exposure and development (**Figure 4b**). Subsequently, buffered oxide etch (BOE) solutions are used to strip off the exposed SiO_2 (**Figure 4c**), and the remanent PR is removed by a cleaning step (**Figure 4d**). Then, some micro-grooves with trapezoidal cross sections are created by wet etching (**Figure 4e**). For flow visualization, a Pyrex 7740 glass is finally bonded with the silicon wafer after removing the SiO_2 layer using HF solution (**Figure 4f**). Before silicon-to-glass bonding, the laser drill technology is employed to create the inlet/outlet holes for evacuating and charging. After the completion of the MEMS fabrication process, the wafer is sliced into individual dice.

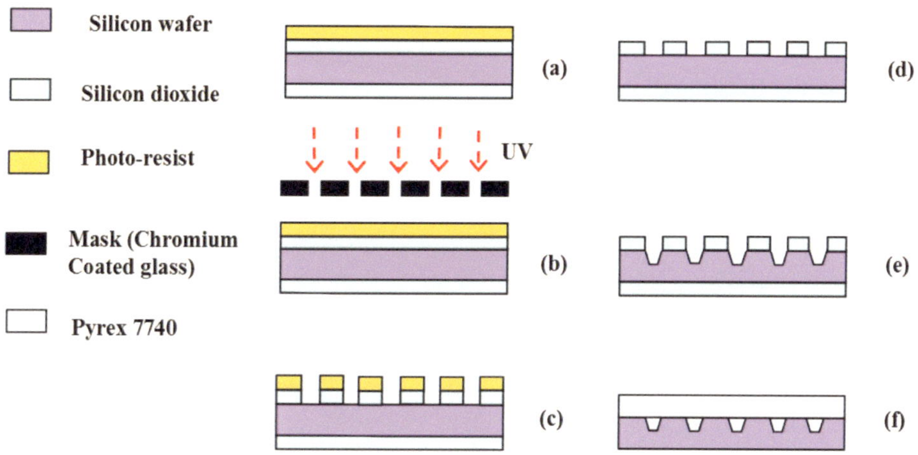

Figure 4. Fabrication processes of a MEMS-based MHP: (a) spin coating photoresist, (b) UV exposure, (c) BOE etching (d) wet etching, (e) HF etching silicon layer, and (f) silicon-to-glass anodic bonding.

In addition to the orientation-dependent etching processes, a more elaborate technique was developed that utilizes the multi-source vapor deposition process [31, 32] to create an array of long, narrow channels of triangular cross-section lined with a thin layer of copper. This process begins with the fabrication of a series of square or rectangular grooves in a silicon wafer. Then, the grooves are closed using a dual E-beam vapor deposition process, creating an array of long narrow channels of triangular cross section with two open ends. **Figure 5** gives a SEM image of the end view of a vapor deposited MHP which has not quite been completely closed at the top. Clearly, the MHPs are lined with a thin layer of copper, and thus the migration of the working fluid throughout the semiconductor material could be significantly reduced.

Figure 5. A vapor-deposited micro-grooved heat pipe [17].

3. State-of-the-art of research on MEMS-based micro-grooved heat pipes

3.1. Experimental investigation

The original conception of micro-grooved heat pipes fabricated in silicon substrate was first introduced by Cotter, but the first experimental test results on these micro-devices were not published until somewhat later by Peterson and coworkers [26]. In their investigation, several silicon wafers as shown in **Figure 6** were fabricated with distributed heat sources on one side and an array of MHPs on the other. As an intermediary step in the development process, experimental tests were conducted by Babin et al. [8] on two individual micro-grooved heat pipes, one copper and one silver, approximately 1 mm^2 in cross-section area and 57 mm in length. Distilled and deionized water were used as the working fluid.

Figure 6. Array of micro-grooved heat pipes fabricated on silicon wafer [26].

After that, Peterson's group carried out several experimental and numerical investigations [28, 31, 33, 34] to verify the feasibility of MHPs as an integral part of semiconductor devices, and then a large number of experimental investigations have been conducted by other researchers to extend the MHP array concept and determine the potential advantages of MEMS-based MHPs.

In 1993, Peterson et al. [28] carried out the experiment on MHP arrays fabricated in silicon chips. As compared to a plain silicon wafer, their experiment demonstrated that the silicon chips of the same size integrated with rectangular and triangular MHP arrays charged with methanol could obtain reductions in the maximum temperature of 14.1 and 24.9°C, respectively, at a power input of 4 W. The effective thermal conductivities of these two MHP arrays were increased by 31 and 81%, respectively. Due to the higher capillary pumping effect, it is found that the thermal performance of a triangular MHP is better than that of a rectangular one. However, the experimental investigation by Badran et al. [35] shown an indistinctive increase in effective thermal conductivity after using MHP arrays fabricated on silicon substrate. Compared to plain silicon, the effective thermal conductivities were only increased by about 6 and 11% at high power levels using methanol and water as working fluids, respectively, which are far less than the predicted values based on a theoretical model. This result was found to be similar to the experimental results conducted by Berre et al. [36], according to whom that there was only a systematic slight temperature decrease in the charged MHP array of 55 parallel triangular-shaped channels for filling ratios between 6 and 66% as

http://dx.doi.org/10.5772/62786

compared with the empty MHP array at a heat input range between 0.5 and 4 W. However, this temperature discrepancy was found to be comparable to the experimental uncertainty and therefore no significant heat transfer enhancement could be clearly identified. These authors believed that it is mainly attributed to the large thermal conductivity of silicon, and therefore, a large part of heat is transferred by conduction through the silicon material and that the improvement due to the MHP array is negligible.

To enhance performance of MHPs, Kang and Huang [37] proposed two silicon MHPs with star and rhombus grooves, as illustrated in **Figures** 7a, b, respectively. The heat transfer performance of these MHPs was improved due to better capillarity provided by more acute angles and micro-gaps. Experimental results demonstrate that for the silicon wafer with an array of 31 star-grooved MHPs (340 μm in hydraulic diameter) filled with 60% methanol at a power input of 20 W, reduction in the maximum wafer temperature was 32°C. For the silicon wafer with an array of 31 rhombus-grooved MHP (55 μm in hydraulic diameter) filled with 80% methanol at a power input of 20 W, reduction in the maximum wafer temperature was 18°C. The best thermal conductivities of star and rhombus grooves MHPs were found to be 277.9 and 289.4 W/(m K), respectively.

Berre et al. [36] fabricated two sets of MHP arrays in silicon wafers. The first array, as illustrated in **Figure** 8a, was made from two silicon wafer with 55 triangular parallel micro-channels (230 μm in width and 170 μm in depth); and the second array, as illustrated in **Figure** 8b, was made from three silicon wafers having two sets of 25 parallel micro-channels, with the larger ones placed on the top of the smaller ones. The smaller triangular channels were used as arteries drain the liquid to the evaporator, so the liquid returns via independently etched channels to the evaporator rather than common liquid–vapor counter-current flow as occurred in **Figure** 8a, and thus significantly reducing the liquid–vapor interactions and enhancing the heat transport limitation. Ethanol and methanol were used as the working fluids. Filling ratios ranging from 0 to 66% were tested. The effective thermal conductivity evaluated by a 3D simulation was found to be 600 W/(m K), which represented an increase of 300% of the silicon thermal conductivity at high heat flux, demonstrating remarkable heat transfer enhancement.

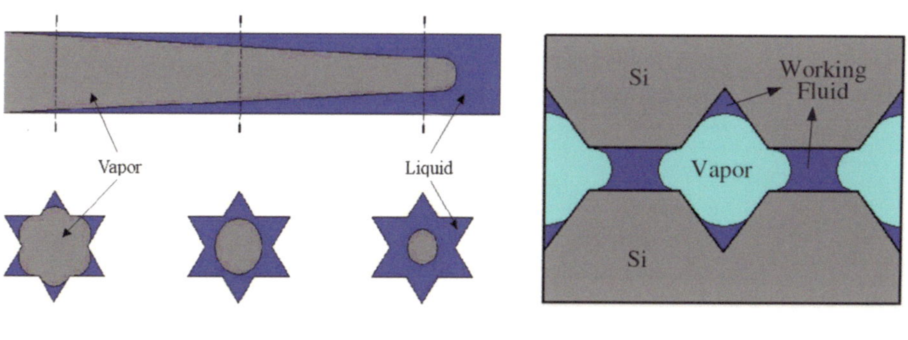

Figure 7. Schematic diagram of star grooves MHP (a) and rhombus grooves MHP (b) [37].

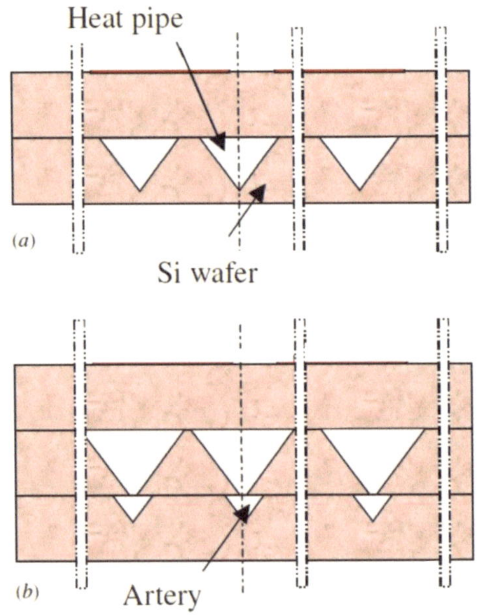

Figure 8. Transverse cross-sections of a MHP array (a) with triangular channels and (b) with triangular channels coupled with arteries [36].

Recently, a novel artery MHP array as illustrated in **Figure 9** was proposed by Kang et al. [38] to enhance the liquid backflow. Two smaller channels serving as arteries are positioned on both sides of one vein channel which acts as the ordinary MHP, and these channels are connected together at both ends by two connecting channels. Because of the two ends' pressure difference of the V-shape grooves in the MHP array, the working liquid gathered at the

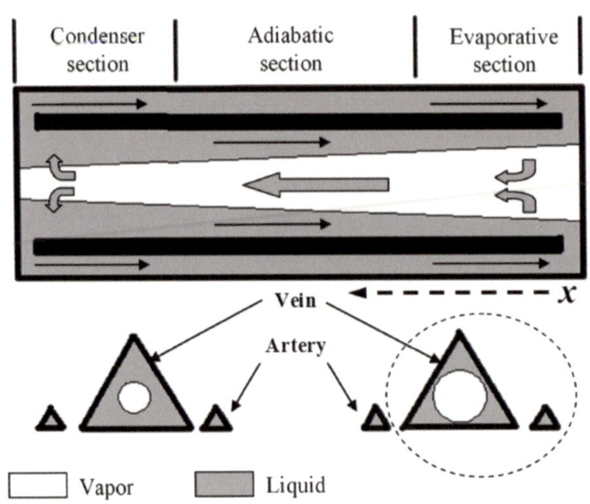

Figure 9. Schematic diagram of the MHP and artery and working principle [38].

http://dx.doi.org/10.5772/62786

condenser could be transported to the evaporator both through the MHPs' grooves and arteries. Soon afterward, the same group [39] stated that implanted arteries can effectively enhance the capillarity thus improving the capability to transport the liquid from the cold end back to the hot end, and limiting the propagation of dry-out region.

In addition to the artery MHPs, micro-grooves with non-parallel cross section were also utilized to enhance capillary effect and then heat transport capability of MHPs by Luo et al. [40]. A silicon-glass MHP with non-parallel micro-channel structure was put forward, having larger dimension of grooves in the evaporator section in comparison with that in the condenser section. Besides, a vapor chamber was wet etched onto the Pyrex 7740 glass and then bonded with the channel-etched silicon wafer as illustrated in **Figure 10**. The depths of the micro-grooves and vapor chamber in the silicon wafer and Pyrex 7740 were about 160 and 200 μm, respectively. Experimental results show that the non-parallel micro-channels could enhance the capillarity of liquid back flow from the condenser to the evaporator of the MHP and then improve the thermal performance. Also, it reveals that the vapor chamber influenced the performance of the MHP and a suitable design could reduce the vapor flow resistance and hence enhancing the liquid back flow. The novel MHPs demonstrate 10.6 times higher in the maximum equivalent thermal conductivity than that of the pure silicon wafer.

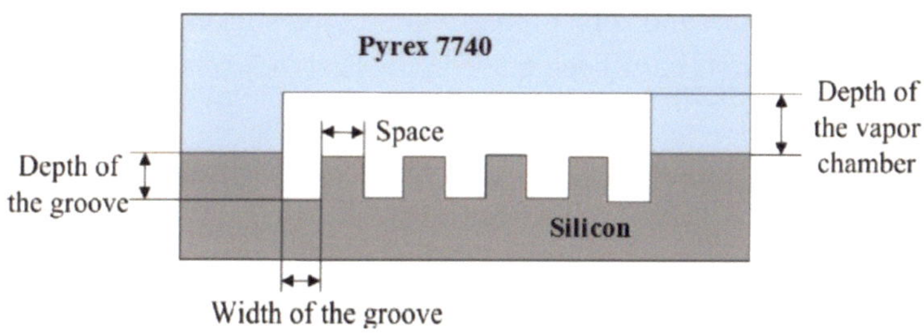

Figure 10. Schematic diagram of a micro-heat pipe with a vapor chamber [40].

In order to comprehensively understand the thermal performance of MHPs, micro-temperature sensors including poly-silicon integrated thermistors [36, 41–44] and platinum resistance temperature detectors (RTDs) [45] were used to obtain temperature profile along the longitudinal axis of a MHP array precisely.

3.2. Theoretical analysis

While some analytical models that predict the heat transfer limitations and operating characteristics of individual MHPs have been developed [46–49], it is unclear how the incorporation of an array of these MHPs on a silicon wafer might affect the temperature distribution and the resulting thermal performance. Hence, Mallik et al. [31] developed a three-dimensional numerical model capable of predicting the thermal performance of an array of parallel MHPs constructed as an integral part of semiconductor chips. In order to determine the potential advantages of this concept, several different thermal loading configurations were analyzed. The reduction in maximum chip temperature, localized heat fluxes, and maximum temperature gradient across the chip as a function of the number of MHPs in the array was determined. Besides, the 3D numerical model was further extended to determine transient response characteristics of an array of MHPs integrated on silicon wafers. Numerical results show significant reductions in the transient response time, indicating the effectiveness of an array of these MHPs in dissipating heat over the entire chip surface and improving the heat removal capability. The transient thermal response was measured and compared with the calculations based on the numerical model proposed by the same group [33].

Suman and Kumar [50] and Suman and Hoda [51, 52] developed several one-dimensional models, which include the substrate effect, to predict the thermal characteristics of MHPs embedded in a silicon chip. These models are considerable simpler in form and easier to implement than those developed by other, while less accurate since only the fluid phase were took into account and neglected the liquid–vapor interface shear effect.

3.3. Novel designs for performance improvement

According to the working principles of a MHP, the liquid back flow is derived from a difference in the radius of curvature between the hot part and the cold part. Therefore, its heat transfer capacity is less than that of a conventional heat pipe having wicking structures. Owning to its advantages of simple design and direct integration on the silicon wafers, suitable for many applications, several attempts have been made in the past to increase the transport capability of MHPs.

By applying electric field at the liquid–vapor interface, pressure difference can be increased if the working fluid is dielectric in nature. This research is based on the assumption that both augmentation of the heat transport capability and active thermal control of MHPs can be achieved through the application of a static electric field. Yu et al. [53] conducted experimental and theoretical analyses to evaluate the potential benefits of electrohydrodynamic (EHD) forces on the operation of MHPs. In their experiments, the electric fields were used to orient and guide the flow of the dielectric liquid within the MHP from the condenser to the evaporator, and then a six time increase in the heat transport capability was obtained. The application of an electric field to MHPs not only can enhance the heat transfer capacity but also permits active thermal control of sources subject to transient heat loads and thus making the temperature control more precise [54].

Using EHD-assisted MHPs, the substrate temperature can be controlled more precise by varying the field strength. But the model developed by Yu et al. [53, 54] are semi-empirical in nature. The effect of electrical field has not been directly incorporated into flow of fluid. Therefore, a model developed from the first principle and its experimental validation is required to understand the effect of an electrical field in the performance of MHPs. Such an attempt has been presented by Suman [55] that developed a model for the fluid flow and heat transfer in an EHD-assisted MHP considering the coulomb and dielectrophoretic forces. The analytical expressions for the critical heat input and for the dry-out length have been obtained. It was found that the critical heat input could be increased by 100 times using EHD.

To provide enough capillary pressure to collect more working fluid at the evaporator region passively and enlarge the capillary limitation, surface wettability treatment of inner wall along the longitudinal direction of a MHP offers a possible solution. Qu et al. [56] proposed a triangular MHP characterized by a gradient inner surface, with the evaporator, adiabatic section, and condenser having different surface wettabilities and hence contact angles. The contact angle decreases from the condenser to the evaporator, thereby enhancing heat transfer capacity. The results revealed that the surface with a gradient wettability increased the maximum heat input of the MHP up to 49.7%, compared with that of uniform surface wettability. The effect of surface-tension gradient on the thermal performance of a MHP has been numerically investigated by Suman [57]. Results show that the liquid pressure drop across the MHP can be decreased by about 90%, and the maximum heat throughput can be increased by about 20% with a favorable surface-tension gradient. A mixture of water and normal alcohol with carbon chain ranging 4–7 (like water-butanol mixture) was suggested to

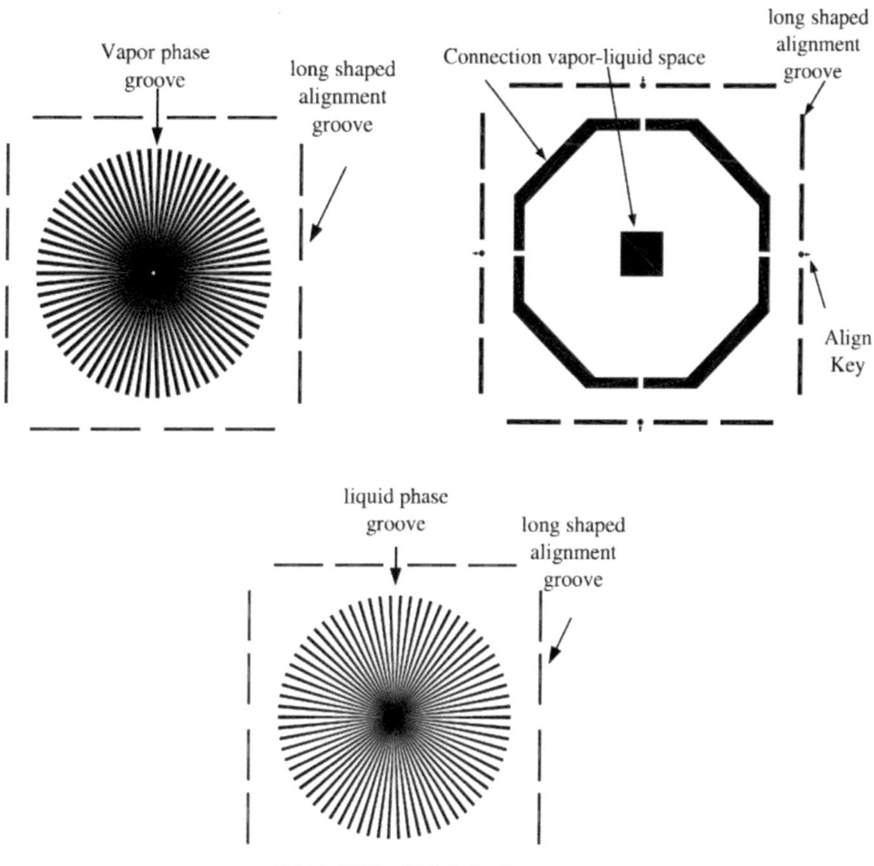

Figure 11. A radial-grooved micro-heat pipe: vapor-phase grooves (top left); interface (top right); liquid phase grooves (bottom) [58].

use as a liquid solution whose surface tension increases with the increase of temperature. The favorable effects will promote the fluid flow from the cold end to the hot end resulting in the heat transfer enhancement of a MHP.

A radial-grooved MHP as illustrated in **Figure 11** was designed and fabricated in silicon wafer by Kang et al. [58]. This radial-grooved MHP consisted of a three-layer structure, with the middle layer serving as the interface between liquid and vapor phases flowing in the upper and bottom layers, respectively. The separation of the liquid and vapor flow was designed to reduce the viscous shear force. This MHP with a size of 5 cm × 5 cm was fabricated by bulk micro-machining and eutectic bonding techniques. Both the vapor and liquid phase grooves were 23 mm in length and trapezoidal in shape, with 70 grooves spreading in a radial manner from the center outward. For the vapor phase grooves, the widths at the inner and outer ends of the grooves were 350 and 700 μm, respectively. The corresponding widths for the liquid phase grooves at inner and outer end are 150 and 500 μm, respectively. The best heat transfer performance of 27 W at a filling rate of 70% was obtained for this micro-device. Later, Kang et al. [59] presented two wick designs of MHPs with three copper foil layers. The first design has almost the same structures as depicted in **Figure 11** and worked based on the same principle and advantages of liquid–vapor separation, whereas the second one had 100-mesh copper screens as wicking structure (**Figure 12**). It was found that the radial grooved MHP, filled with methanol at a filling ratio of 82%, showed better performance at a heat input of 35 W than that using mesh screens as wicking structure.

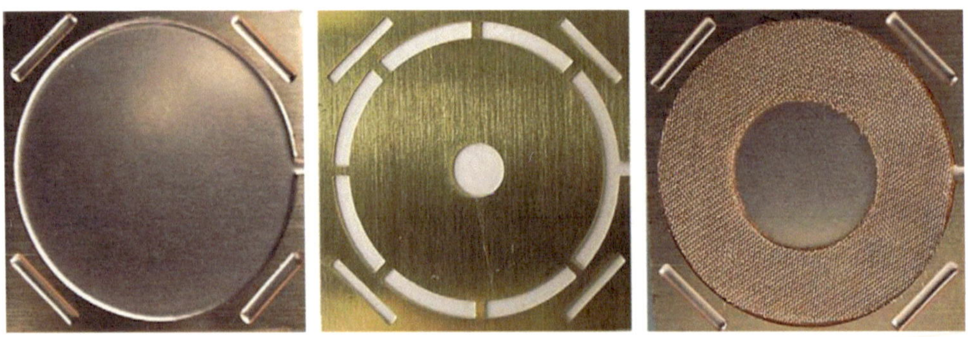

Figure 12. The diagram about the structures of each layer of a copper-screen-styled micro-heat pipe heat spreader: gas phase (left); partition panel (central); liquid phase (right) [59].

4. Other emerging MEMS-based MHPs

In addition to MEMS-based micro-grooved heat pipes, some other mini- or micro-scale heat pipes, such as capillary pumped loops (CPLs) [60–64], loop heat pipes (LHPs) [65–69], oscillating heat pipes (OHPs) [70–75], and vapor chambers (VCs) [76–80] as shown **Figure 13**, were also successfully constructed on silicon substrates by means of micro-fabrication technique recent years and became two-phase passive micro-coolers for electronic cooling.

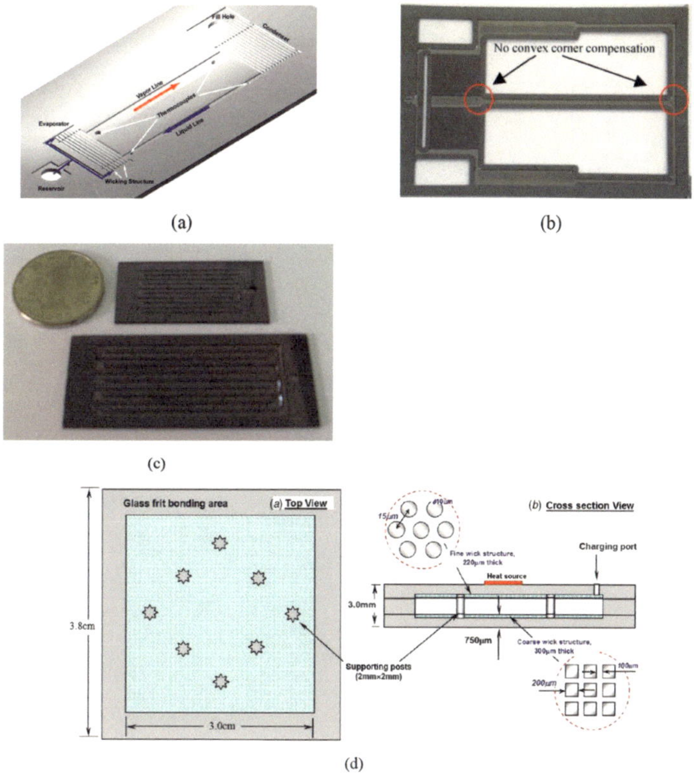

Figure 13. Novel MEMS-based micro-heat pipes: (a) micro-CPL [62], (b) micro-LHP [65], (c) micro-OHP [72], and (d) micro-vapor chamber [77].

Similar to MEMS-based micro-grooved heat pipes, these novel MEMS-based MHPs could be considered as small versions of corresponding conventional prototypes and work at the related mechanism. Although some of these micro-devices have more complicated structures in comparison with micro-grooved heat pipes, especially the micro-CPLs and micro-LHP consisting of additional wicking structures, the heat cooling capability is much higher and the maximum allowable heat fluxes could be up to 185.2 W/cm^2 [63] and 300 W/cm^2 [68] for micro-CPLs and micro-LHP, respectively.

In addition to MEMS-based loop-type heat pipes as shown in Figure 13a–c, MEMS-based VCs are also utilized for spreading high local heat flux and act as silicon heat spreaders. A silicon VC illustrated in **Figure 13**d based on a unique three-layer silicon wafer-stacking fabrication process demonstrated an maximum effective thermal conductivity about 2700 W/(m K) [77], indicating excellent performance to attain temperature uniformity.

To further increase the heat transport capability of micro-VCs, recently micro-/nano-hierarchical wicking structures are proposed by researches. The materials of carbon nanotube, Ti, and Cu as shown in Figure 14 are available due to the easy-fabrication feasibility and material compatibility. As compared to the micro-wicking structures, the micro-/nano-biwick structure shows better wettability [82, 83] and can sustain ultra-high localized heat flux over 700 W/cm^2 [81].

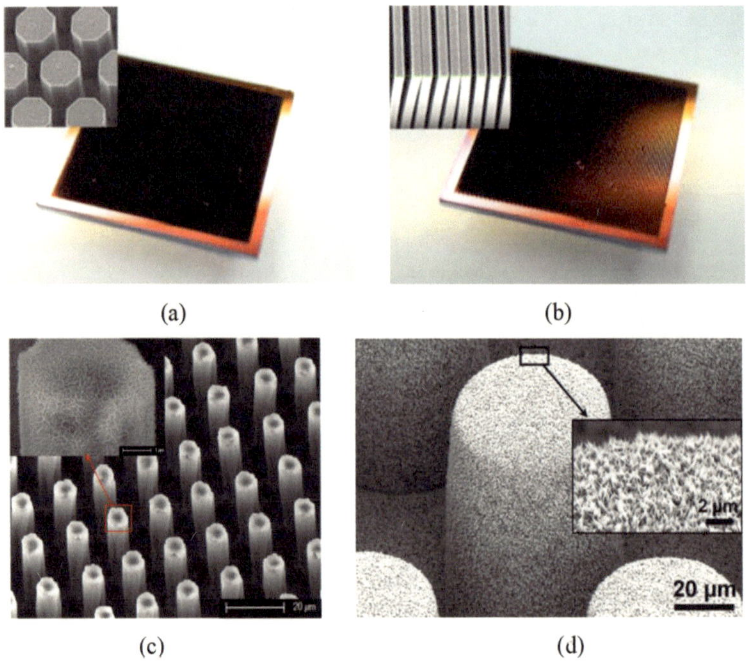

Figure 14. SEM images of micro-/nano-hierarchical wicking structures for micro-vapor chamber: (a) biwick structure composed of cylindrical CNT pillars [81]; (b) biwick structure composed of straight CNT stripes [81]; (c) Ti pillar array with oxidized hairlike NST(nanostructured titania) [82]; (d) nanostructured Cu micro-posts [83].

5. Applications of MEMS-based MHPs

The most ongoing and potential application of MEMS-based MHPs is in the thermal management of electronics [84, 85]. Adkins et al. [86] discussed the use of a "heat-pipe heat spreader" embedded in a silicon substrate as an alternative to the conductive cooling of integrated circuits using diamond films. These MHPs function as highly efficient heat spreaders, collecting heat from the localized hot spots and dissipating the heat over the entire chip surface. Incorporation of these MHPs as an integral part of silicon wafers has been shown to significantly reduce the maximum wafer temperature and reduce the temperature gradients occurring across these devices [28, 32]. Currently, mobile electronics, such as smart phones and tablet PCs, are widely used and becoming an alternate solution of traditional PCs or notebooks. These devices comprise many high-heat-generating components and have been miniaturized and designed for high-density packaging. The complex thermal behavior due to their usage under various circumstances affects the reliability and usability. The ultra-compact cooling space demands of these mobile electronics make the MEMS-based MHPs a good alternative solution as compared to other cooling schemes.

The biological field associated with human disease remedy is another potential application of MEMS-based MHPs. MHPs can provide a controllable heat rate at constant temperature and may be matched to the thermal conductivity of live tissue and the degree to which a cancerous tumor is perfused. They may be useful in treating cancerous tumors in body regions that cannot be treated by other means [87, 88].

In addition to the above applications, the thermal management of localized heat generating devices such as concentrated solar cells, MEMS-based infrared detectors and micro-fuel cells as well as thermal energy harvesting devices is also possible fields that MEMS-based MHPs can be used.

6. Summary

In this chapter, a generalized concept of MEMS-based MHPs is proposed on the basis of the initial description of MHP by Cotter as an integral part of semiconductor devices. The working principle, capillary limitation, fabrication process as well as the state-of-the-art of MEMS-based micro-grooved heat pipes have been introduced firstly and discussed in detail. Some new MEMS-based MHPs, including micro-CPLs, micro-LHPs, micro-OHPs, and micro-VCs, and some of their structures and thermal characteristics have been presented. In view of the continued trend in miniaturization of electronic/optoelectronic devices and circuits and explosive growth of MEMS products, MEMS-based MHPs exhibit advantages and will find increasing applications in related engineering and medical fields. More research work is needed to provide rational tools for optimal designs and fabrications of these micro-devices.

Acknowledgements

This work was supported by the National Natural Science Foundation of China (Nos. 51206065 and 51576091) and China Postdoctoral Science Special Foundation (No. 2015T80523).

Nomenclature

A	Cross-sectional area (m^2)
Bo	Bond number
C	Constant
f	Fanning friction factor
g	Gravitational acceleration ($m\ s^{-2}$)
h_{fg}	Vaporization latent heat ($J\ kg^{-1}$)

K	Permeability (m^2)
L	Length (m)
Ma	Mach number
Δp	Pressure difference (Pa)
Q	Heat transfer rate (W)
r	Radius of curvature (m)
Greek symbols	
μ	Dynamic viscosity (kg $m^{-1}s^{-1}$)
ρ	Density (kg m^{-3})
σ	Surface tension (N m^{-1})
Subscripts	
a	Adiabatic section
c	Condenser section, capillary radius
e	Evaporator section
eff	Effective
g	Gas
h	Hydraulic radius
l	Liquid
v	Vapor

Author details

Qu Jian* and Wang Qian

*Address all correspondence to: rjqu@mail.ujs.edu.cn

School of Energy and Power Engineering, Jiangsu University, Zhenjiang, China

References

[1] He YL, Tao WQ. Convective heat transfer enhancement: Mechanisms, techniques, and performance evaluation. Advances in Heat Transfer. 2014; 46: 88–186.

[2] Agostini B, Fabbri M, Park JE, Wojtan L, Thome JR, Michel B. State of the art of high heat flux cooling technologies. Heat Transfer Engineering. 2007; 28(4): 258–281.

http://dx.doi.org/10.5772/62786

[3] Garimella SV, Fleischer AS, Murthy JY, Keshavarzi A, Prasher R, Patel C, Bhavnani SH, Venkatasubramanian R, Mahajan R, Joshi Y, Sammakia B, Myers BA, Chorosinski L, Baelmans M, Sathyamurthy P, Raad PE. Thermal challenges in next-generation electronic systems. IEEE Transactions on Components and Packaging Technologies. 2008; 31(4): 801–815.

[4] Ebadian MA, Lin CX. A review of high-heat-flux heat removal technologies. Journal of Heat Transfer. 2011; 133(11): 110801.

[5] Marcinichen JB, Olivier JA, Lamaison N, Thome JR. Advances in electronics cooling. Heat Transfer Engineering. 2013; 34(5–6): 434–446.

[6] Cotter TP. Principles and prospects of micro-heat pipes. Proceedings of the 5th International Heat Pipe Conference. 1984.

[7] Suman B. Microgrooved heat pipe. Advanced in Heat Transfer. 2009; 41: 1–80.

[8] Babin BR, Peterson GP, Wu D. Steady-state modeling and testing of a micro heat pipe. Journal of Heat Transfer. 1990; 112(3): 595–601.

[9] Cao Y, Faghri A. Micro/miniature heat pipes and operating limitations. Journal of Enhanced Heat Transfer. 1994; 1(3): 265–274.

[10] Zaghdoudi MC, Maalej S, Mansouri J, Sassi MBH. Flat miniature heat pipes for electronics cooling: state of the art, experimental and theoretical analysis. International Journal of Engineering and Applied Sciences. 2011; 7(3): 166–189.

[11] Cao Y, Faghri A, Mahefkey ET. Micro/Miniature Heat Pipes and Operating Limitations. ASME-PUBLICATIONS-HTD. 1993.

[12] Mohamed GH. The MEMS Handbook. Boca Raton: CRC. 2002.

[13] Gerner FM, Longtin JP, Henderson HT, Hsieh WM, Ramadas P, Chang WS. Flow and heat transfer limitations in micro heat pipes. ASME, HTD-Vol. 206-3, 1992, San Diego, CA, USA.

[14] Peterson GP. Modeling, fabrication, and testing of micro heat pipes: An update. Applied Mechanics Reviews. 1996; 49: S175–83.

[15] Sobhan CB, Rag RL, Peterson GP. A review and comparative study of the investigations on micro heat pipe. International Journal of Energy Research. 2007; 31: 664–688.

[16] Suman B. Modeling, experiment, and fabrication of micro-grooved heat pipes: An update. Applied Mechanics Reviews. 2007; 60(3): 107–119.

[17] Peterson GP. An Introduction to Heat Pipes: Modeling, Testing and Applications. New York: John Wiley & Sons, INC. 1994.

[18] Faghri A. Review and advances in heat pipe science and technology. Journal of Heat Transfer. 2012; 134(12): 123001.

[19] Chakraborty S. Microfluidics and Microscale Transport Processes. Boca Raton: CRC Press, Taylor & Francis Group. 2012.

[20] Faghri A. Performance characteristics of a concentric annular heat pipe part II: Vapor flow analysis. Journal of Heat Transfer. 1989; 111(4): 851–857.

[21] Kim BH, Peterson GP. Analysis of the critical Weber number at the onset of liquid entrainment in capillary-driven heat pipes. International Journal of Heat and Mass Transfer. 1995; 38(8): 1427–1442.

[22] Suman B, De S, DasGupta S. A model of the capillary limit of a micro heat pipe and prediction of the dry-out length. International Journal of Heat and Fluid Flow. 2005; 26(3): 495–505.

[23] Shukla KN. Heat transfer limitation of a micro heat pipe. Journal of Electronic Packaging. 2009; 131(2): 024502.

[24] Zohar Y. Heat convection in micro ducts. Springer Science & Business Media, Netherlands, 2013.

[25] Ma HB. Micro heat pipes. Encyclopedia of Microfluidics and Nanofluidics. 2015; 1813–1825.

[26] Peterson GP, Duncan AB, Ahmed AS, Mallik AK, Weichold MH. Experimental investigation of micro heat pipes in silicon wafers. Winter Annual Meeting of the American Society of Mechanical Engineers. 1991.

[27] Gerner FM. Micro Heat Pipes. AFSOR Final Report No. S-210-10MG-066. 1990.

[28] Peterson GP, Duncan AB, Weichold MH. Experimental investigation of micro heat pipes fabricated in silicon wafers. Journal of Heat Transfer. 1993; 115(3): 751–756.

[29] Laermer F, Urban A. Challenges, developments and applications of silicon deep reactive ion etching. Microelectronic Engineering. 2003; 67: 349–355.

[30] Marty F, Rousseau L, Saadany B, Mercier B, Français O, Mita Y, Bourouina T. Advanced etching of silicon based on deep reactive ion etching for silicon high aspect ratio microstructures and three-dimensional micro-and nanostructures. Microelectronics Journal. 2005; 36(7): 673–677.

[31] Mallik AK, Peterson GP, Weichold MH. On the use of micro heat pipes as an integral part of semiconductor devices. Journal of Electronic Packaging. 1992; 114(4): 436–442.

[32] Weichold MH, Peterson GP, Mallik A. Vapor deposited micro heat pipes. US Patent 5, 1993.

[33] Peterson GP, Mallik AK. Transient response characteristics of vapor deposited micro heat pipe arrays. Journal of Electronic Packaging. 1995; 117(1): 82–87.

[34] Mallik AK, Peterson GP. Steady-state investigation of vapor deposited micro heat pipe arrays. Journal of Electronic Packaging. 1995; 117(1): 75–81.

[35] Badran B, Gerner FM, Ramadas P, Henderson T, Baker KW. Experimental results for low-temperature silicon micromachined micro heat pipe arrays using water and methanol as working fluids. Experiment Heat Transfer. 1997; 10: 253–272.

[36] Berre ML, Launay S, Sartre V, Lallemand M. Fabrication and experimental investigation of silicon micro heat pipes for cooling electronics. Journal of Micromechanics and Microengineering. 2003; 13(3): 436.

[37] Kang SW, Huang D. Fabrication of star grooves and rhombus grooves micro heat pipe. Journal of Micromechanics and Microengineering. 2002; 12(5): 525.

[38] Kang J, Fu X, Liu W, Dario P. Investigation on Microheat Pipe Array with Arteries. Journal of Thermophysics and Heat Transfer. 2010; 24(4): 803–810.

[39] Liu W, Kang J, Fu X, Stefanini C, Dario P. Analysis on heat resistance of the micro heat pipe with arteries. Microelectronic Engineering. 2011; 88(8): 2255–2258.

[40] Luo Y, Liu G, Zou LL, Yu BK, Wang XD. Thermal behavior investigation of silicon-Pyrex micro heat pipe. AIP Advances. 2014; 4(3): 031305.

[41] Lee M, Wong M, Zohar Y. Characterization of an integrated micro heat pipe. Journal of Micromechanics and Microengineering. 2003; 13(1): 58.

[42] Launay S, Sartre V, Lallemand M. Experimental study on silicon micro-heat pipe arrays. Applied Thermal Engineering. 2004; 24(2): 233–243.

[43] Berre ML, Pandraud G, Morfouli P, Lallemand M. The performance of micro heat pipes measured by integrated sensors. Journal of Micromechanics and Microengineering. 2006; 16(5): 1047.

[44] Lee M, Wong M, Zohar Y. Integrated micro-heat-pipe fabrication technology. Journal of Microelectromechanical Systems. 2003; 12(2): 138–146.

[45] Harris DK, Palkar A, Wonacott G, Dean R, Simionescu F. An experimental investigation in the performance of water-filled silicon microheat pipe arrays. Journal of Electronic Packaging. 2010; 132(2): 021005.

[46] Babin BR, Peterson GP, Wu D. Steady-state modeling and testing of a micro heat pipe. Journal of Heat Transfer. 1990; 112(3): 595–601.

[47] Longtin JP, Badran B, Gerner FM. A one-dimensional model of a micro heat pipe during steady-state operation. Journal of Heat Transfer. 1994; 116(3): 709–715.

[48] Khrustalev D, Faghri A. Thermal analysis of a micro heat pipe. Journal of Heat Transfer. 1994; 116(1): 189–198.

[49] Peterson GP, Ma HB. Theoretical analysis of the maximum heat transport in triangular grooves: A study of idealized micro heat pipes. Journal of Heat Transfer. 1996; 118(3): 731–739.

[50] Suman B, Kumar P. An analytical model for fluid flow and heat transfer in a micro-heat pipe of polygonal shape. International Journal of Heat and Mass Transfer. 2005; 48(21–22): 4498–4509.

[51] Suman B, Hoda N. Effect of variations in thermophysical properties and design parameters on the performance of a V-shaped micro grooved heat pipe. International Journal of Heat and Mass Transfer. 2005; 48(10): 2090–2101.

[52] Suman B, Hoda N. On the transient analysis of a V-shaped microgrooved heat pipe. Journal of Heat Transfer. 2007; 129(11): 1584–1591.

[53] Yu Z, Hallinani K, Bhagat W, Kashani RA. Electrohydrodynamically augmented micro heat pipes. Journal of Thermophysics and Heat Transfer. 2002; 16(2): 180–186.

[54] Yu Z, Hallinan K P, Kashani RA. Temperature control of electrohydrodynamic micro heat pipes. Experimental Thermal and Fluid Science. 2003; 27(8): 867–875.

[55] Suman B. A steady state model and maximum heat transport capacity of an electrohydrodynamically augmented micro-grooved heat pipe. International Journal of Heat and Mass Transfer. 2006; 49(21): 3957–3967.

[56] Qu J, Wu H, Cheng P. Effects of functional surface on performance of a micro heat pipe. International Communications in Heat and Mass Transfer. 2008; 35(5): 523–528.

[57] Suman B. Effects of a surface-tension gradient on the performance of a micro-grooved heat pipe: an analytical study. Microfluidics and Nanofluidics. 2008; 5(5): 655–667.

[58] Kang SW, Tsai SH, Chen HC. Fabrication and test of radial grooved micro heat pipes. Applied Thermal Engineering. 2002; 22(14): 1559–1568.

[59] Kang SW, Tsai SH, Ko MH. Metallic micro heat pipe heat spreader fabrication. Applied Thermal Engineering. 2004; 24(2): 299–309.

[60] Kirshberg J, Yerkes K, Liepmann D. Micro-cooler for chip-level temperature control. SAE Aerospace Power Systems Conference. 1999.

[61] Kirshberg J, Yerkes K, Trebotich D, Liepmann D. Cooling effect of a MEMS based micro capillary pumped loop for chip-level temperature control. ASME MEMS. 2000.

[62] Liepmann D. Design and fabrication of a micro-CPL for chip-level cooling. Proceedings of ASME International Mechanical Engineering Congress and Exposition. 2001.

[63] Wang CT, Leu TS, Lai TM. Micro capillary pumped loop system for a cooling high power device. Experimental Thermal and Fluid Science. 2008; 32(5): 1090–1095.

[64] Moon SH, Hwang G. Development of the micro capillary pumped loop for electronic cooling. THERMINIC. 2007.

[65] Hsu C, Kang S, Hou T. Performance testing of micro loop heat pipes. Tamkang Journal of Science and Engineering. 2005; 8: 123–32.

[66] Cytrynowicz D, Hamdan M, Medis P, Shuja A, Henderson HT, Gerner FM, Golliher E. MEMS Loop Heat Pipe Based on Coherent Porous Silicon Technology. Proceedings of Space Technology and Applications International Forum. 2002.

[67] Cytrynowicz D, Medis P, Parimi S, Shuja A, Henderson HT, Gerner FM. The MEMS loop heat pipe based on coherent porous silicon-The modified system test structure. AIP Conference Proceedings. 2004.

[68] Ghajar M, Darabi J, and Jr NC. A hybrid CFD-mathematical model for simulation of a MEMS loop heat pipe for electronics cooling applications. Journal of Micromechanics and Microengineering. 2005; 15(2): 313–321.

[69] Ghajar M, Darabi J. Evaporative heat transfer analysis of a micro loop heat pipe with rectangular grooves. International Journal of Thermal Sciences. 2014; 79: 51–59.

[70] Qu J, Wu H Y. Flow visualization of silicon-based micro pulsating heat pipes. Science China Technological Sciences. 2010; 53(4): 984–990.

[71] Qu J, Wu H, Wang Q. Experimental investigation of silicon-based micro-pulsating heat pipe for cooling electronics. Nanoscale and Microscale Thermophysical Engineering. 2012; 16(1): 37–49.

[72] Qu J, Wu H, Cheng P. Start-up, heat transfer and flow characteristics of silicon-based micro pulsating heat pipes. International Journal of Heat and Mass Transfer. 2012; 55(21): 6109–6120.

[73] Youn YJ, Kim SJ. Fabrication and evaluation of a silicon-based micro pulsating heat spreader. Sensors and Actuators A: Physical. 2012; 174: 189–197.

[74] Yang KS, Cheng YC, Liu MC, Shyu JC. Micro pulsating heat pipes with alternate microchannel widths. Applied Thermal Engineering. 2015; 83: 131–138.

[75] Kwon GH, Kim SJ. Experimental investigation on the thermal performance of a micro pulsating heat pipe with a dual-diameter channel. International Journal of Heat and Mass Transfer. 2015; 89: 817–828.

[76] Cai Q, Chen BC, Tsai C, Chen CL. Development of scalable silicon heat spreader for high power electronic devices. Journal of Thermal Science and Engineering Applications. 2009; 1(4): 041009.

[77] Cai Q, Chen B, Tsai C. Design, development and tests of high-performance silicon vapor chamber. Journal of Micromechanics and Microengineering. 2012; 22(3): 035009.

[78] Cai Q, Bhunia A, Tsai C, Kendig MW. DeNatale JF. Studies of material and process compatibility in developing compact silicon vapor chambers. Journal of Micromechanics and Microengineering. 2013; 23(6): 065003.

[79] Wei M, Somasundaram S, He B, Liang Q, Tan CS, Wang EN. Experimental characterization of Si micropillar based evaporator for advanced vapor chambers. IEEE 16th Electronics Packaging Technology Conference. 2014.

[80] Yang KS, Lin CC, Shyu JC, Tsenga CY, Wang CC. Performance and two-phase flow pattern for micro flat heat pipes. International Journal of Heat and Mass Transfer. 2014; 77: 1115–1123.

[81] Cai Q, Chen YC. Investigations of biporous wick structure dryout. Journal of Heat Transfer. 2012; 134(2): 021503.

[82] Ding C, Soni G, Bozorgi P, Piorek BD, Meinhart CD, MacDonald NC. A flat heat pipe architecture based on nanostructured titania. Journal of Microelectromechanical Systems. 2010; 19(4): 878–884.

[83] Nam Y, Ju YS. A comparative study of the morphology and wetting characteristics of micro/nanostructured Cu surfaces for phase change heat transfer applications. Journal of Adhesion Science and Technology. 2013; 27(20): 2163–2176.

[84] Vasiliev LL. Micro and miniature heat pipes–electronic component coolers. Applied Thermal Engineering. 2008; 28(4): 266–273.

[85] Chen X, Ye H, Fan X, Ren T, Zhang G. A review of small heat pipes for electronics. Applied Thermal Engineering. 2016; 96: 1–17.

[86] Adkins DR, Shen DS, Palmer DW, Tuck MR. Silicon heat pipes for cooling electronics. Sandia National Labs., Albuquerque, NM (United States), 1994.

[87] Fletcher LS, Peterson GP. Micro-heat-pipe catheter: US Patent 5, 1993.

[88] Fletcher LS, Peterson GP. Method of treating diseased tissue: US Patent 5, 1997.

http://dx.doi.org/10.5772/62786

Chapter 6

Performance Evaluation of Nanofluids in an Inclined Ribbed Microchannel for Electronic Cooling Applications

Mohammad Reza Safaei, Marjan Gooarzi,
Omid Ali Akbari, Mostafa Safdari Shadloo and
Mahidzal Dahari

Additional information is available at the end of the chapter

http://dx.doi.org/10.5772/62898

Abstract

Nanofluids are liquid/solid suspensions with higher thermal conductivity, compared to common working fluids. In recent years, the application of these fluids in electronic cooling systems seems prospective. In the present study, the laminar mixed convection heat transfer of different water–copper nanofluids through an inclined ribbed microchannel—as a common electronic cooling system in industry—was investigated numerically, using a finite volume method. The middle section of microchannel's right wall was ribbed, and at a higher temperature compared to entrance fluid. The modeling was carried out for Reynolds number of 50, Richardson numbers from 0.1 to 10, inclination angles ranging from 0° to 90°, and nanoparticles' volume fractions of 0.0–0.04. The influences of nanoparticle volume concentration, inclination angle, buoyancy and shear forces, and rib's shape on the hydraulics and thermal behavior of nanofluid flow were studied. The results were portrayed in terms of pressure, temperature, coefficient of friction, and Nusselt number profiles as well as streamlines and isotherm contours. The model validation was found to be in excellent accords with experimental and numerical results from other previous studies.

The results indicated that at low Reynolds' flows, the gravity has effects on the heat transfer and fluid phenomena considerably; similarly, with inclination angle and nanoparticle volume fraction, the heat transfer is enhanced by increasing the Richardson number, but resulting in a less value of friction coefficient. The results also represented that for specific Reynolds (Re) and Richardson (Ri) numbers, heat transfer and pressure drop augmented by increasing the inclination angle or volume fraction of nanoparticles. With regard to the coefficient of friction, its value decreased by adding less nanoparticles to the fluid or by increasing the inclination angle of the microchannel.

Keywords: mixed convection heat transfer, inclined ribbed microchannel, nanofluid, finite volume method, friction factor

1. Introduction

Electronics have turned smaller, quicker, and more powerful due to the current development in computing technology during the past few decades, resulting in a dramatic rise in the rate of heat generation from electronic appliances. One way to keep the heat generated by different parts of electronic devices within safety zone is to cool the chips via forced air flow. However, standard cooling procedures seem insufficient to deal with the parts which are comprised of billions of transistors functioning at high frequency, considering the fact that the temperature can rise up to a critical point. Thus, microscale cooling appliances like microchannel heat sinks have vital roles in heat removal applications in appliances including high-energy mirrors and laser diode arrays [1]. In 1981, Tuckerman and Pease brought up the concept of a microchannel heat exchanger first [2]. The major advantage of a microchannel heat sink is the fact that its heat transfer coefficient is much higher than the traditional heat exchangers [3]. This causes microchannels to become useful for being employed in semiconductor power devices, very large-scale integrated (VLSI) circuits, etc. [4]. The first idea was to utilize water as a coolant in microchannels as cooling systems [5, 6]. Nevertheless, water is subjected to weak thermophysical properties. The convective heat transfer rate of these types of working fluids can be enhanced by improving their thermophysical properties. Nanofluids prepared through dispersing nanosized particles into the base fluid for the sake of enhancing the thermophysical properties of the working fluid are considered to support higher heat transfer compared to conventional fluids, such as water [7], ethylene glycol [8], kerosene [9], etc.

Recently, heat transfer and nanofluid flow in microchannels have drawn enormous interests by researchers. However, most of the researches are concerned with the forced convection heat transfer in smooth microchannels. The laminar forced convection heat transfer of γ-Al_2O_3/deionized water nanofluid through a rectangular microchannel heat sink was studied by Kalteh et al. [10], using a finite volume method. Moreover, they carried out experimental study to make comparison between the outcomes with numerical results. Their findings demonstrated that average Nusselt number rises with a growth in Re and vol. % of nanofluid besides a reduction in the nanoparticle size.

The theoretical study of laminar forced convection heat transfer of Al_2O_3/H_2O nanofluid inside a circular microchannel accompanied by a uniform magnetic field was carried out by Malvandi and Ganji [11]. Due to the nonadherence of the fluid–solid interface accompanied by nanoparticle migration, considered as a slip condition, and also the microscopic roughness in circular microchannels, the Navier's slip boundary condition was applied to the walls. The results of this research showed that the near-wall velocity gradients rise by applying the magnetic field, improving the slip velocity, and therefore, the pressure drop and heat transfer rate rise.

The heat transfer and fluid flow of MWCNT/water-based nanofluids in a microchannel, with frequent change of heat flux and slip boundary condition, were studied by Nikkhah et al. [12]. Based on their results, local Nusselt number, along the length of the microchannel, changes periodically and enhances with the rising of Reynold's number. Furthermore, it was pointed out that an increase in the weight percentage of nanoparticles and slip coefficient results in the rise of Nusselt number, which is higher in upper Reynolds numbers.

The experimental investigation of forced convection of various nanofluids in a 500 μm width, 800 μm height, and 40 mm length microchannel was conducted by Nitiapiruk et al. [13]. Pure water and TiO_2-water with 0.5–2 vol.% were studied in this research. According to the outcomes of this research, the use of nanofluid with a volume fraction of 2 vol.% and minimum rate of heat flux and Reynold's number is more beneficial than other conditions.

An analytical approach was taken to study the entropy generation of alumina–water nanofluid inside circular microchannels and minichannels by Hassan et al. [14]. In their research, the Reynolds number was maintained constant at 1500, while the nanoparticle volume fraction and the diameter of channels differed from 0 to 0.14, and 3 mm (minichannel) to 0.05 mm (microchannel), respectively. They realized that water/Al_2O_3 nanofluid is an excellent coolant in minichannels under laminar flow regime. Nonetheless, employing high-viscous H_2O/Al_2O_3 nanofluid for laminar flow in microchannels is undesirable. Therefore, it is necessary to develop low-viscous Al_2O_3/water nanofluids in order to apply in microchannels under laminar flow condition.

Rimbault et al. [15] investigated convection heat transfer of nanofluids in a rectangular microchannel heat sink. The nanofluids were comprised of CuO nanoparticles combined with water as the base fluid in 0.24–4.5 volume fractions. The findings reveal that employment of copper oxide/water nanofluid for microchannel under the examined conditions does not offer great heat transfer improvement, compared to water. Such results were inconsistent with the experimental results reported by Zhang et al. [16] for alumina–water nanofluid flow through a circular microchannel, who indicated a significant increase in heat transfer rate and Nusselt number while using 0.25–0.75 vol.% nanofluid. While employing non-Newtonian Al_2O_3 nanofluid of up to 4% in a rectangular microchannel, the findings of Esmaeilnejad et al. [17] were consistent with those of Zhang et al. [16].

The literature survey reveals that combined use of nanofluids with microchannels gives higher heat transfer performance compared to the use of common, traditional fluids in conventional systems [18–20]. However, fulfilling the requirements from other applications of the micro-channels needs additional advancement. A particular still uncomprehending case is the natural and mixed convection heat transfer of nanofluids in vertical and inclined ribbed microchannel heat sinks. In this work, dilute mixture of Cu nanoparticles and water has been analyzed in an inclined microchannel with four rectangular shaped ribs. Laminar mixed convection heat transfer was studied by the use of FLUENT software. Properties of nanofluids have been extracted from the available formulations in literature and introduced in the software. Model validation has been performed by the comparison of the simulation results and the existing literature. The focus was on the heat transfer of water-based nanofluids with variable volume fractions of solid nanoparticles in microchannels with different angles of inclination. Results of this study may be applied in the use of coolants in various electronic devices such as high-power light-emitting diodes (LED), VLSI circuits, and micro-electro mechanical system (MEMS) [21].

2. Governing equations for laminar nanofluids

Dimensionless governing equations comprised of continuity, momentum, and energy equations, which are solved for laminar, steady-state flow in Cartesian coordinate system, are as follows [22, 23]:

$$\frac{\partial U}{\partial X}+\frac{\partial V}{\partial Y}=0 \tag{1}$$

$$U\frac{\partial U}{\partial X}+V\frac{\partial U}{\partial Y}=-\frac{\partial P}{\partial X}+\frac{\mu_{nf}}{\rho_{nf}v_{nf}}\frac{1}{\mathrm{Re}}\left(\frac{\partial^2 U}{\partial X^2}+\frac{\partial^2 U}{\partial Y^2}\right) \tag{2}$$

$$\mathrm{U}\frac{\partial V}{\partial X}+V\frac{\partial V}{\partial Y}=-\frac{\partial P}{\partial Y}+\frac{\mu_{nf}}{\rho_{nf}\upsilon_{nf}}\frac{1}{\mathrm{Re}}\left(\frac{\partial^2 V}{\partial X^2}+\frac{\partial^2 V}{\partial Y^2}\right)+\left(\frac{Gr}{\mathrm{Re}^2}\theta\right) \tag{3}$$

$$\mathrm{U}\frac{\partial \theta}{\partial X}+V\frac{\partial \theta}{\partial Y}=\frac{\alpha_{nf}}{\alpha_f}\frac{1}{\mathrm{Re}\,\mathrm{Pr}}\left(\frac{\partial^2 \theta}{\partial X^2}+\frac{\partial^2 \theta}{\partial Y^2}\right) \tag{4}$$

In the above equations, the following dimensionless parameters are used [24, 22]:

$$\begin{gathered}\mathrm{X}=\frac{\mathrm{x}}{\mathrm{h}},\ \mathrm{Y}=\frac{\mathrm{y}}{\mathrm{h}}, U=\frac{u}{u_{in}}, V=\frac{v}{u_{in}}, \mathrm{Pr}=\frac{\upsilon_f}{\alpha_f},\\ \theta=\frac{T-T_c}{T_h-T_c},\ \mathrm{Re}=\frac{u_{in}L_1}{\upsilon_f},\ \mathrm{P}=\frac{\overline{p}}{u_{in}^2\rho_{nf}}, Gr=\frac{g\beta(T_h-T_c)L_1^3}{\upsilon^2}\end{gathered} \tag{5}$$

To calculate the local Nusselt number along the lower wall, the following relation is used [22]:

$$\mathrm{Nu(X)}=-\frac{k_{\mathrm{nf}}}{k_{\mathrm{f}}}\left(\frac{\partial\theta}{\partial Y}\right)_{Y=0} \tag{6}$$

The local Nusselt number across the ribs is given as

http://dx.doi.org/10.5772/62898

$$\mathrm{Nu(Y)} = -\frac{k_{\mathrm{nf}}}{k_{\mathrm{f}}}\left(\frac{\partial\theta}{\partial X}\right)_{X=0} \tag{7}$$

The local Nusselt number along each horizontal and vertical part of the lower wall can be expressed as follows:

$$\mathrm{Nu}_{\mathrm{m,x}} = \frac{1}{L_H}\int_0^{L_H} Nu(x)dx \tag{8}$$

$$\mathrm{Nu}_{\mathrm{m,y}} = \frac{1}{L_v}\int_0^{L_v} Nu(y)dy \tag{9}$$

Total **N**usselt number on the surface of each rib is calculated by

$$\mathrm{Nu}_{\mathrm{m,\,total}} = \mathrm{Nu}_{\mathrm{m,x}} + \mathrm{Nu}_{\mathrm{m,y}} \tag{10}$$

To calculate the local friction factor along the lower wall, the following relation is used:

$$C_f = \frac{\mu\frac{\partial u}{\partial y}}{0.5\rho u_{in}^2} \tag{11}$$

Substituting dimensionless parameters of Eq. (5) in Eq. (11), relation (12) and (13) are obtained as follows:

$$C_f(X) = \frac{2}{\mathrm{Re}}\left(\frac{\partial U}{\partial Y}\right)_{Y=0} \tag{12}$$

$$C_f(Y) = \frac{2}{\mathrm{Re}}\left(\frac{\partial V}{\partial X}\right)_{X=0} \tag{13}$$

The average friction factor along each horizontal part of the lower wall can be calculated as

$$C_{f_{\mathrm{m,x}}} = \frac{1}{L_H}\int_0^{L_H} C_f(x)dx \tag{14}$$

The average friction factor across each rib is defined as

$$C_{f_{m,y}} = \frac{1}{L_v}\int_0^{L_v} C_f(y)dy \tag{15}$$

Total friction factor:

$$C_{f_{m,total}} = C_{f_{m,x}} + C_{f_{m,y}} \tag{16}$$

2.1. Nanofluid properties

Table 1 shows the thermophysical properties of copper (as nanoparticles) and water (as base fluid). The thermophysical properties of the nanofluid can be acquired from the nanoparticles' characteristics as well as that of the base fluid.

	Copper (Cu)	Water
$\rho\left(\mathrm{Kg\ m^{-3}}\right)$	8933	997.1
$k\left(\mathrm{W\ m^{-1}\ K^{-1}}\right)$	400	0.613
$C_p\left(\mathrm{J\ Kg^{-1}\ K^{-1}}\right)$	385	4179
$\beta\left(\mathrm{K^{-1}}\right)$	0.0000167	0.00021
$\mu\left(\mathrm{Pa\ s}\right)$	–	0.000891

Table 1. Thermophysical properties of the base fluid and Cu nanoparticles [26].

Density and heat capacity of nanofluids can be computed through the recommended expressions by Goodarzi et al. [25], Togun et al. [26] and Safaei et al. [27]:

$$\rho_{nf} = \phi\rho_s + (1-\phi)\rho_f \tag{17}$$

$$\left(\rho c_p\right)_{nf} = (1-\phi)(\rho c_p)_f + \phi(\rho c_p)_s \tag{18}$$

For nanofluid thermal conductivity, Chon et al. [28] suggested a model for Al_2O_3–water which includes the influences of Brownian motion, viscous sublayer thickness, and temperature [29]:

$$\frac{k_{nf}}{k_f} = 1 + 64.7\phi^{0.746}\left(\frac{d_f}{d_s}\right)^{0.369}\left(\frac{k_s}{k_f}\right)^{0.7476} \mathrm{Pr}^{0.9955}\,\mathrm{Re}^{1.2321} \tag{19}$$

where $\mathrm{Re}=\frac{\rho_f k_b T}{3\pi\mu^2 l_f}$ and $\mathrm{Pr}=\frac{\mu_f}{\rho_f \alpha_f}$ are the Brownian Reynolds and Prandtl numbers, l_f is the mean free path of base fluid (0.17 nm for water), and μ is the temperature-dependent viscosity of the base fluid, represented as

$$\mu = Q \times 10^{\frac{O}{T-J}} \tag{20}$$

where O, J, and Q are constants. For water, they are equal to 247.8, 140, and 2.414×10^{-5}, respectively [29]. However, based on the previous studies by Karimipour et al. [30], the aforementioned correlation can be used with confidence for copper–water nanofluids.

Dynamic nanofluid viscosity is evaluated based on the recommendations of Brinkman [31]:

$$\mu_{nf} = \frac{\mu_f}{(1-\phi)^{2.5}} \tag{21}$$

The thermal expansion coefficient can be obtained from the suggested formula by Khanafer et al. [32] and Abouali and Ahmadi [33]:

$$\beta_{nf} = \beta_f\left[\frac{1}{1+\frac{(1-\phi)\rho_f}{\phi\rho_s}}\frac{\beta_s}{\beta_f} + \frac{1}{1+\frac{\phi\rho_s}{(1-\phi)\rho_f}}\right] \tag{22}$$

3. Boundary conditions

A 2-D microchannel with four same rectangular ribs was selected for the analysis. Investigation of heat transfer and fluid dynamics, including the study of velocity, thermal field, and friction effects, was performed in different angles of inclination. The schematic of the investigated microchannel is illustrated in **Figure 1**. The microchannel is 1350 μm long and 90 μm high. The length of the lower wall of the microchannel was divided into three parts. The temperature of 290.5 K was set at the inlet. The temperature of 305.5 K was considered in the middle part of the microchannel with the length of 450 μm, consisting of four ribs. The channel was insulated on the total length of the upper wall (L_1) as well as on the length of 450 μm of both left and right sides of the lower wall. Rectangular ribs in all the studied cases were considered to have a pitch, width, and height of 90, 15, and 30 μm (one-third of the microchannel's height), respectively. In all cases, inclination angle between the microchannel and the horizon line was changed from 0° (horizontal case) to 90° (vertical case). A Reynolds number equal to 50 was selected to investigate the laminar flow, and Richardson number was varied between 0.1 and 10. Water as the base fluid was mixed with 0, 2, and 4% volume fractions of Cu nanoparticles (φ = 0.00, 0.02, and 0.04).

In this investigation, flow is considered to be incompressible, Newtonian, laminar, and single-phase. Thermophysical properties of nanofluid are assumed to remain unchanged with temperature.

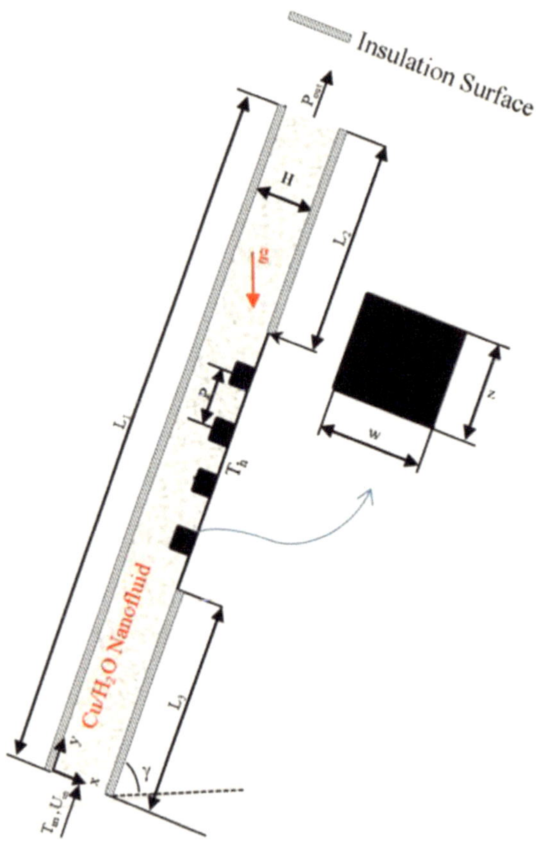

Figure 1. Schematic of the analyzed configuration.

4. Numerical method

The FLUENT commercial code was used to solve the partial differential equations that govern to the flow. The software applies the finite volume method, which is a particular case of the residual weighting method. This procedure is based on dividing the computational domain into finite control volumes, each node of which surrounds with a control volume. The partial differential equation is afterward integrated over each finite volume [34].

The QUICK scheme [35] was applied for the discretization of all convective terms, while the SIMPLEC algorithm [36] was employed for pressure/velocity coupling. At one point, when the residuals for all equations fell under 10^{-7}, the calculation reached the convergence [37]. Heat transfer and fluid dynamics parameters can be assessed, after solving the governing equations.

5. Numerical procedure validation

5.1. Comparison with numerical and experimental study of water

Results of this study were compared with those of Salman et al. [38] for validation purposes. Validation has been performed with numerical and experimental data, considering fluid flow of water in a smooth microtube with Reynolds number equal to 90. **Figure 2** shows an excellent agreement between the simulation results of this work with both experimental and numerical results.

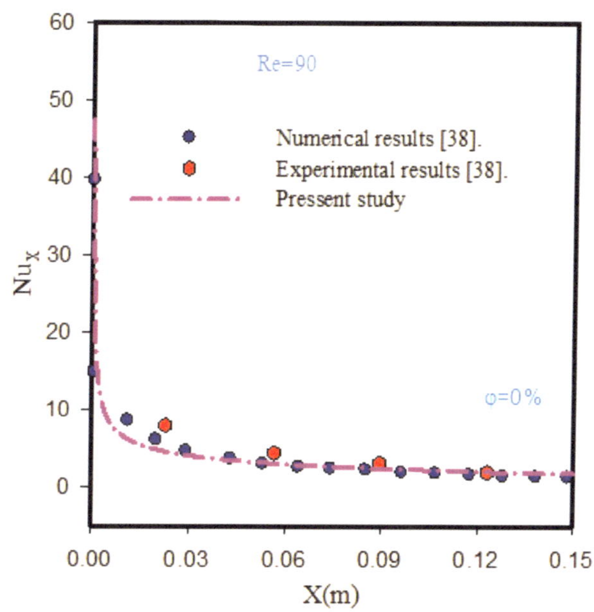

Figure 2. Local Nusselt number variation—comparison with the work of Salman et al. [38].

5.2. Comparison with numerical study of nanofluid

Aminossadati et al. [24] numerically investigated forced convection of water/Al_2O_3 in a horizontal microchannel. Middle part of the microchannel was exposed to a constant magnetic field and heated by a constant heat flux. The effect of parameters such as Reynolds number, volume fraction of solid nanoparticles, and Hartmann number on the flow field and thermal performance of the microchannel was studied.

Figure 3 demonstrates excellent agreement between the present model's predictions and the numerical results of Aminossadati et al. [24] in different Reynolds numbers and volume fractions, in terms of average Nusselt number. This comparison shows that the present numerical method is reliable and is useful in predicting forced convection heat transfer inside a microchannel for nanofluids.

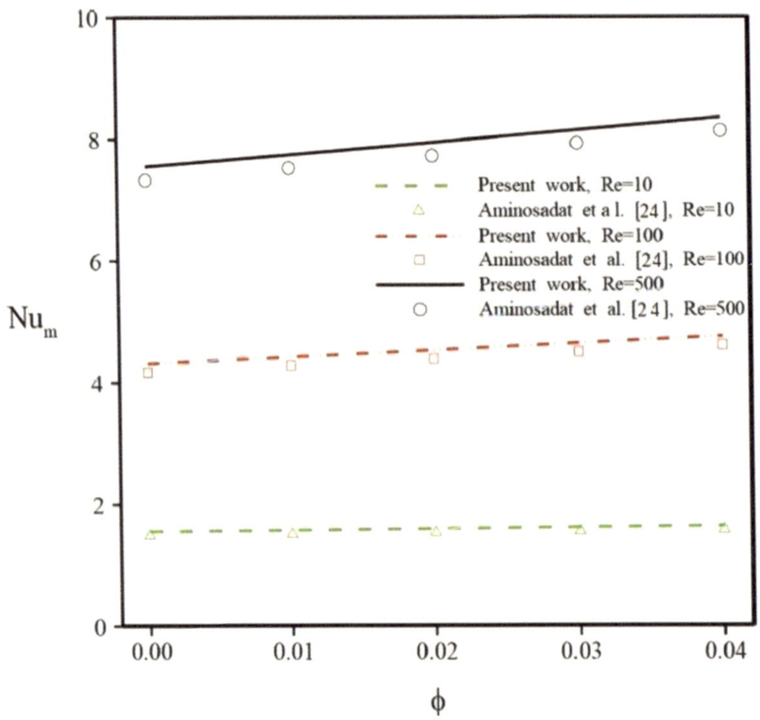

Figure 3. Averaged Nusselt number from present work versus that of Aminossadati et al. [24] for different values of Re and φ.

5.3. Grid independence

A structured, nonuniform grid has been chosen for the discretization of the computational domain. A more refined grid was applied near the walls, where temperature and velocity gradients are sensitive. Grid independency of the computational domain was tested by using various grid distributions. Average Nusselt number and dimensionless pressure drop for each number of grids are shown in **Figure 4(A, B)**, from which a grid of 60 × 900 was chosen for all the simulation cases.

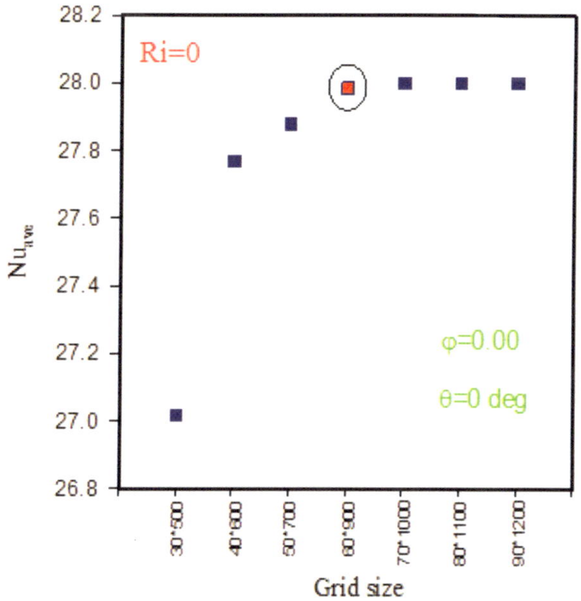

(A) Average Nusselt number

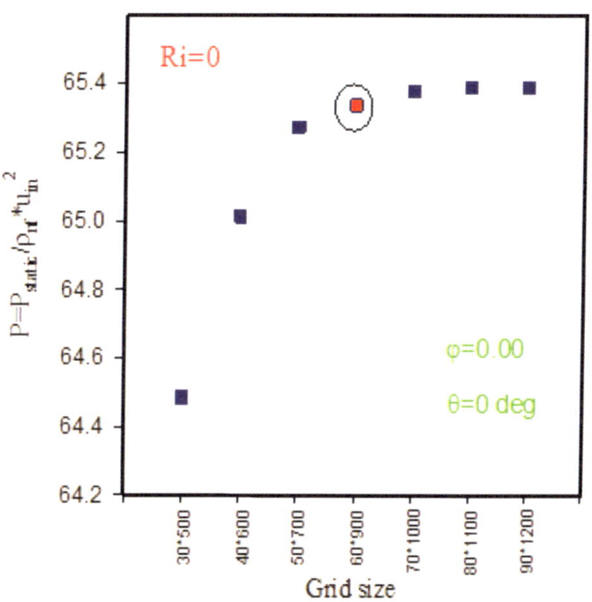

(B) Pressure drop

Figure 4. Grid independence tests for the present study by comparison of average Nusselt number and dimensionless pressure drop in various mesh concentrations: (A) average Nusselt number and (B) pressure drop.

6. Results and discussion

Inside an inclined microchannel with four rectangular ribs, mixed convection heat transfer of water–coppernanofluid is studied, utilizing finite volume method (**Figure 1**). The distances between the ribs and their lengths and widths are supposed to be constant. The simulation results are plotted in the form of contours and diagrams.

The isotherm contours and streamlines for $\gamma = 90°$, Re = 50, different Richardson numbers, and volume fraction of 4% are shown in **Figure 5 (A, B)**. After the microchannel's entry, the flow attains a fully developed hydrodynamic regime. When the fluid reaches the ribs, its direction is diverted and will result in an increased vertical component of the velocity. Yet, increased Richardson number does not lead to any change in the streamlines' variations. In case of isotherms' illustrations along the microchannel, once fluid with temperature of T_h arrives in the rib-roughened areas with T_c(surface temperature), temperature of fluid decreases, and heat is transferred between the rib-roughened surfaces and fluid. Along the microchannel, ribs function as a mixer and reduce the temperature gradient between the surface and the fluid, and afterwards, the rate of heat transfer increases. These variations in heat transfer improve as the inclination angle (γ) or Richardson number increases. The first influential factor is the resultant from the gravity and variations in its components—perpendicular to and in line with the flow fluid—along the microchannel. Once γ increases from 0 to 90°, the terms of diffusion and advection in natural convection heat transfer strengthen, which leads to isothermal line variations.

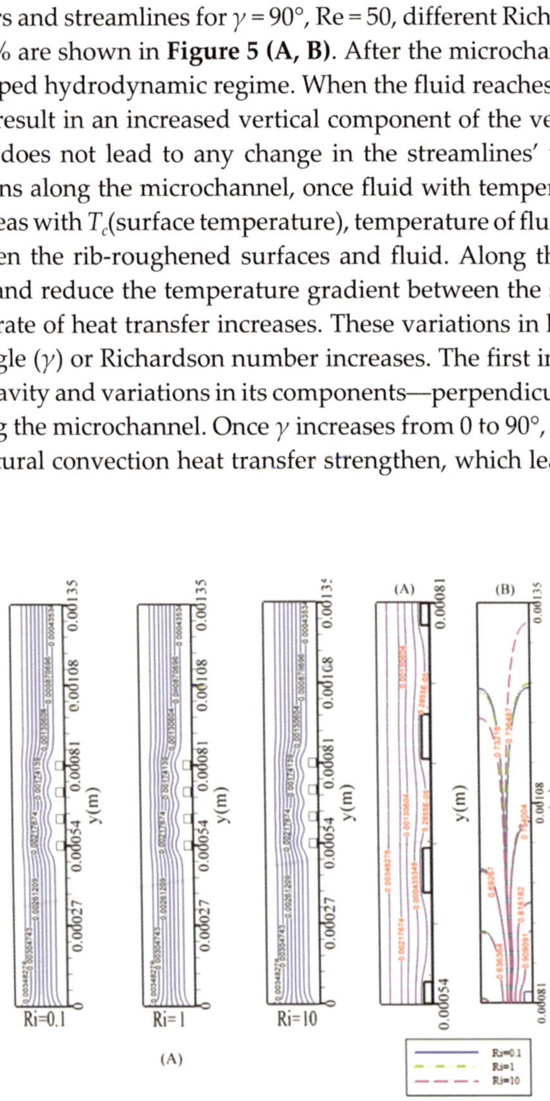

Figure 5. (A) Streamlines and (B) Isotherm contours for 4% volume fraction and $\gamma = 90°$.

The dimensionless velocity contours for Ri = 10, 2% volume fraction, and 30°, 45°, 60°, and 90° inclination angles, in line with (A) and perpendicular (B) to the flow are demonstrated in **Figure**

6 (A, B). The increasing γ exerts a significant effect on fluid flow behavior and heat transfer. The velocity components (perpendicular to and along with the flow) vary by flowing the fluid along the microchannel, because of the ribs. Increased inclination angle intensifies these variations. The outcomes showed that the perpendicular velocity component exhibited more variation, which causes vortexes and reverse flows in the flow field. Consequently, this velocity component is deemed more effective, because its intensification can improve flow mixing and rate of heat transfer.

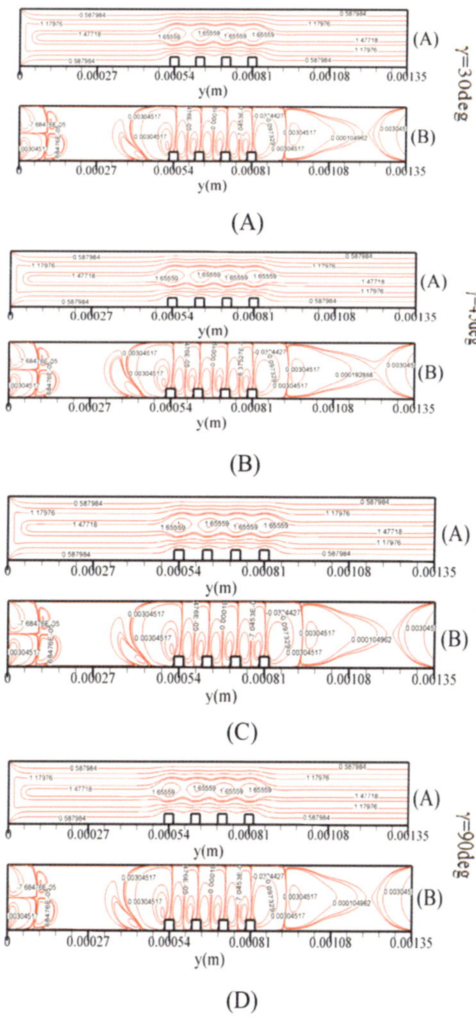

Figure 6. Dimensionless velocity contours for 2% volume fraction, different inclination angles, and Ri = 10: (A) along the flow and (B) perpendicular to the flow.

The average Nusselt number for a ribbed microchannel with various volume fractions, different Ri, and inclination angles is depicted in **Figure 7**. The results endorse that the average

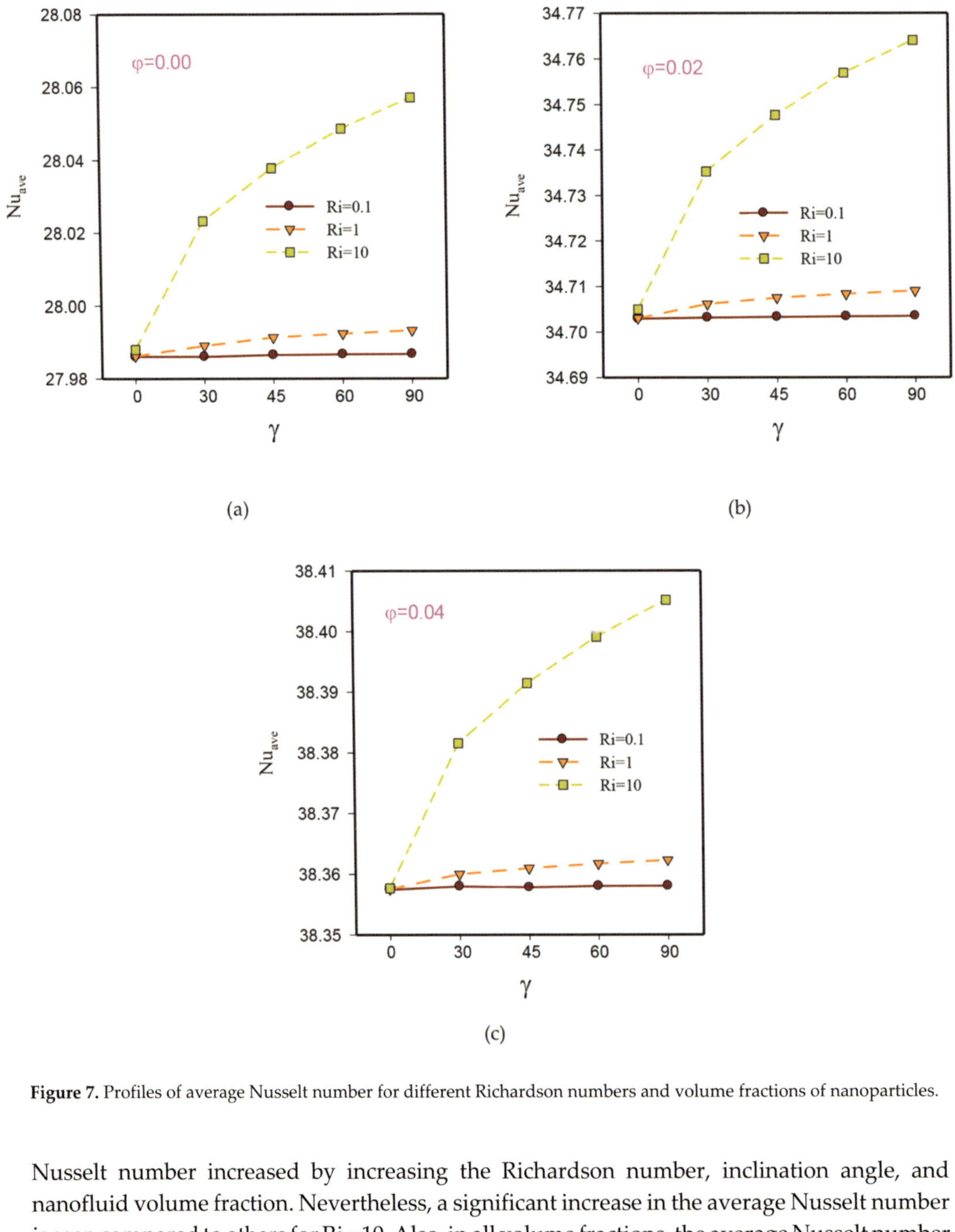

Figure 7. Profiles of average Nusselt number for different Richardson numbers and volume fractions of nanoparticles.

Nusselt number increased by increasing the Richardson number, inclination angle, and nanofluid volume fraction. Nevertheless, a significant increase in the average Nusselt number is seen compared to others for Ri = 10. Also, in all volume fractions, the average Nusselt number is higher when Ri = 1 compared with Ri = 0.1. This can be attributed to the fact that as the Richardson number increases, the effective terms in natural convection heat transfer are strengthened. Moreover, increased volume fraction of nanoparticles significantly affects fluids' thermal conductivity, which enhances the rate of nanofluid heat transfer. Even though

http://dx.doi.org/10.5772/62898

when Ri = 0.1, the increment of average Nusselt number is nearly independent of γ, the heat transfer is increased with an increase in γ in higher Richardson numbers. The reason can be the velocity component variations, which rise mixing of the fluid layers.

The local Nusselt number for the distillated water and nanofluids on the lower wall of the microchannel, $\gamma = 90°$, and different Richardson numbers is compared in **Figure 8**. As can be seen, nanofluid has a greater Nusselt number than the distillated water, because of the existence of nanoparticles with greater thermal conductivity and also the effect of Brownian motion on the nanofluid's thermal conductivity. Other factors that increase the Nusselt number are the ribs, which lead to abrupt upsurge of the heat transfer rate in the rib-roughened parts. It is primarily due to improved mixing of the fluid layers between cold fluid and hot area. Thermal boundary layer is altered and reformed when the fluid hits the ribs, which eventually increases the rate of heat transfer.

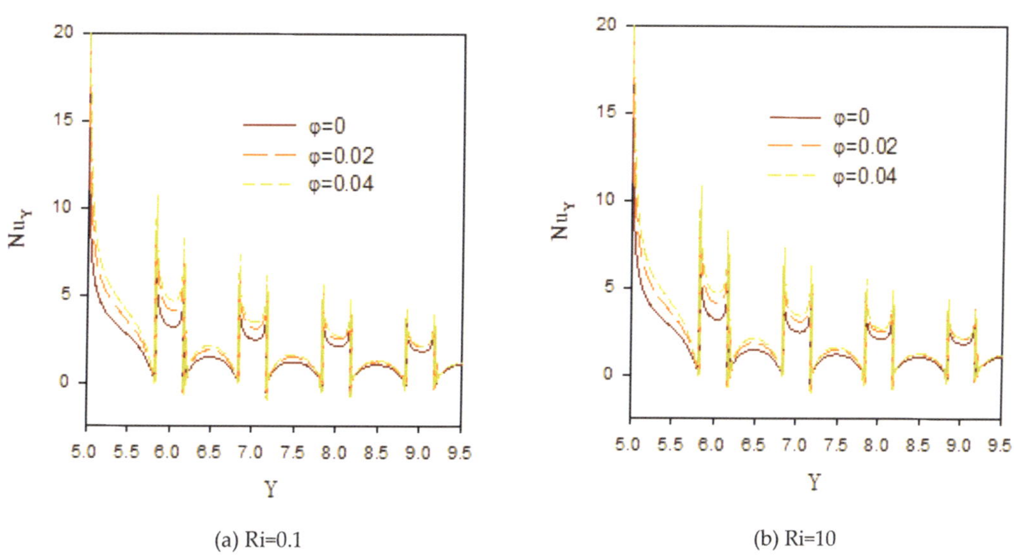

Figure 8. Local Nusselt number on lower rib-roughened wall for $\gamma = 90°$: (A) Ri = 0.1; (B) Ri = 10.

The pressure drop values for different Richardson numbers and volume fractions are shown in **Figure 9**. It was observed that in all studied cases, pressure drop augments as the volume fractions of nanoparticles, Richardson number, or inclination angle increase. In the cooling fluid, solid nanoparticles cause a significant drop in pressure owing to the flow of denser, high-viscous fluid, compared with the fluid with lower density and viscosity. More vortexes are created as a result of increased inclination angle of the microchannel and the flow is reversed, which necessitate more energy to increase the pressure drop. Likewise, the pressure drop increases by transition from forced convection domination to free convection one, as a result of high variations of gravity components in higher Richardson numbers.

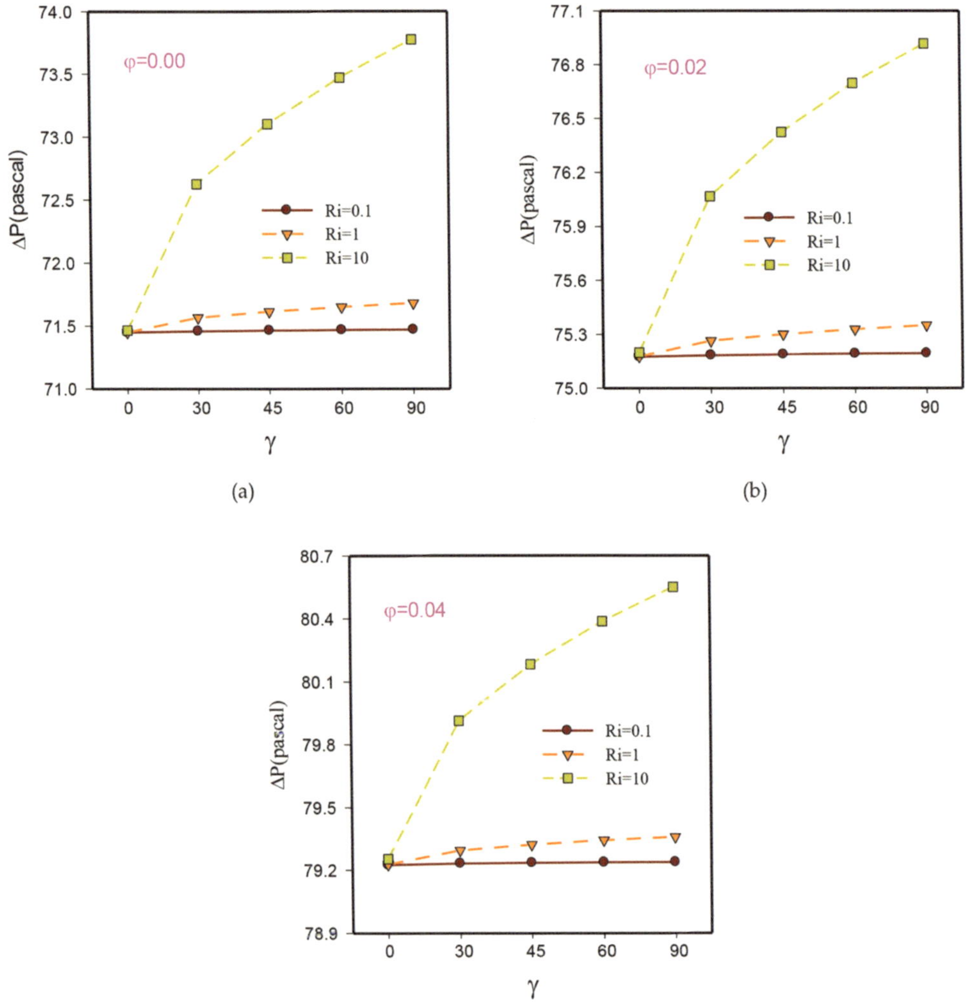

Figure 9. Pressure drop diagram for different Richardson numbers and volume fractions of nanoparticles.

The average friction factor for different Richardson numbers and volume fractions on the upper wall of the microchannel are shown in **Figure 10**. The average friction factor drops as the nanoparticle volume fraction decreases, and Richardson number and inclination angle increase. The density and dynamic viscosity of the fluid are intensified as the nanoparticle volume fraction increases, which leads to an increment in the average friction factor. Also, collision of particles with the microchannel's surface increases in higher nanoparticle volume fraction, which raises the friction factor. The friction factor is more or less independent from γ for the case of forced convection domination. Nevertheless, with an increase in inclination angle or Richardson number, the friction factor on the upper wall drops because of gradient reduction in axial velocity in line with the upper wall of the microchannel.

http://dx.doi.org/10.5772/62898

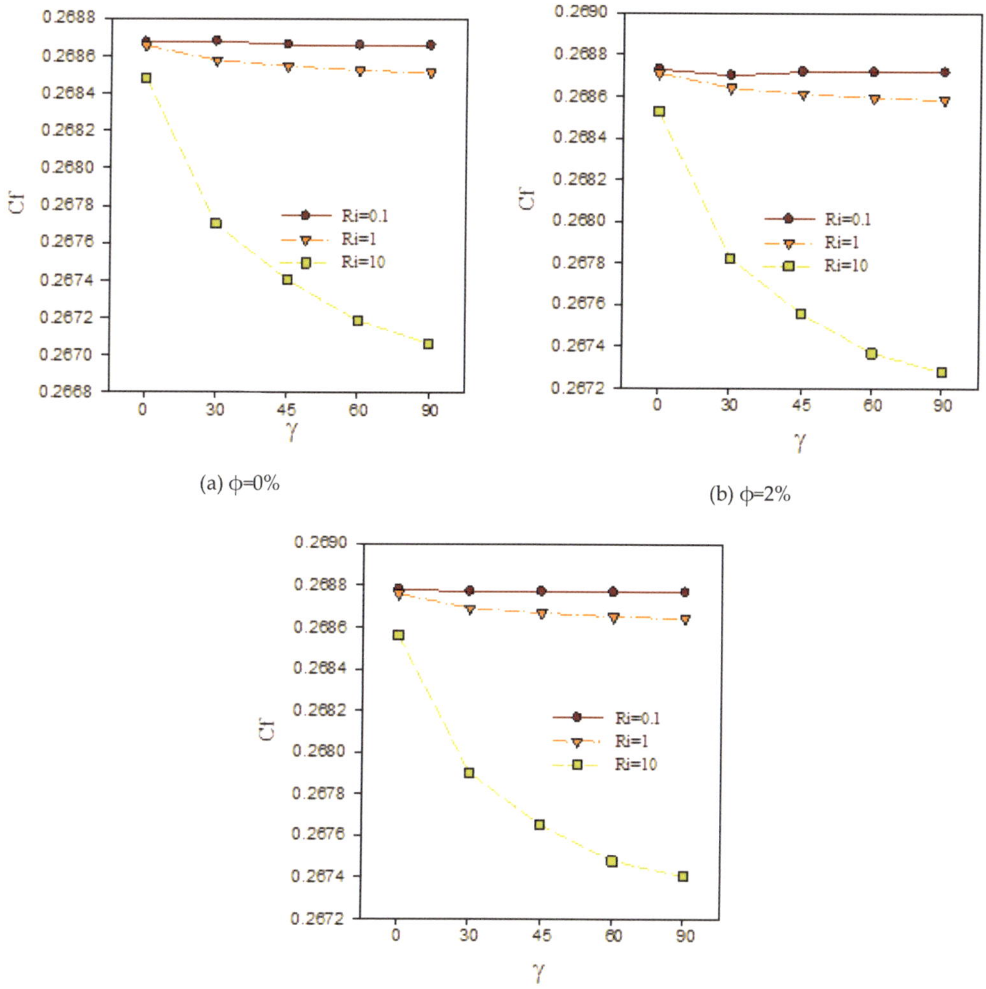

Figure 10. Average friction factor on microchannel's top wall. (A) φ=0%; (B) φ=2%; (C) φ=4%.

The dimensionless temperature profiles in different inclination angles and microchannel cross sections for $\varphi = 0.04$ and $\mathrm{Ri} = 1$ are demonstrated in **Figure 11**. It can be seen that approaching microchannel's outlet cross section or increasing inclination angle of microchannel decreases the dimensionless temperature of hot fluid for all cases. This results in better mixing of fluid layers, and lastly, increase of heat transfer.

Higher inclination angles result in development of intensive vortexes and better fluid mixing, which significantly decrease the dimensionless temperature, particularly in near-inlet cross sections. Thus, the dimensionless temperature for the vertical microchannel has the least value in all cross sections, meaning that this microchannel angle has the maximum rate of heat transfer.

At sections near to the entry, the dimensionless temperature profile drops, because the thermal boundary layer has not been developed yet. The thermal boundary layer becomes fully developed as the entry length is increased, which increases the dimensionless temperature.

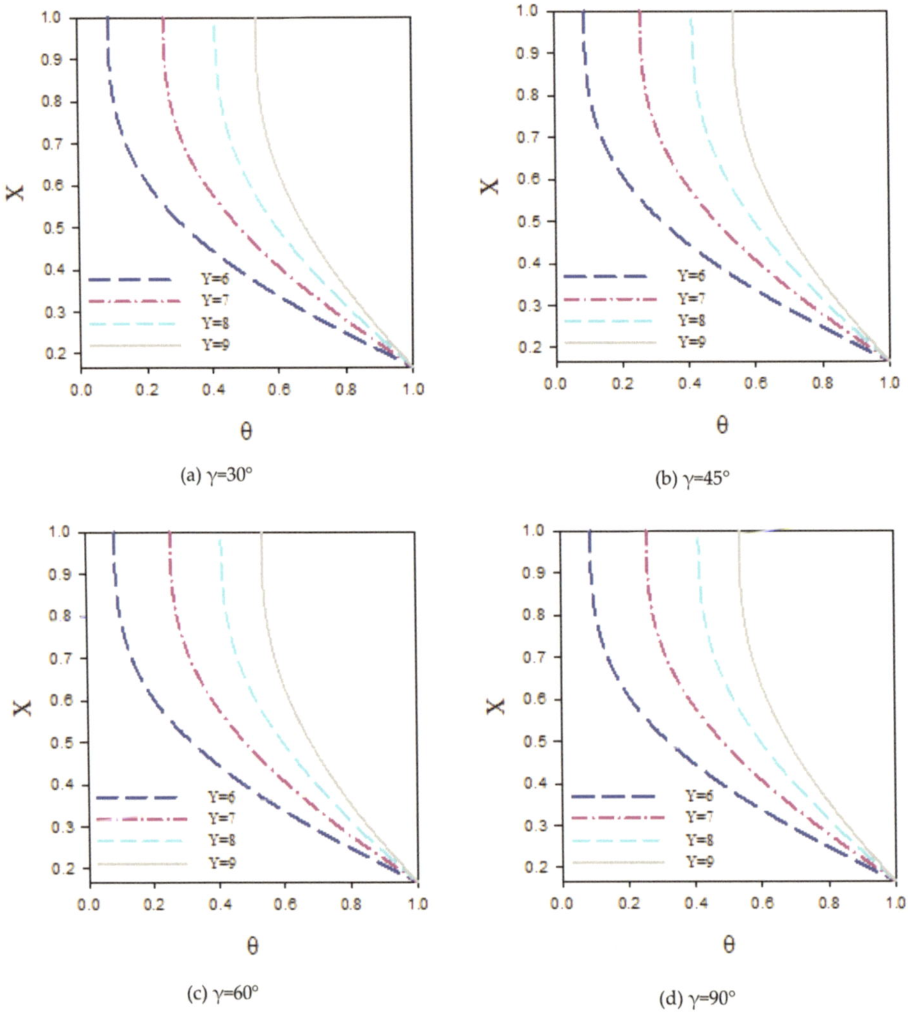

Figure 11. Profiles of dimensionless temperature in different microchannel cross sections for Ri = 1 and φ = 0.04. (A) γ=30°; (B) γ=45°; (C) γ=60°; (D) γ=90°.

7. Conclusions

In this work, the fluid flow and heat transfer of laminar Cu–water nanofluid in a 2D rectangular ribbed microchannel with different inclination angles and Richardson numbers were investigated. Simulation of the problem was performed by the use of finite volume method. Reynolds

http://dx.doi.org/10.5772/62898

number of 50 and Richardson numbers between 0.1 and 10 were applied to the simulation. Solid nanoparticles were chosen to have a volume fraction of 0.0–4.0%.

The results of this research revealed that increasing the inclination angle of microchannel or volume fraction of solid particles enhances the heat transfer rate. Existence of ribs through the flow path results in velocity gradient and increases the fluid contact with the surfaces of the microchannel, which in turn enhances heat transfer, while increasing the average friction factor. Addition of nanoparticles to the base fluid does not majorly affect the hydrodynamic parameters of the flow such as fluid velocity. Of all the studied cases, maximum heat transfer can be seen in a vertical microchannel, dominated by natural convection, because of the significant effect of gravity on the fluid structure and enhanced mixing of the fluid layers; and the lowest Nusselt number belongs to the horizontal microchannel dominated by forced convection.

Acknowledgements

The authors gratefully acknowledge High Impact Research Grant UM.C/HIR/MOHE/ENG/23 and Faculty of Engineering, University of Malaya, Malaysia for support in conducting this research work.

Nomenclature

x, y	Cartesian coordinates (m)
D	Diameter (m)
X, Y	Dimensionless coordinates
U, V	Dimensionless flow velocity in x–y direction
H, L	Dimensionless microchannel height and length
P	Fluid pressure (Pa)
C_f	Friction factor
Gr	Grashof number
G	Gravity acceleration (m/s^2)
C_p	Heat capacity (J/kg K)
u_{in}	Inlet flow velocity (m/s)
h, l	Microchannel height and length (m)
Nu	Nusselt number
Pr	Prandtl number
Re	Reynolds number
T	Temperature, K

K	Thermal conductivity, W/m K
u, v	velocity components in x, y directions, m/s

Greek symbols

κ_b	Boltzmann constant (J/K)
ρ	Density (kg/m^3)
θ	Dimensionless temperature
μ	Dynamic viscosity (Pa s)
υ	Kinematics viscosity (m^2/s)
φ	Nanoparticles volume fraction
Γ	The angle between ribs and horizon line (°)
α	Thermal diffusivity (m^2/s)
β	Thermal expansion coefficient (1/ K)

Superscripts and subscripts

F	Base fluid (distillated water)
C	Cold
H	Hot
H	Horizontal
In	Inlet
M	Mean
Nf	Nanofluid
S	Solid nanoparticles
total	Total
V	Vertical

Author details

Mohammad Reza Safaei[1*], Marjan Gooarzi[2], Omid Ali Akbari[3,4], Mostafa Safdari Shadloo[5] and Mahidzal Dahari[6]

*Address all correspondence to: cfd_safaei@um.edu.my; cfd_safaei@yahoo.com

1 Department of Mechanical Engineering, Faculty of Engineering, University of Malaya, Kuala Lumpur, Malaysia

2 Young Researchers and Elite Club, Mashhad Branch, Islamic Azad University, Mashhad, Iran

3 Department of Mechanical Engineering, Aligoudarz Branch, Islamic Azad University, Aligoudarz, Iran

4 Department of Mechanical Engineering, Azna Branch, Islamic Azad University, Azna, Iran

5 CORIA-UMR 6614, Normandie University, CNRS-University & INSA of Rouen, Rouvray, France

6 Department of Electrical Engineering, Faculty of Engineering, University of Malaya, Kuala Lumpur, Malaysia

References

[1] Sakanova A, Keian CC, Zhao J. Performance improvements of microchannel heat sink using wavy channel and nanofluids. International Journal of Heat and Mass Transfer. 2015;89:59–74. doi:http://dx.doi.org/10.1016/j.ijheatmasstransfer.2015.05.033.

[2] Tuckerman DB, Pease R. High-performance heat sinking for VLSI. Electron Device Letters, IEEE. 1981;2(5):126–129.

[3] Sohel M, Saidur R, Sabri MFM, Kamalisarvestani M, Elias M, Ijam A. Investigating the heat transfer performance and thermophysical properties of nanofluids in a circular micro-channel. International Communications in Heat and Mass Transfer. 2013;42:75–81.

[4] Nimmagadda R, Venkatasubbaiah K. Conjugate heat transfer analysis of micro-channel using novel hybrid nanofluids (Al_2O_3+Ag/water). European Journal of Mechanics - B/Fluids. 2015;52:19–27. doi:http://dx.doi.org/10.1016/j.euromechflu.2015.01.007.

[5] Khaled ARA, Vafai K. Cooling augmentation using microchannels with rotatable separating plates. International Journal of Heat and Mass Transfer. 2011;54(15–16):3732–3739. doi:http://dx.doi.org/10.1016/j.ijheatmasstransfer.2011.02.054.

[6] Vafai K, Khaled ARA. Analysis of flexible microchannel heat sink systems. International Journal of Heat and Mass Transfer. 2005;48(9):1739–1746. doi:http://dx.doi.org/10.1016/j.ijheatmasstransfer.2004.11.020.

[7] Goodarzi M, Amiri A, Goodarzi MS, Safaei MR, Karimipour A, Languri EM et al. Investigation of heat transfer and pressure drop of a counter flow corrugated plate heat

exchanger using MWCNT based nanofluids. International Communications in Heat and Mass Transfer. 2015;66:172–179.

[8] Sarafraz MM, Hormozi F. Experimental study on the thermal performance and efficiency of a copper made thermosyphon heat pipe charged with alumina–glycol based nanofluids. Powder Technology. 2014;266:378–387. doi:http://dx.doi.org/10.1016/j.powtec.2014.06.053.

[9] Goshayeshi HR, Goodarzi M, Safaei MR, Dahari M. Experimental study on the effect of inclination angle on heat transfer enhancement of a ferrofluid in a closed loop oscillating heat pipe under magnetic field. Experimental Thermal and Fluid Science. 2016;74:265–270. doi:http://dx.doi.org/10.1016/j.expthermflusci.2016.01.003.

[10] Kalteh M, Abbassi A, Saffar-Avval M, Frijns A, Darhuber A, Harting J. Experimental and numerical investigation of nanofluid forced convection inside a wide microchannel heat sink. Applied Thermal Engineering. 2012;36:260–268. doi:http://dx.doi.org/10.1016/j.applthermaleng.2011.10.023.

[11] Malvandi A, Ganji DD. Brownian motion and thermophoresis effects on slip flow of alumina/water nanofluid inside a circular microchannel in the presence of a magnetic field. International Journal of Thermal Sciences. 2014;84:196–206. doi:http://dx.doi.org/10.1016/j.ijthermalsci.2014.05.013.

[12] Nikkhah Z, Karimipour A, Safaei MR, Forghani-Tehrani P, Goodarzi M, Dahari M et al. Forced convective heat transfer of water/functionalized multi-walled carbon nanotube nanofluids in a microchannel with oscillating heat flux and slip boundary condition. International Communications in Heat and Mass Transfer. 2015;68:69–77.

[13] Nitiapiruk P, Mahian O, Dalkilic AS, Wongwises S. Performance characteristics of a microchannel heat sink using TiO_2/water nanofluid and different thermophysical models. International Communications in Heat and Mass Transfer. 2013;47:98–104. doi:http://dx.doi.org/10.1016/j.icheatmasstransfer.2013.07.001.

[14] Hassan M, Sadri R, Ahmadi G, Dahari MB, Kazi SN, Safaei MR et al. Numerical study of entropy generation in a flowing nanofluid used in micro-and minichannels. Entropy. 2013;15(1):144–155.

[15] Rimbault B, Nguyen CT, Galanis N. Experimental investigation of CuO–water nanofluid flow and heat transfer inside a microchannel heat sink. International Journal of Thermal Sciences. 2014;84:275–292. doi:http://dx.doi.org/10.1016/j.ijthermalsci.2014.05.025.

[16] Zhang H, Shao S, Xu H, Tian C. Heat transfer and flow features of Al_2O_3–water nanofluids flowing through a circular microchannel—Experimental results and correlations. Applied Thermal Engineering. 2013;61(2):86–92. doi:http://dx.doi.org/10.1016/j.applthermaleng.2013.07.026.

[17] Esmaeilnejad A, Aminfar H, Neistanak MS. Numerical investigation of forced convection heat transfer through microchannels with non-Newtonian nanofluids. Interna-

tional Journal of Thermal Sciences. 2014;75:76–86. doi:http://dx.doi.org/10.1016/j.ijthermalsci.2013.07.020.

[18] Karimipour A, Hossein Nezhad A, D'Orazio A, Hemmat Esfe M, Safaei MR, Shirani E. Simulation of copper–water nanofluid in a microchannel in slip flow regime using the lattice Boltzmann method. European Journal of Mechanics - B/Fluids. 2015;49, Part A: 89–99. doi:http://dx.doi.org/10.1016/j.euromechflu.2014.08.004.

[19] Hedayati F, Malvandi A, Kaffash MH, Ganji DD. Fully developed forced convection of alumina/water nanofluid inside microchannels with asymmetric heating. Powder Technology. 2015;269:520–531. doi:http://dx.doi.org/10.1016/j.powtec.2014.09.034.

[20] Salman BH, Mohammed HA, Munisamy KM, Kherbeet AS. Characteristics of heat transfer and fluid flow in microtube and microchannel using conventional fluids and nanofluids: a review. Renewable and Sustainable Energy Reviews. 2013;28:848–880. doi:http://dx.doi.org/10.1016/j.rser.2013.08.012.

[21] Hadadian M, Samiee S, Ahmadzadeh H, Goharshadi EK. Nanofluids for heat transfer enhancement—A review. Physical Chemistry Research. 2013;1(1):1–33.

[22] Raisi A, Ghasemi B, Aminossadati S. A numerical study on the forced convection of laminar nanofluid in a microchannel with both slip and no-slip conditions. Numerical Heat Transfer, Part A: Applications. 2011;59(2):114–129.

[23] Sharif M. Laminar mixed convection in shallow inclined driven cavities with hot moving lid on top and cooled from bottom. Applied Thermal Engineering. 2007;27(5): 1036–1042.

[24] Aminossadati S, Raisi A, Ghasemi B. Effects of magnetic field on nanofluid forced convection in a partially heated microchannel. International Journal of Non-Linear Mechanics. 2011;46(10):1373–1382.

[25] Goodarzi M, Safaei MR, Vafai K, Ahmadi G, Dahari M, Kazi SN et al. Investigation of nanofluid mixed convection in a shallow cavity using a two-phase mixture model. International Journal of Thermal Sciences. 2014;75:204–220. doi:http://dx.doi.org/10.1016/j.ijthermalsci.2013.08.003.

[26] Togun H, Ahmadi G, Abdulrazzaq T, Shkarah AJ, Kazi S, Badarudin A et al. Thermal performance of nanofluid in ducts with double forward-facing steps. Journal of the Taiwan Institute of Chemical Engineers. 2015;47:28–42.

[27] Safaei MR, Togun H, Vafai K, Kazi S, Badarudin A. Investigation of heat transfer enhancement in a forward-facing contracting channel using FMWCNT nanofluids. Numerical Heat Transfer, Part A: Applications. 2014;66(12):1321–1340.

[28] Chon CH, Kihm KD, Lee SP, Choi SUS. Empirical correlation finding the role of temperature and particle size for nanofluid (Al_2O_3) thermal conductivity enhancement. Applied Physics Letters. 2005;87(15):153107—153107-3.

[29] Mintsa HA, Roy G, Nguyen CT, Doucet D. New temperature dependent thermal conductivity data for water-based nanofluids. International Journal of Thermal Sciences. 2009;48(2):363–371.

[30] Karimipour A, Nezhad A, Behzadmehr A, Alikhani S, Abedini E. Periodic mixed convection of a nanofluid in a cavity with top lid sinusoidal motion. Proceedings of the Institution of Mechanical Engineers, Part C: Journal of Mechanical Engineering Science. 2011;225:2149–2160.

[31] Brinkman H. The viscosity of concentrated suspensions and solutions. The Journal of Chemical Physics. 1952;20(4):571–.

[32] Khanafer, Vafai K, Lightstone M. Buoyancy-driven heat transfer enhancement in a two-dimensional enclosure utilizing nanofluids. International Journal of Heat and Mass Transfer. 2003;46(19):3639–3653.

[33] Abouali O, Ahmadi G. Computer simulations of natural convection of single phase nanofluids in simple enclosures: a critical review. Applied Thermal Engineering. 2012;36:1–13.

[34] Patankar SV. Numerical Heat Transfer and Fluid Flow, Series in Computational Methods in Mechanics and Thermal Sciences. Hemisphere Publishing Corporation; 1980.

[35] Rahmanian B, Safaei MR, Kazi SN, Ahmadi G, Oztop HF, Vafai K. Investigation of pollutant reduction by simulation of turbulent non-premixed pulverized coal combustion. Applied Thermal Engineering. 2014;73(1):1222–1235.

[36] Goodarzi M, Safaei M, Karimipour A, Hooman K, Dahari M, Kazi S et al. Comparison of the finite volume and lattice Boltzmann methods for solving natural convection heat transfer problems inside cavities and enclosures. Abstract and Applied Analysis. 2014;2014(Article ID 762184):1–15. doi:10.1155/2014/762184.

[37] Goodarzi M, Safaei M, Oztop HF, Karimipour A, Sadeghinezhad E, Dahari M et al. Numerical study of entropy generation due to coupled laminar and turbulent mixed convection and thermal radiation in an enclosure filled with a semitransparent medium. The Scientific World Journal. 2014;2014:1–8.

[38] Salman B, Mohammed H, Kherbeet AS. Numerical and experimental investigation of heat transfer enhancement in a microtube using nanofluids. International Communications in Heat and Mass Transfer. 2014;59:88–100.

Chapter 7

Reciprocating Mechanism–Driven Heat Loop (RMDHL) Cooling Technology for Power Electronic Systems

Olubunmi Popoola, Soheil Soleimanikutanaei and Yiding Cao

Additional information is available at the end of the chapter

http://dx.doi.org/10.5772/62518

Abstract

The most significant hindrances to the technological advances in high power electronics (HPE) and digital computational devices (DCD) has always been the issue of effective thermal management. Energy losses during operation cause heat to build up in these components, resulting in temperature rise. Finding effective thermal solutions will become a major constraint for the reduction of cost and time-to-market, two governing factors between success and failure in commercial evolution of technology. Even when high temperatures are not reached, high thermal stresses because of temperature variations are major causes of failure in electronic components mounted on circuit boards. An effective electronic cooling technique, which is based on reciprocating heat pipe, is the so-called reciprocating mechanism–driven heat loop (RMDHL) that has a heat transfer mechanism different from those of traditional heat pipes. Experimental results show that the heat loop worked very effectively and a heat flux as high as 300 W/cm^2 in the evaporator section could be handled. In addition to eliminating the cavitation problem associated with traditional two-phase heat loops, the RMDHL also provides superior cooling advantage with respect to temperature uniformity. Considering the other advantages of coolant leakage free and the absence of cavitation problems for aerospace-related applications, the single phase RMDHL could be an alternative of a conventional liquid cooling system (LCS) for electronic cooling applications. This chapter will provide insight into experimental, numerical and analytical study undertaken for RMDHL in connection with high heat and high heat flux thermal management applications and electronic cooling. In addition to clarifying the fundamental physics behind the working mechanism of RMDHLs, a working criterion has also been derived, which could provide a guidance for the design of a reciprocating mechanism–driven heat loop.

Keywords: power electronic cooling, high heat flux, reciprocating flow, temperature uniformity, single and two-phase heat transfer

1. Introduction

Thermal management and related design problems continue to be identified by the Semiconductor Industries Association Roadmap [1] as one of the five key challenges during the next decade to achieve the projected performance goals of the industry. Finding effective thermal solutions will become a major constraint for the reduction of cost and time-to-market, two governing factors between success and failure in commercial evolution of technology [2]. In addition to the time urgency, the heat generation problem is further compounded by the increasing trend of miniaturization of these chips. It has been observed over the years, these chips have gotten smaller and more compact and the smaller they get the higher the heat flux associated with their operation. Microelectronic chips may dissipate heat fluxes as high as 10 W through a 5 mm x 5 mm side (400 W/cm^2) [3–5] and heat fluxes over 1,000 W/cm^2 have been projected [6]. As a result, there is a need to create a capability to effectively remove these high heat fluxes. An effective thermal management system must also find a solution to non-uniform system temperature or heat flux distribution across the surfaces [7]. Even when high temperatures are not reached, high thermal stresses because of temperature variations are major causes of failure in electronic components mounted on circuit boards [8]. Non-uniform heat flux distribution leads to local hot spots and elevated temperature gradients across the silicon die, excessive thermal stresses on the device, and ultimately device failure.

For a cooling system, there are several design options to have a larger rate of heat removal. The first option is the passive two-phase heat transfer systems [9, 10]. Some typical passive heat transfer systems are heat pipes, gravity-assisted heat pipes, capillary pumped loops, and vapor chambers (a flat-plate type heat pipe). The passive systems can function without requiring any mechanical power input. However, heat pipe or capillary pumped loop are capable of handling the maximum heat flux of 20 W/cm^2. In some cases for a higher heat flux, a special wick structure design may handle it better but the temperature uniformity requirement may not be held as the temperature drop across the heat pipe could be on the order of 5–10 °C. The capillary pumped loop has an advantage over the heat pipe as it transports heat over a longer distance [11], which is also may considered as a special type of heat pipe. But it may also have the same drawbacks of temperature uniformity and heat flux as heat pipe. The most significant challenge that the above passive heat transfer devices are facing is the tolerance of a substantial body force. In passive heat transfer system, the working fluid could be thrown out of the evaporator because of the inertial force that results in liquid reduction in the evaporator section.

The second option is the single-phase forced convection cooling, which is an active cooling system. This cooling system is the most popular method that uses a pumping system to circulate a liquid coolant for extracting heat from a heat generating device.

The third design option is a two-phase pumped cooling loop to simultaneously satisfy the temperature uniformity and high heat flux requirements [9]. In this case, the coolant is still circulated by a pumping device and the boiling/evaporation are allowed to occur over the heated surface, which could provide an enhanced capability to remove a larger amount of heat and achieve a higher level of temperature uniformity over the system. However, the pumping

http://dx.doi.org/10.5772/62518

reliability is always a serious concern. First, the problem of a large the body force (pΔv stress because of phase change of the coolant) may be experienced during the operation, which may be a significant challenge on the design of a cooling system [12]. Second, the space within the cold plate must be reserved for boiling and vaporization and the two-phase loop cannot be filled completely with the liquid, as a result, vapor or liquid–vapor two-phase mixture may enter the pump, which could cause so-called cavitation problem and render the pump ineffective [13].

There is another heat transfer mechanism different from those of traditional heat pipes called reciprocating heat pipe. Cao et al. [14, 15] developed a reciprocating heat pipe, the so-called reciprocating mechanism–driven heat loop (RMDHL) that worked very effectively. As experimental results show that it can handle a heat flux as high as 300 W/cm^2 in the evaporator section. A RMDHL (**Figure 1**) is normally composed of a hollow loop having an interior flow passage, an amount of working fluid filled within the loop, and a reciprocating driver. The hollow loop has an evaporator section, a condenser section, and a liquid reservoir. The reciprocating driver is integrated with the liquid reservoir and facilitates a reciprocating flow of the working fluid within the loop. It supplies liquid from the condenser to the evaporator under a substantially saturated condition that avoids the cavitation problem associated with a conventional pump. For electronics cooling and high-temperature applications, the reciprocating driver could be a solenoid-operated reciprocating driver (**Figure 1a**) and a bellows-type reciprocating driver (**Figure 1b**), respectively. RMDHL not only eliminates the cavitation problem associated with traditional two-phase heat loops, but also provides superior cooling advantage with respect to temperature uniformity.

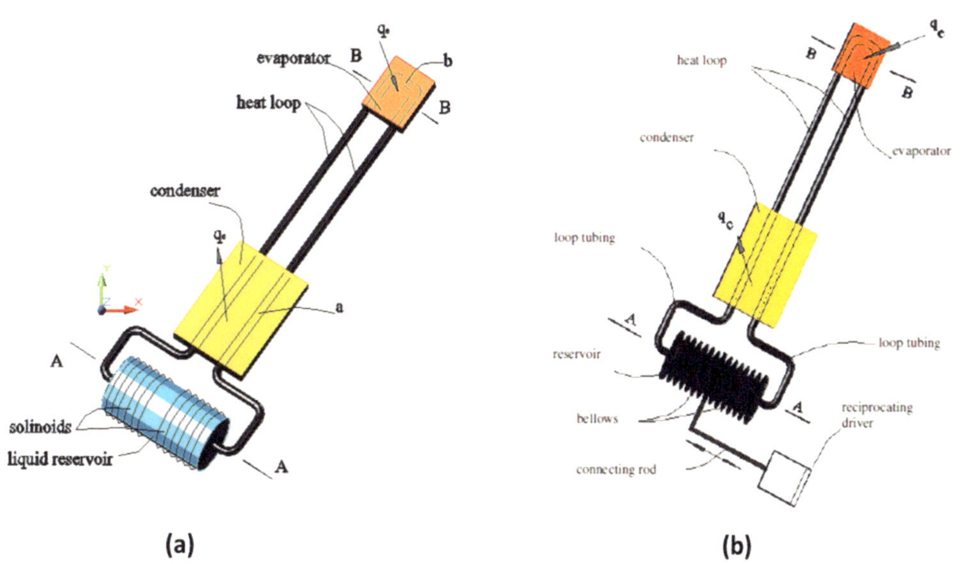

Figure 1. Schematic of a (a) solenoid-driven reciprocating mechanism–driven heat loop and (b) bellows-type reciprocating mechanism–driven heat loop [12].

To facilitate the assembling of the bellows and reciprocating driver, a bellows stand has been constructed and is schematically shown in **Figure 2a**. As seen in the figure, two bellows are placed side by side in a bellows housing. A partition plate between the two bellows holds the two bellows together. The other sides of the two bellows are fixed to the housing plates, respectively, on the frontal and rear sides of the bellows housing. The partition plate is connected to the reciprocating driver through a four-arm rack and four connecting rods that run through the frontal hosing plate. During the operation, the reciprocating motion of the driver arm generates a reciprocating motion of the partition plate, which would then create a reciprocating motion of the working fluid hermetically enclosed within the bellows-type RMDHL. A photo of assembled heat loop under evacuation is shown in **Figure 2b**.

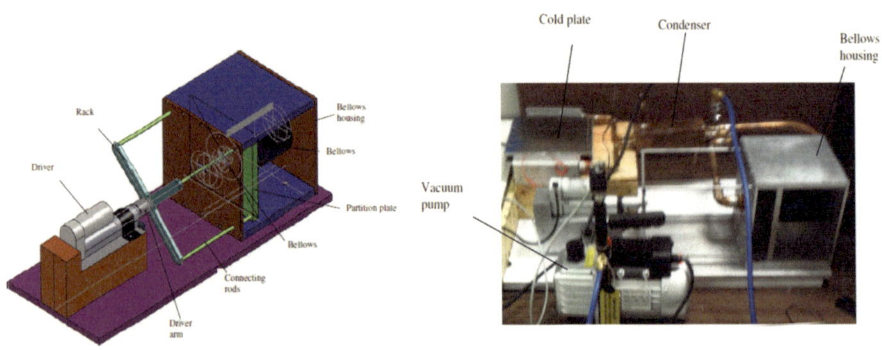

(a) (b)

Figure 2. (a) Configuration of the designed bellows/driver assembly. (b) A photo of the assembled bellows-type heat loop being evacuated [9].

Figure 3 illustrates solenoid-operated electromagnetic driver (line A-A in **Figure 1a**), which is composed of a piston of magnetic metal disposed movably inside the reservoir. The circuit of the right-hand solenoid is closed through a switch, whereas the circuit of the left-hand solenoid is opened through a switch associated with it. As a result, the magnetic field generated by the solenoid attracts the piston toward the right that provides a counterclockwise flow of the working fluid within the loop. As the piston approaches the right end of the liquid reservoir, the left-hand switch is closed while the right-hand switch is opened. As a result, the piston is no longer attracted by the right-hand solenoid and instead attracted by left-hand solenoid toward the left which provides a clockwise working fluid flow within the loop. A reciprocating motion of the piston is induced as the circuits of the two solenoids being opened and closed alternately opposite to each other, which produces a reciprocating flow of the working fluid within the heat loop. As the liquid reservoir has a substantially larger inner diameter than that of the loop tubing (or the volume of the reservoir is large compared with the remainder of the interior volume of the loop) and that, a sufficient fraction of the interior volume of the loop is occupied by liquid, with a sufficiently large piston stroke, liquid is effectively supplied to the evaporator section from the condenser section.

http://dx.doi.org/10.5772/62518

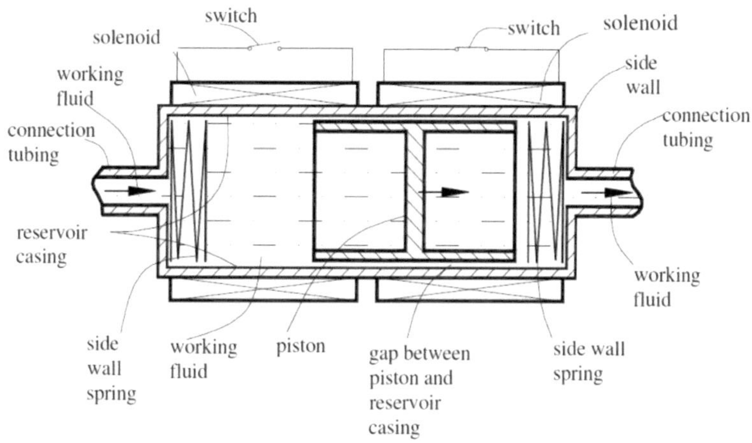

Figure 3. Schematic of a solenoid driver integrated with the liquid reservoir [12].

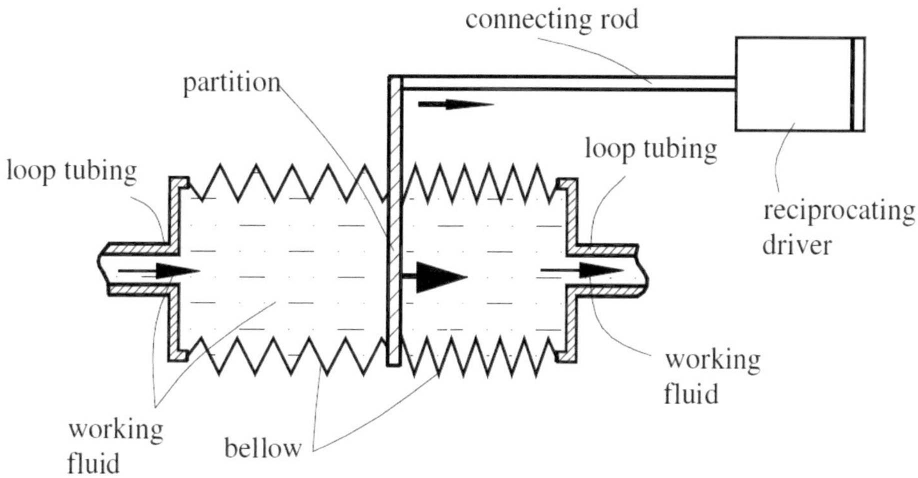

Figure 4. Schematic axial cross-sectional view of a bellows-type reciprocating driver [12].

Figure 4 shows a bellows-type reciprocating heat loop that employs an external reciprocating mechanism as the working temperature of the heat loop is high. As shown in the figure, the bellows is coupled with a reciprocating mechanism through a connecting rod, which could produce a reciprocating motion with a sufficiently large reciprocating stroke. **Figure 1b** shows a detailed description of the aforementioned bellows-type driver in which part or substantially entire circumferential casing of the liquid reservoir is a bellows. A partition is disposed near the mid-section of the bellows. The partition is coupled with an external reciprocating mechanism through a connecting rod. The external reciprocating mechanism can be a solenoid-operated electromagnetic driver or a mechanical reciprocating mechanism driven by an electric motor. As the external reciprocating mechanism is in operation, it generates a reciprocating motion of the partition that produces a reciprocating flow of the heat-carrying fluid enclosed within the loop. The bellows-type reciprocating heat loop can work at a much higher temperature as it does not contain any contacting surfaces having a relative motion in the high-temperature region. Additionally, the bellows can be maintained at a sufficiently low temperature for its reliability during the operation as the outer surface of the bellows can be adequately cooled. Moreover, a non-condensable gas can be filled within the bellows to further reduce the bellows temperature.

From the application point of view, a bellows-type RMDHL loop has the advantages over the solenoid-based RMDHL:

1. The bellows-type RMDHL has successfully overcome the weakness of small displacement of a solenoid-based RMDHL, and enabled a RMDHL for applications involving large heat transfer rates and over a large surface area.

2. The tests show that the bellows-type RMDHL has the potential to maintain a heat-generating surface at an exceedingly uniform temperature. Although in some cases, the maximum temperature difference over the cold plate has exceeded 1.5oC, this temperature difference may be significantly reduced with a more powerful actuator working at a higher frequency.

3. The power consumption of the bellows driver was less than 5 W in all cases, resulting in a ratio of the driver power input to the heat input of the cold plate being less than 1%, which is a ten-fold improvement over that of the solenoid-based RMDHL.

In general, a unique advantage offered by the RMDHL is "coolant leakage" free and the absence of cavitation problems for aerospace-related applications. The single-phase RMDHL could also be an alternative of a conventional liquid cooling system (LCS) for electronic cooling applications. We wish to find a relation that could describe this critical requirement for the operation of the heat loop. Parameters to be determined will include the liquid displacement volume of the piston, effective displacement volume of the heat loop, and terminology to describe the mean performance parameters of the RMDHL.

2. Fluid flow specifications

For all cases of the RMDHL, the displacement of the piston $x_p(t)$ with time is [16]:

$$x_p(t) = -\tfrac{1}{2}S - \tfrac{1}{2}\,S\,cos\,(\omega t) \tag{1}$$

where ω is the pump frequency in radians per second. Differentiating Equation (2) with respect to time we have the mean velocity for the oscillating flow:

$$u = u_{max} \sin(\omega t) \tag{2}$$

The stroke frequency n (in strokes or cycles per second) then follows from:

$$n = \omega / (2\pi) \tag{3}$$

The average volume flow rate q_{av} is equal to the product of stroke volume and pump frequency [16]:

$$q_{av} = \omega / (2\pi) S A_p \tag{4}$$

The pressure gradient takes the form:

$$-\frac{1}{\rho}\frac{\partial p}{\partial x} = a e^{i\omega t} \tag{5}$$

There are several fundamental differences between the reciprocating flow and the continuous flow. First the velocity profiles are completely different. Although the maximum axial velocity for the continuous flow at the center of the channel is of the so-called parabolic effect, the maximum axial velocity for a fast oscillating flow occurring close to the wall is of the so-called annular effect [17]. Also the transition from laminar to turbulence in reciprocating flow is different for that of continuous flow. Even though the categorization of reciprocating flow regime as either laminar or turbulent is based on the Reynolds number, the definition of the critical Reynolds number for the reciprocating flow in the main pipe is given by:

$$Re_\omega = \frac{\omega D^2}{\nu} \tag{6}$$

While the Reynolds number for the reciprocating flow in the rectangular channels for the cold plate is determined as:

$$(Re_\omega)_x = \frac{\omega x_{\max}^2}{\nu} \tag{7}$$

where $x_{\max}$ represents the maximum displacement of the fluid defined by assuming that the fluid moves as a plug flow. In this case, it is equal to the minimum theoretical length of the channel. This value of the Reynolds number in the pipe indicates that the flow in the pipe is turbulent. As the hydraulic diameter of the cold plate is small than the diameter of the pipe, it follows that the flow in the rectangular channels in the cold plate is turbulent.

The second basic parameters dictating the effect of the oscillating fluid flow frequency [18] is the Wimberley (α) number and the depth of penetration of the flow (δ). At low, the flow is quasi-steady, i.e., the fluid particles everywhere respond instantaneously to the applied pressure gradient. When α is large as in the case of this study case, the motion of the boundary layer follow the pressure gradient more closely than the laminae of fluid in the tube core, which shows phase lags to the imposed pressure gradient. Based on the fluid flow in the cold plate, the two terms are defined as follows:

$$\alpha = \frac{D}{2}\sqrt{\frac{\omega}{\nu}} \tag{8}$$

$$\delta = \sqrt{\frac{2\nu}{\omega}} = \frac{D\sqrt{2}}{\alpha} = depth\,of\ penetration \tag{9}$$

For a given reciprocating mechanism-driven heat loop, the volume displacement of the reciprocating driver must be sufficiently large so that the liquid can be supplied from the condenser section to the evaporator section. We wish to find a relation that could describe this critical requirement for the operation of the heat loop. Consider a reciprocating mechanism–driven heat loop under a two-phase working condition (liquid and vapor coexist) similar to that shown in **Figure 5(a)**. The heat loop is assumed to have a condenser section on each side of the reciprocating driver, and the loop is symmetric about the line connecting the midpoints of the evaporator and reservoir. Because of this geometric symmetry, we would like to concentrate on the right half of the loop, as shown in **Figure 5(b)**. The length and average interior cross-sectional area of the evaporator are denoted by L_e and A_e, respectively, the length and average interior cross-sectional area of the connection tubing between the evaporator and the condenser are L_t and A_t, the length and interior cross-sectional area of each condenser section are L_c and A_c, the interior volume of the section between the end of the condenser and the piston right dead center is $V_d/2$, and the piston cross-sectional area and reciprocating stroke are A_p and S, respectively.

2.1. Critical displacement of the reciprocating driver

Consider initially the circuits of both solenoids are open and the piston is stationed in the mid-section of the liquid reservoir, and the vapor generated in the evaporator section pushes the liquid toward the condenser section with a liquid–vapor interface as indicated in the figure. Although there could be thin liquid films at the interior surface of the evaporator, the amount of liquid associated is neglected in the current analysis. In the derivation of the critical liquid displacement, the critical working condition is assumed to be reached when the liquid at the center of condenser, denoted by A, can just reach the mid-section of the evaporator when the right-hand solenoid is turned on and the piston reaches the right dead center in the reservoir.

This condition means that the liquid initially at the condenser center would move to or pass the center of the evaporator as indicated in **Figure 5b**, if the reciprocating mechanism–driven heat loop would work properly. A liquid balance between these two states would give the following relation:

$$A_p.\frac{S}{2}+\frac{V_d}{2}+A_cL_c+A_tL_i\geq\frac{V_d}{2}+A_cL_c+A_tL_t+\frac{1}{2}A_eL_e+\frac{1}{2}A_cL_c+A_tL_i \tag{10}$$

Canceling out the common terms on both sides of the equation and multiplying the resulting equation by 2, we have

$$A_p.S\geq A_cL_c+2A_tL_t+A_eL_e \tag{11}$$

The above equation can be rewritten as follows:

$$A_p.S\geq 2\left(\frac{1}{2}A_cL_c+A_tL_t+\frac{1}{2}A_eL_e\right) \tag{12}$$

The terms in the parentheses on the right-hand side of Equation (12) is the interior volume from the center of the condenser to the center of the evaporator on each side of the heat loop, which reflects one of the essential geometric characteristics of the heat loop in connection with

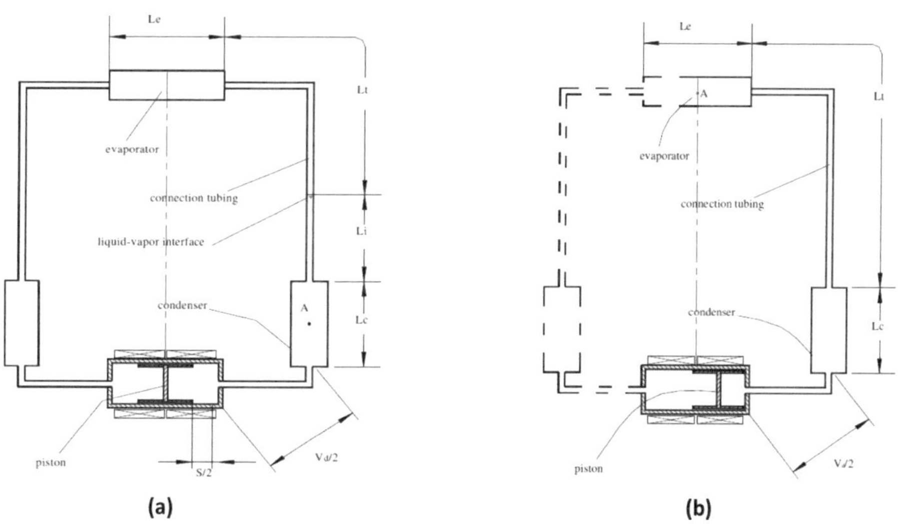

Figure 5. (a) The initial state of the heat loop for the derivation of the working criterion and (b) final state of the heat loop for the derivation of the working criterion [12].

the heat transfer distance and fluid displacement volume. If an effective displacement volume is defined for the entire heat loop as follows:

$$V_{eff} = 2\left(\frac{1}{2}A_cL_c + A_tL_t + \frac{1}{2}A_eL_e\right) \tag{13}$$

Equation (12) can be written as

$$A_p.S \geq V_{eff} \tag{14}$$

Equation (5) indicates that the liquid displacement volume of the piston as represented by A_p.S must be equal to or greater than the effective displacement volume of the heat loop if the heat loop is to work properly. Equation (5), however, is true only for a single-phase heat transfer mode. For a two-phase heat transfer mode, the criterion as represented by Equation (4) or (5) is too conservative because of several reasons. Since the cross-sectional area of the reservoir is usually much greater than that of the rest of the heat loop, the liquid velocity exiting the liquid reservoir should be relatively high. Even if after the piston has reached the dead center in the reservoir, the liquid would continue to move toward the evaporator until the kinetic energy associated with it is exhausted. Additionally, once the liquid enters the evaporator section, some liquid will be evaporated into vapor. The evaporation will drastically change the volume of the flow stream and the liquid/vapor two-phase mixture will expand vigorously into the evaporator section. As a result, the section between the piston right dead center and the center of the evaporator would be filled with both liquid and vapor and the flow is in a two-phase flow condition. It is understood that the liquid fraction would change substantially along the loop. For the derivation of a more concise relation, an effective liquid fraction, ∅, is used. By taking into account the two-phase flow condition, the liquid balance as represented by Equation (1) should be modified as follows:

$$A_p.\frac{S}{2} + \frac{V_d}{2} + \varnothing A_cL_c + \varnothing A_tL_i \geq \frac{V_d}{2} + \varnothing\left(A_cL_c + A_tL_t + \frac{1}{2}A_eL_e + \frac{1}{2}A_cL_c + A_tL_i\right) \tag{15}$$

Following the same deriving procedure, the following relation is obtained:

$$A_p.S \geq 2\varnothing\left(\frac{1}{2}A_cL_c + A_tL_t + \frac{1}{2}A_eL_e\right) \tag{16}$$

or

$$A_p.S \geq \varnothing V_{eff} \tag{17}$$

The value of ∅, by definition, is greater than zero and less than unity. An actual value of ∅, however, has to be determined experimentally for most practical applications because of the complex heat transfer process in the heat loop. Still, Equation (3) or (7) provides a concise criterion that could be used for the design of a heat loop. It should be pointed out that during the derivation of above relations, the liquid reservoir is assumed to contain pure liquid and the back flow through the gap between the outer surface of the piston and the inner surface of the reservoir casing is neglected. If the reservoir would deal with a two-phase liquid–vapor mixture and the back flow effect is taken into account, the term A_p.S in the above equations may need to be multiplied by a driver efficiency η that is less than unity:

$$\eta A_p.S \geq 2\varnothing\left(\frac{1}{2}A_cL_c + A_tL_t + \frac{1}{2}A_eL_e\right) \tag{18}$$

2.2. Velocity profile

Considering the oscillating motion of the fluid in a pipe that is driven by the sinusoidal varying pressure gradient given by Equation (6), the exact solution of the axial velocity profile for a fully developed laminar reciprocating flow in a circular in a circular pipe is given as [17]:

$$\mathbf{u(r,\ t)} = \frac{\mathbf{A_t}}{\omega}(\mathbf{A}\cos(\omega \mathbf{t}) - (1 - \mathbf{A})\sin(\omega \mathbf{t})) \tag{19}$$

$$\mathbf{A} = \frac{\mathbf{ber}\lambda\mathbf{bei}(2\lambda\mathbf{R}) + \mathbf{bei}\lambda\mathbf{ber}(2\lambda\mathbf{R})}{\mathbf{ber}^2\lambda + \mathbf{bei}^2\lambda} \tag{20}$$

$$\mathbf{B} = \frac{\mathbf{ber}\lambda\mathbf{bei}(2\lambda\mathbf{R}) - \mathbf{bei}\lambda\mathbf{ber}(2\lambda\mathbf{R})}{\mathbf{ber}^2\lambda + \mathbf{bei}^2\lambda} \tag{21}$$

$$\overline{\overline{V}} = \frac{V_{max}}{\tau R}\int_0^R\int_0^\tau\left(\frac{32}{r\sigma Re_\omega}\left[\sin t - \left(e^{-E}\right)\sin\left(t - E\right)\right]\right) \tag{22}$$

And

$$E = \left[1 - \left(\frac{r}{R}\right)^2\right]\sqrt{\frac{Re_\omega}{8}} \tag{23}$$

$$\sigma = \frac{8}{\alpha^3}\sqrt{(\alpha - 2C_1)^2 + 4C_2^2} \tag{24}$$

$$C_1 = \frac{ber\alpha bei'\alpha - bei\alpha ber'\alpha}{ber^2\alpha + bei^2\alpha} \tag{25}$$

$$C_2 = \frac{ber\alpha bei'\alpha + bei\alpha ber'\alpha}{ber^2\alpha + bei^2\alpha} \tag{26}$$

ber( ), bei( ), ber'( ), and *bei'( )* are Kelvin functions [19].

2.3. Bulk temperature on the cold plate

An effective tool for comparing the performance of the both of the RMDHL is the value of the bulk temperature on the cold plate. The classical definition of the bulk fluid temperature is given as follows:

$$\boldsymbol{T_b} = \frac{\frac{1}{\boldsymbol{H}}\int_{-H/2}^{H/2} \boldsymbol{V}(\boldsymbol{y.t})\boldsymbol{T}(\boldsymbol{x},\boldsymbol{y},\boldsymbol{z})\,\boldsymbol{dy}}{\frac{1}{\boldsymbol{H}}\int_{-H/2}^{H/2} \boldsymbol{V}(\boldsymbol{y.t})\,\boldsymbol{dy}} \tag{27}$$

$$\overline{\boldsymbol{T_b}} = \frac{\frac{1}{\boldsymbol{\tau H}}\int_{-H/2}^{H/2}\int_0 \boldsymbol{V}(\boldsymbol{y.t})\boldsymbol{T}(\boldsymbol{x},\boldsymbol{y},\boldsymbol{z})\,\boldsymbol{dy}\,\boldsymbol{dt}}{\overline{\overline{V}}} \tag{28}$$

2.4. Pressure drop friction coefficients

The friction coefficient in Equation (19) needs to be evaluated. For the sake of simplicity, the study is restricted to fully developed steady flow and assumes that the two-phase gas flow is incompressible. There are two components to the wall because of the mixture flow and the interfacial shear stresses, hence the pressure loss friction coefficient.

$$\frac{1}{\sqrt{c_{fW}}} = 3.48 - 4\log_{10}\left[\frac{2k_w}{Dh} + \frac{9.35}{\mathrm{Re}\sqrt{c_{fW}}}\right] \tag{29}$$

We use the single-phase flow relationship to predict the wall friction factor for the gas and liquid phase. If we accept that the momentum transfer across a rough liquid surface is governed by the same mechanism as for a rough wall, it is possible to define the pressure loss friction coefficient as [20]:

$$\frac{1}{\sqrt{c_{fW}}} = 3.48 - 4\log_{10}\left[\frac{2k_W}{D_h} + \frac{9.35}{\mathrm{Re}\sqrt{c_{fW}}}\right] \tag{30}$$

in which k_W is the sand roughness of the wall. If we assume a smooth wall,

$$\frac{1}{\sqrt{c_{fW}}} = 3.48 - 4\log_{10}\left[\frac{9.35}{\mathrm{Re}\sqrt{c_{fW}}}\right] \tag{31}$$

where is the friction coefficient that is related to the friction factor by $f = 4c_f$. The Reynolds number in Equation (20) is based on the mixture density and viscosity:

$$\mathrm{Re} = \frac{VD_h\rho}{\mu} \tag{32}$$

$$\frac{1}{\rho} = \frac{x}{\rho_v} + \frac{1-x}{\rho_l} \tag{33}$$

$$\mu = \frac{x}{\mu_v} + \frac{1-x}{\mu_l} \tag{34}$$

The interfacial pressure drop friction coefficients are determined using the correlation below [20]:

$$\frac{1}{\sqrt{c_{fi}}} = 3.48 - 4\log_{10}\left[\gamma Fr_G f_i + \frac{9.35}{\mathrm{Re}_G\sqrt{c_{fi}}}\right] \tag{35}$$

where Fr_G is a Froude number defined as:

$$Fr_G = \frac{\left(u_g - u_l\right)^2}{gD_{hg}} \tag{36}$$

If we assume that $u_g = u_l$, the equation reduces to

$$\frac{1}{\sqrt{c_{fi}}} = 3.48 - 4\log_{10}\left[\frac{9.35}{\mathrm{Re}_G \sqrt{c_{fi}}}\right] \tag{37}$$

2.5. Heat transfer coefficient

Zhao and Cheng [21] obtained the following correlation for a space cycled averaged Nusselt number for a reciprocating laminar flow as:

$$\overline{Nu} = .02\left(\frac{x_{\max}}{D}\right)^{0.85} \mathrm{Re}_{\omega}^{0.58} \tag{38}$$

where $x_{\max}$ is the maximum fluid displacement within the pipe, and

$$\overline{Nu} = \frac{qD_i}{k_f\left(\overline{T_w} - \overline{T_m}\right)} \tag{39}$$

$\overline{T_w}$ and $\overline{T_m}$ are the bulk temperatures for the cold plate and coolant, respectively.

3. Performance comparison of RMDHL to CONTINUOUS cooling system

In this section heat transfer and fluid flow aspects of the reciprocating mechanism–driven heat loops (RMDHL) have been studied numerically using the available commercial software, Ansys Fluent [22]. The main objective of the present study is to compare the performance of a RMDHL with the conventional continuous cooling loops in terms of temperature, uniformity, and heat removal from the surface of the heat source. For the current study, 3D setup of CONTINUOUS and RMDHL cooling loops are provided. The 3D setup, which is based on the previous experimental studies, can be used for future development and optimization of a real industrial product.

3.1. Numerical study of continuous cooling loops

Figure 6 shows the geometrical and boundary conditions of the cooling loops. Both loops are consisting of a single passage with two 90′ elbows. The inner loop is the condenser loop and the other loop forms the evaporator loop. The condenser and evaporator loops are enclosed with solid wall.

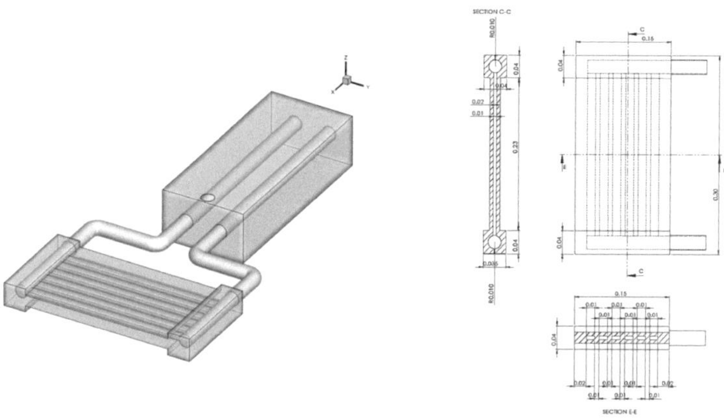

(a) (b)

Figure 6. (a) 3D geometry of the cooling loops and (b) key dimensions.

The two loops are the main challenge in the present simulation to setup a closed loop in Ansys fluent. Based on the Navier Stokes equation, the continuity and momentum equations are coupled and for an incompressible flow, and the SIMPLE algorithm indicates the coupling of pressure and momentum fields inside the computational domain. Hence introducing a cross section with a constant velocity in a closed loop would result in a discontinuity in the velocity field, which makes the solution unstable and leads to inaccurate results. **Figure 7** shows the grid distribution for the present simulation.

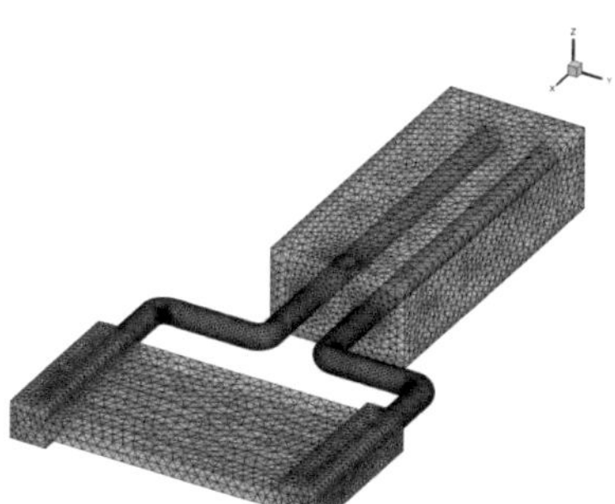

Figure 7. Mesh distribution for a 3D.

Hence, the CONTINUOUS loops are simulated using the following setups:

For continues loop:

a. Instead of a closed loop, an open loop is simulated.

b. Constant velocity is applied on the inlet boundary to obtain the same flow rate.

c. Using a User Defined Function (UDF), the inlet temperature of the loop is set as the average outlet.

Temperature of the loop should mimic the temperature and velocity of a closed loop. The solid walls are copper, and their thermophysical properties are obtained from the fluent database. The working liquid in the both loops is water.

3.2. Governing equations and boundary condition

In the present study for the CONTINUOUS loop the following assumptions are made:

1. Both fluid flow and heat transfer are in steady-state.
2. Fluid is in single phase and flow and laminar.
3. Properties of both fluid and heat sink materials are temperature independent.
4. All the surfaces of heat sink exposed to the surroundings are assumed to be insulated except the walls of evaporator where constant heat flux simulating the heat generation from different components.

Based on above assumptions, the governing equations for fluid and energy transport are:

Fluid flow:

$$\nabla \cdot \vec{V} = 0 \tag{40}$$

$$\rho\left(\vec{V} \cdot \nabla V\right) = -\nabla p + \mu \nabla^2 \vec{V} \tag{41}$$

Energy in fluid flow:

$$\rho c_p\left(\vec{V} \cdot \nabla T\right) = k \nabla^2 T \tag{42}$$

Based on the operating conditions described above, the boundary conditions for the governing equations are given as:

Inlet:

http://dx.doi.org/10.5772/62518

$$V = V_{in}, \quad T_{in} = \left(T_{out}\right)_{ave} \tag{43}$$

Outlet:

$$P = P_{out}, \quad \frac{\partial T}{\partial n} = 0 \tag{44}$$

Fluid–solid interface:

$$\vec{V} = 0, \quad T = T_s, \quad -k_s \frac{\partial T_s}{\partial n} = -k \frac{\partial T}{\partial n} \tag{45}$$

At the top wall:

$$q_w = -k_s \frac{\partial T_s}{\partial n} \tag{46}$$

In Equation (44), V_{in} and T_{in} are the fluid inlet pressure and temperature, respectively; p_{out} is the pressure at the outlet, n is the direction normal to the wall or the outlet plane, and q_w is the heat flux applied at the top wall of the heat sink.

3.3. Numerical studies of RMDHL cooling loops

The geometry and grid distribution for RMDHL is as same as CONTINOUS loop. To simulate a closed RMDHL loop, the following setup is used:

For RMDHL loop:

a. Instead of a closed loop, an open loop is simulated.

b. A UDF is used to generate the sinusoidal inlet velocity for the evaporator loop.

c. Using a UDF, the inlet temperature of the loop is set as the average outlet temperature of the loop and the backflow temperature of the outlet is set to the average temperature of the inlet boundary to mimic the temperature and velocity in distribution of a closed loop.

4. Performance of CONTINOUS and RMDHL loops

Temperature profiles on the evaporator walls (left and right walls) are also shown in **Figure 8b**, **d**, **f**, and **h**. The figures clearly show the non-uniformity of the temperature contours for the CONTINOUS loop. As seen in these figures, the temperature is minimum at the inlet of the evaporator and gradually increases toward the outlet of the outlet. Moreover, these figure clearly indicate that the temperature increases with increase in heat flux on the walls.

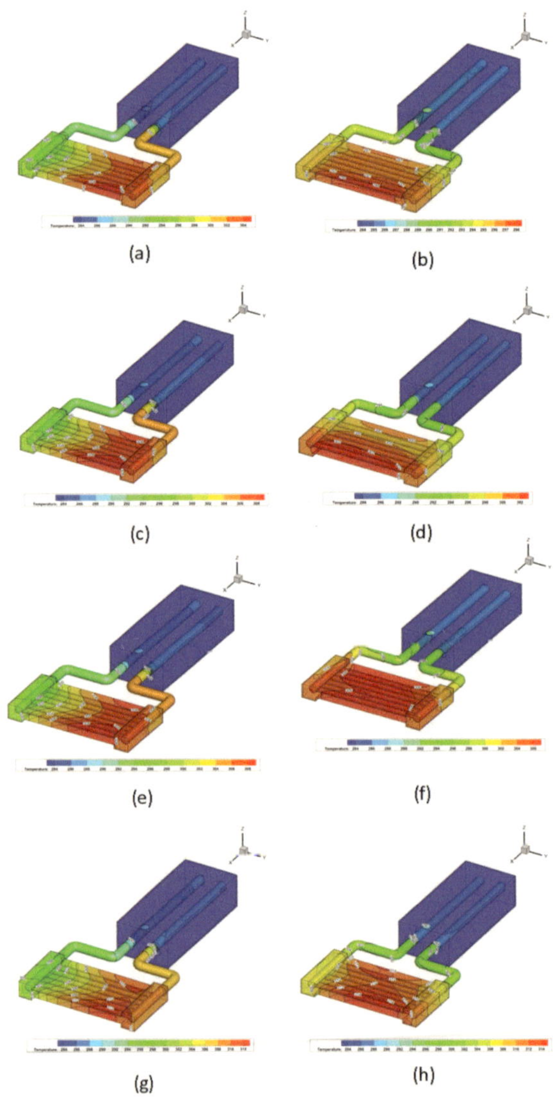

Figure 8. Temperature profile on the evaporator surface, T = 30 s for heat fluxes (a), (b) 11594.2 W/m^2 (c), (d) 13043.48 W/m^2, (e),(f) 14492.75 W/m^2, and (g),(h) 15971.01 W/m^2.

Contrary to the CONTINOUS loop, the temperature contour is in symmetry for a RMDHL system. The temperature distributions of both the RMDHL and CONTINOUS cold plates are obtained at a condenser inlet velocity of 1.23 m/s, heat transfer rate range from 11594 W/m^2, and 15971 W/m^2 and a condenser inlet temperature of 283 K. The results of unsteady simulation in **Figures 8a, c, e,** and **g** indicate the following important point:

http://dx.doi.org/10.5772/62518

1. Frequency of the inlet velocity has a very important effect on the rate of heat removal from the evaporator. In fact, it can be concluded the optimum loop time should be equal or more than:

$$\Delta T = 2 \times \Delta T_{half} \tag{47}$$

Where

$$\Delta T_{half} = \frac{L_{half}}{U_{max}} \tag{48}$$

Where L_{half} is the half of the evaporator loop length and U_{max} is the maximum velocity of the fluid in evaporator loop. The numerical results also show that choosing the duration time less than the above value results in much higher temperature on the evaporator walls because the fluid could not transfer the heat from the evaporator to the condenser well.

2. In this study a sinusoidal velocity profile is used, but there is no guarantee that this profile is the best choice to obtain the maximum heat transfer rate. The authors believe that a velocity profile with longer residence time and shorter circulation time will have a better performance for the RMDH loops.3. In this study a reciprocating velocity profile has been applied on the inlet boundary and out let boundary is set to constant pressure boundary.

Figures 8 a–h clearly show that the uniformity of the temperature profiles of the RMDHL shown in the left column is much better than that of the CONTINOUS. As seen in **Figures 8**, there are two temperature gradients: one gradient along the evaporator width and the another gradient across the evaporator thickness. The gradient along the evaporator width is similar for both the CONTINOUS and the RMDHL and is because of the pressure drop along the grooves in the evaporator. The effect of this gradient can be reduced if a different groove configuration is adopted. However, it is observed that the pressure gradient along the evaporator is more pronounced for the CONTINOUS loop than the RMDHL loop. For the temperature gradient along the fluid flow path, **Figure 8** shows that the CONTINOUS (the column of the right) has up to 13 distinct temperature bands where observed for the 15,971.01 W/m^2 cold plate. It was also observable that temperature band increases with increasing heat flux, whereas for the RMDHL the number of bands is much fewer and independent of heat flux. As much as 80% of the cold plate of the RMDHL was maintained at a within a temperature difference of 0.5 °C.

5. Conclusion

In this chapter the concept of bellows-type and solenoid-based RMDHL cooling mechanism has been demonstrated. This novel type of cooling system has several advantages over the conventional cooling system in power electronic cooling industries. The experimental results clearly showed that the heat loop worked very effectively and a heat flux in the evaporator section could be handled. Moreover, it has been proven both numerically and theoretically that the RMDHL provides superior cooling advantage with respect to temperature uniformity compared with CONTINOUS cooling loops; hence it could be an alternative of a conventional liquid cooling system (LCS) for electronic cooling applications. The results also proved that the bellows-type RMDHL has successfully overcome the weakness of small displacement of a solenoid-based RMDHL, and enabled a RMDHL for applications involving large heat transfer rates and over a large surface area. The tests also show that the bellows-type RMDHL has the potential to maintain a heat-generating surface at an exceedingly uniform temperature. Although in some cases, the maximum temperature difference over the cold plate has exceeded, this temperature difference may be significantly reduced with a more powerful actuator working at a higher frequency. The power consumption of the bellows driver was less than 5 W in all cases, resulting in a ratio of the driver power input to the heat input of the cold plate being less than 1%, which is a ten-fold improvement over that of the solenoid-based RMDHL. Using numerical analysis, CONTINOUS and RMDHL loops are simulated as well. The numerical simulations have been conducted using different parameters and boundary conditions for a 3D setup. The results show that the temperature increases with an increase in heat flux on the walls or decrease of the flow rate. The results also indicate that the temperature profiles are more uniform for an RMDHL loop compared with a CONTINOUS loop.

Nomenclature

A Area [m^2]

C_p Specific heat [J/kg K]

D_i Inside tube diameter [m]

D_o Tube outside diameter [m]

D_h Hydraulic diameter [m]

H Height of rectangular channel [m]

h Heat-transfer coefficient [W/m^2 K]

k Thermal conductivity [W/m^{2}K]

L Length

n Reciprocating pump stroke frequency[cycles/s]

$\dot{m}$ Mass flow rate [kg/s]

Nu Nusselt number: $h/(k/D_h)$

p Pressure [Pa]

$\dot{Q}$ Heat transfer rate [W]

σ_T Standard deviation

α Surface effectiveness: $\sqrt{2\nu/\omega}$

μ Dynamic viscosity [kg/ms]

ρ Density [kg/m^3]

ω pump frequency [rad/s]

τ Cycle period [s]

σ Constant: $(8/\alpha^3)\sqrt{(\alpha-2C_1)^2+4C_2^2}$

Subscript

ave Average value

c Condenser

e Evaporator

in Inlet

m Mean value

min Minimum value

Nomenclature

q	Volume flow rate [m^3/s]	*max*	Maximum value
Re	Reynolds number: $(\rho VD)/\mu$	n	Direction normal to the wall
Re_ω	Kinetic Reynolds number: $\omega x_{max}^2 / v$ [m]	*out*	Outlet
r	Tube inside radius [m]	p	Pump piston
S	Stroke [m]	s	Surface
T	Temperature [°C]	t	Tubing
U	Overall heat-transfer coefficient[W/m^2 K]	w	Wall
t	Time[s]	**Superscript**	
Greek Letters		= -	Time-averaged quantity
s	Flow penetration	→	Vector

Author details

Olubunmi Popoola, Soheil Soleimanikutanaei* and Yiding Cao

*Address all correspondence to: ssole016@fiu.edu

Department of Mechanical Materials Engineering, Florida International University, Miami, Florida, USA

References

[1] Semiconductor Industry Association. International Technology Roadmap for Semiconductors. Austin, TX: International SEMATECH; 1999.

[2] Zuo Z, Hoover L, and Phillips A. Thermal Challenges in Next Generation Electronic Systems, 317–336. Joshi, Y.K., Garimella, S.V. An integrated thermal architecture for thermal management of high power electronics, Millpress, 2002, 416. http://www.iospress.nl/book/thermal-challenges-in-next-generation-electronic-systems/978-90-77017-03-6

[3] Vafai K. High heat flux electronic cooling apparatus, devices and systems incorporating same. US 20020135980A1. 2002.

[4] Bergles AEA. High-flux processes through enhanced heat transfer. 2003; http://dspace.mit.edu/handle/1721.1/5564.

[5] Liu Z, Tan S, Wang H, Hua Y, and Gupta A. Compact thermal modelling for packaged microprocessor design with practical power maps. Integration the VLSI Journal. 2014;47(1):71–85.

[6] Hetsroni G, Mosyak A, and Segal Z. Nonuniform temperature distribution in electronic devices cooled by flow in parallel microchannels. IEEE Transactions on Components and Packaging Technologies. 2001;24(1):16–23.

[7] Krishnamoorthy S. Modeling and Analysis of Temperature Distribution in Nanoscale Circuits and Packages. Chicago: University of Illinois; 2008.

[8] Jeakins W and Moizer W. Cooling of electronic equipment. US Pat; 2003. 1–70.

[9] Cao Y, Xu D, and Gao M. Experimental study of a bellows-type reciprocating-mechanism driven heat loop. International Journal of Energy Research. 2013;37(6):665–672.

[10] Faghri A. Heat pipe science and technology. Washington, DC: Taylor & Francis; 1995.

[11] Kosoy B. Heat Pipes. Kirk-Othmer Encyclopedia of Chemical Technology. 19 Nov 2004. 1–20. http://onlinelibrary.wiley.com/doi/10.1002/0471238961.0805012002090514.a01.pub2/abstract DOI: 10.1002/0471238961.0805012002090514.a01.pub2.

[12] Cao Y and Gao M. Experimental and analytical studies of reciprocating-mechanism driven heat loops (RMDHLs). Journal of Heat Transfer. 2008;130(7):1–20.

[13] Munson B, Young D, and Okiishi T. Fundamentals of Fluid Mechanics. 6th edition. Danvers: Wiley; 2009.

[14] Cao Y and Wang Q. Engine Piston. U.S. Patent No. 5,454,351. 3 October 1995.

[15] Cao Y and Gao M. Reciprocating-mechanism driven heat loops and their applications. ASME 2003 Heat Transfer Summer Conference. 2003.

[16] De-Jongh J and Rijs R. Pump Design. Arrakis; 2004.

[17] Zhao TS and Cheng P. Heat transfer in oscillatory flows. Annual Review of Heat Transfer. 1998;4(35):359–419.

[18] Menon AS, Weber ME, and Chang HK. Model study of flow dynamics in human central airways. Part III: Oscillatory velocity profiles. Respiration Physiology. 1984;55(2):255–275.

[19] Uchida S. The pulsating viscous flow superposed on the steady laminar motion of incompressible fluid in a circular pipe. J Zeitschrift für Angew. Math. und Phys ZAMP. 1964;19(1):117–120.

[20] Line A and Fabre J. Stratified gas–liquid flow. in International Encyclopaedia of Heat and Mass Transfer, Hewitt GF, Shires GL, CRC Press, 1997.1097-1101

[21] Zhao TS and Cheng P. Oscillatory heat transfer in a pipe subjected a periodically reversing flow. ASME Journal of Heat Transfer. 1996;118:592–598.

[22] Available from: http://www.ansys.com/.

Chapter 8

Theoretical Derivation of Junction Temperature of Package Chip

Professor Wei-Keng Lin

Additional information is available at the end of the chapter

http://dx.doi.org/10.5772/62570

Abstract

Junction temperature is the highest operating temperature of the actual semiconductor in an electronic device. In operation, junction temperature is higher than the case temperature and the temperature of the part's exterior. The difference is equal to the amount of heat transferred from the junction to case multiplied by the junction-to-case thermal resistance. When designing integrated circuits, predicting and calculating the chip junction temperature is a very important task. This chapter describes how to derive the junction temperature from the thermal transport model.

Keywords: junction temperature, thermal resistance, thermal conduction, thermal convection, thermal radiation

1. Introduction

From the small integrated circuits in 1960 to the development of today's large and ultra-high-speed integrated circuits, the package density has increased from only several electronic components to billions of electronic components per chip. Because of this high package density, the combination directly causes a serious designing problem, and it will also increase the heat dissipation of the chip per unit volume or area. If the cooling method is not properly designed, this overheated high-density package chip will result in a high junction temperature. As a result, it will have a negative effect on the functions, the reliabilities, and the life of the electronic chip. Usually, a high-speed integrated circuit is the most expensive element of the whole package. If the chip continues to suffer from the effect of high heat, it will cause the speed to slow down or be damaged; therefore, the solution of the heat-dissipated problem should not be underestimated. In electronics manufacturing, integrated circuit packaging is the final stage of semiconductor device fabrication, in which the tiny block of semiconducting material is encased in a supporting case that prevents physical damage and corrosion. The case, known as a "package," supports the electrical contacts that connect the device to a circuit board. The junctions of the chip are used by wire connecting on the package housing. These wires are then connected to other components through the wire on the printed circuit board (PCB). Therefore, for many integrated circuit products, packaging technology is a very important stage. Using chip as the main product such as random access memory (RAM) or dynamic RAM (DRAM), packaging technology not only can guarantee the separation of the chip and the outer world but also can prevent chip circuit from losing its function caused by the corrosion of the impurities in the air; also, the wellness of the packaging technology directly concerns the designing and producing of the PCB connected with the chip. This leads to the deeply influential of the chip's performance. However, if the thermal impedance of the package is too high, the junction temperature will also be raised to a high level. According to the report, once the junction temperature is raised to approximately 10°C, half of the component life will be reduced [1]. if the average life span is 30,000 to 50,000 hours, it is also implied that 15,000 to 25,000 hours of usage time will be decreased and result in the chip efficiency's sharp decline. This chapter is mainly focused on the theoretically export system manufacturers' topmost concern, junction temperature (T_J). Sometime in 1980, PC is still in 386 and 486, and the CPUs' permitted temperature could be up to 90°C; until the 21st century, all the semiconductor chip junction temperature (including LED) has been asked not to surpass 70°C. Some of them are not even allowed to exceed 50°C. Therefore, the purpose of this chapter is how to simply use a theoretical calculation to derive the chip junction temperature (T_J) without using software package (Code).

2. Theoretical derivation of the junction temperature

The following are the logical ways to think of the solutions to counter heat-dissipated problems.

2.1. Questions in Table 1

Step	Questions
A	What is the thermal model in this problem? Is it thermal conduction in [2]? Or thermal convection in [3]? Or thermal radiation in [4]?
B	Fluid? Is liquid? Or gas?
C	Can the fluid be compressed or not [5]? We usually supposed it is not compressible fluid.
D	Are the fluid properties related to the temperature?
E	What is the status of the fluid?

Step	Questions
	Is it laminar flow [6] or period cycle flow in [7]?
	Or turbulent flow in [8]? Or transient in?
F	What is the length of calculating Re's characteristic?
	By tube diameter or by plate length or by obstacle height? Or others
G	What is the effect of the viscosity in this problem [9]?
	How about the boundary layer [10]? What is mechanical loss? And others?

Table 1. Steps of finding the solutions of heat-dissipated problems.

At this step, readers should have a good physical explanation for solving the questions. From steps A to G, we can be closer and see clearly the answer to the question.

2.2. Quantization and removal of unimportant parameters

The goal of this step is to think about every item of the question (or concept) to gain a deeper understanding. For example, $Q=hA(T_s\text{-}T_f)$; in this phase, notice the correct use of the unit (usually in SI unit). Make sure not to compare apple and orange, making correct assumptions necessary. Thus, when making any item negligible, we need to provide a scientific proof. We cannot directly ignore an item because it is small. Take the temperature, for example, when finding the answer to the question on temperature. We need to ask if we are looking for the temperature distribution or the end point. What is the accuracy? Is there anything else that can be simplified?

2.3. Establishment of the governing equation

The definition of the governing equation is using other variables to define an unknown item. If we only consider the heat transfer mechanics of the single chip on the PWB, take **Figures 1** and **2**, for example, during the heat transfer mechanism. The chip and the board both have thermal conductance, thermal convection, and thermal radiation. At this point, we can notice some of the characteristics of the heat transfer processes: (A) Multiple heat transfer processes, a high level of thermal coupling (heat source and sink). (B) Large-scale thermal spreading effect. If we consider all the heat transfer mechanism between each PWB, such as in **Figure 3**, then we need to also consider the thermal conductance coupling problem from the PCB. Among thermal convection, they include (i) material on the board, (ii) thermal convection and thermal radiation between each adjacent boards, and (iii) thermal coupling between the main board and the daughter card. Among radiation coupling, they include (a) material on the board and (b) adjacent boards. What needs to be paid attention of is when there is thermal coupling between the outer heat source and the chip heat itself. The heat received from the critical chip is not less than the heat source chip itself. **Figure 4** presents a schematic diagram between the heat source chip and the critical chip of the motherboard and the outer heat source. Thus, to solve the heat-dissipated problem, we should not only pay attention to the temperature on the heat source of chip itself but also need to know problems such as the heat accumulation locations and the other chip influences.

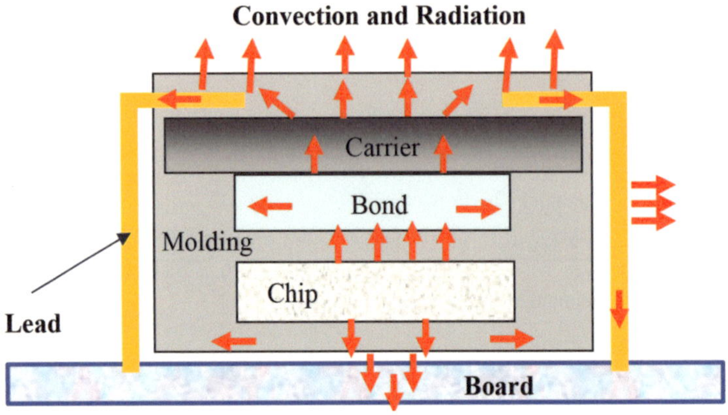

Figure 1. Heat transfer mechanism process of the chip for the upper part.

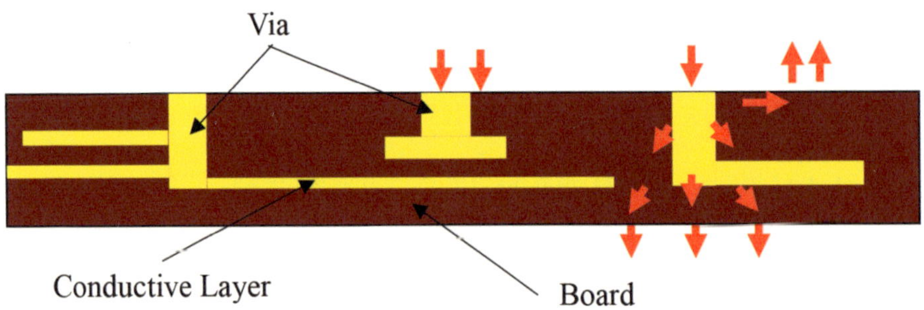

Figure 2. Heat transfer mechanism process of the chip for the lower portion.

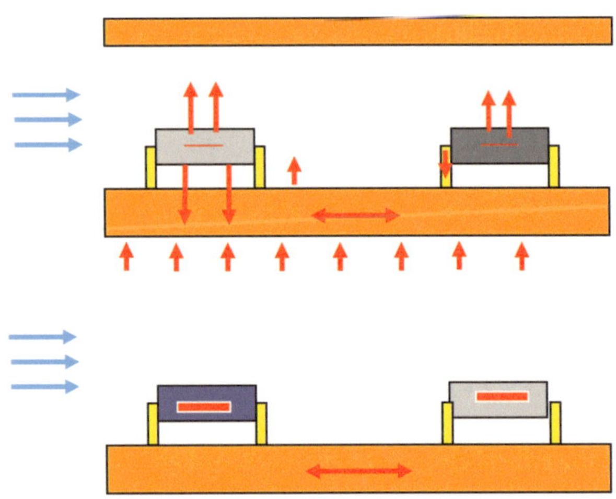

Figure 3. Heat transfer mechanism between each PWB.

http://dx.doi.org/10.5772/62570

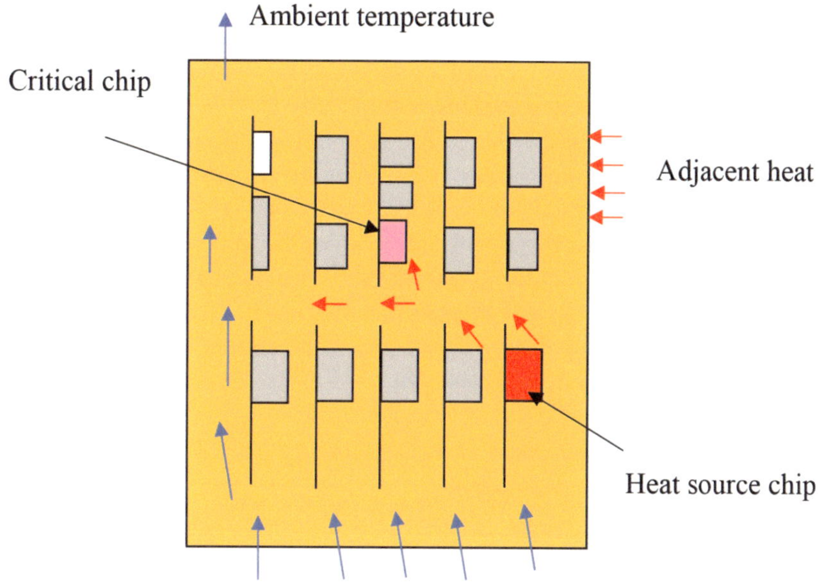

Figure 4. Schematic diagram between the heat source chip and the critical chip of the motherboard and the outer heat source.

2.4. How to analyze the influences of the thermal coupling

Thermal coupling makes it hard to analyze, if we do not include the thermal coupling in the calculation, and the results will not be accurate. Because of the thermal coupling natural properties, we need to consider the environment, chassis, PWB, component (module), chip, and parts (diodes, transistor) etc., when analyzing conducting a solution that can explain the thermal effect. Usually, there are three ways to solve either the key component or the heat source chip's heat-dissipated problem (see **Figure 5**). One of them is using the integral method, that is, a closed-form solution. However, this method can necessarily not be used on every energy conservation. The second method is using the differential method, the so-called numerical analysis. Numerical analysis needs a special mathematical skills technique. It needs someone who has studied numerical analysis to write a program that includes grids definition, module establish, numerical analysis model, converging problem, boundary condition definition, etc. This needs to educate talented people, and most of the companies are unwilling to invest in here. But on the other hand, usually there are also software packages in the market, such as ice pack, fluent, ANSYS, and Flotherm. However, all these software packages cost more than USD 30,000 or 40,000. Not everyone can afford it, and most companies cannot even buy it—these are some of the difficulties what companies are facing. The third solution is measure it by experiment. The experiment is then separated into two kinds. One is the actual measurement that uses the real system with the samples attached to it to measure the data such as temperature. Although this is a very reliable way, it spends a lot of manpower and time, and the cost is expensive. Cooler manufacturers commonly do not use this solution. For example, Intel published the next-generation CPU, but there are supplier problems on these equipment, such as power supply, main board, south bridge, north bridge, hard disk, and DRAM. Cooler manufacturers can only solve the CPU's heat-dissipated problems, and they really cannot wait until all these peripheral accessory devices are ready because it will take too much time and cost too much. Therefore, the actual measurement is only used in system manufacture, such as in HP, DELL, ASUS, ACER, and Lenovo. The second way of the experiment is the Dummy experiment, also known as Dummy heater. It is commonly used by the industry. For example, because we wanted to know what the thermal resistance of the cooler is, we only have to place the cooler on the heating copper block with which it has the same area and then measure the difference temperature between the heat copper block and ambient temperature then divide by the input power to get the thermal resistance of the cooler. The experiment does not have any complex problems. The only thing that we need to be aware of is the sensors' correction, measuring the position and boundary condition.

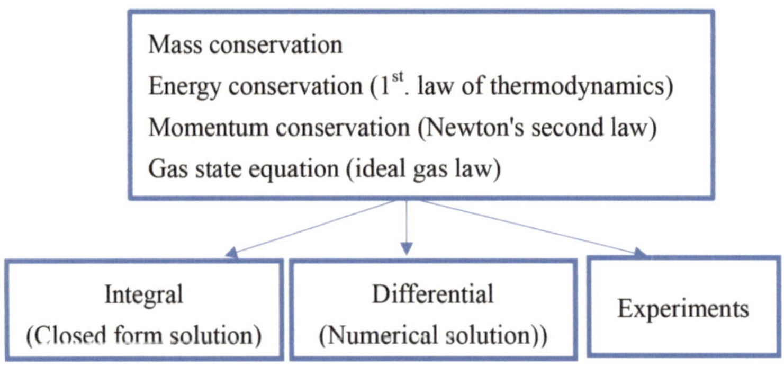

Figure 5. Three methods for solving heat-dissipated problems.

2.5. Theoretical derivation of the junction temperature (T_J)

2.5.1. Consider a control volume around the outside of the component and lead pin

Take the control volume on the external chip and wire as in **Figure 6**.

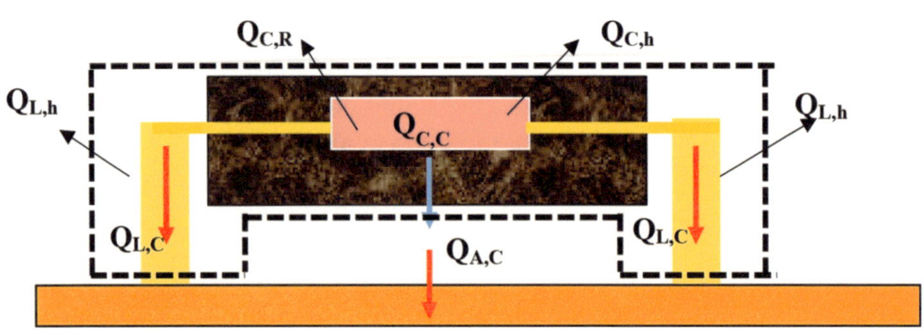

Figure 6. Heat transfer diagram outside the chip.

Let us apply the energy balance equation to the body of the component and device power dissipation is "P_{tot},

$$\begin{aligned} P_{tot} &= Q_{C,R} + Q_{C,h} + Q_{L,h} + Q_{C,C} \\ &= Q_{C,R} + Q_{C,h} + Q_{L,h} + Q_{L,C} + Q_{A,C} \end{aligned} \tag{1}$$

where $Q_{C,R}$=radiation heat transfer from component (W), $Q_{C,H}$=convection heat transfer from component (W), $Q_{L,h}$=convection heat transfer from lead (W), $Q_{C,C}$=conduction heat transfer through component (W), $Q_{L,C}$=conduction heat transfer through lead (W), and $Q_{A,C}$=conduction heat transfer through air gap under the component (W).

Converting all the Q's in Eq. (1) in terms of the temperature definitions, we have

2.5.1.1. Using Stefan-Boltzmann's law to change the thermal radiation of the chip into temperature

$$Q_{C,R} = \sigma \in_C f_{C,ref} A_{C,C}\left(T_C^4 - T_{ref}^4\right) = \left(\frac{1}{R_{th,CR}}\right)\left(T_C^4 - T_{ref}^4\right)$$

$$= \sigma \in_C f_{C,ref} A_{C,C}\left(T_C^4 - T_a^4\right) = \left(\frac{1}{R_{th,CR}}\right)\left(T_C^4 - T_a^4\right) \tag{2}$$

where σ=Stefan-Boltzmann's constant=5.669×10^{-8} W/m^2 K^4,ε=material emissivity, $f_{c,ref}$=shape factor for component, $A_{C,C}$=upper surface area of the chip=bottom surface area of the chip (m^2), T_C=upper surface temperature of the chip (K), h_C=heat transfer coefficient of the chip (W/m^2 K), and T_{ref}=reference temperature where the component radiates to generally can be assumed to be T_a (K).

$$Q_{C,h} = h_C A_{C,C}\left(T_C - T_a\right) \tag{3}$$

$$R_{th,Ch} = \frac{1}{h_C A_{C,C}} = \frac{T_C - T_a}{Q_{C,h}} \tag{4}$$

2.5.1.2. Using Newton's cooling law to change the thermal convection of the chip into temperature

$$Q_{L,h} = h_L A_{L,S}\left(T_L - T_a\right)$$

$$R_{th,Lh} = \frac{1}{h_L A_{L,S}} = \frac{T_L - T_a}{Q_{L,h}} \quad (5)$$

where h_L=heat transfer coefficient of the wire (W/m^2 K) and $A_{L,S}$=surface area of the wire (m^2).

2.5.1.3. Using Newton's cooling law to change the thermal convection of the lead into temperature

$$Q_{L,C} = \frac{k_L A_{L,C}}{L_L}(T_L - T_b)$$

$$R_{th,LC} = \frac{1}{k_L A_{L,S}} = \frac{T_L - T_b}{Q_{L,C}} \quad (6)$$

where $A_{L,C}$=cross-sectional area of the lead (m^2), k_L=lead thermal conductivity (W/m K), L_L=length of the lead outside of the component (m), and T_L=lead average temperature (K).

2.5.1.4. Using Fourier's cooling law to change the thermal conduction of the chip into temperature through air gap between chip and board

$$Q_{A,C} = \frac{k_A A_{C,C}}{t_A}(T_C - T_b)$$

$$R_{th,CA} = \frac{1}{k_A A_{C,C}} = \frac{T_C - T_b}{Q_{A,C}} \quad (7)$$

where k_A=air thermal conductivity (W/m K), t_A=thickness of the layer of air underneath the component (m), T_b=board temperature (K), and $A_{C,C}$=assumed component top surface is the cross-sectional area of the air gap (m^2).

Substitute the above into Eq. (1):

$$\begin{aligned} P_{tot} &= Q_{C,R} + Q_{C,h} + Q_{L,h} + Q_{C,C} \\ &= Q_{C,R} + Q_{C,h} + Q_{L,h} + Q_{C,C} + Q_{L,C} + Q_{A,C} \end{aligned}$$

$$\begin{aligned} &= \sigma \in_C f_{C,ref} A_{C,C}\left(T_C^4 - T_{ref}^4\right) + h_C A_{C,C}\left(T_C - T_a\right) \\ &+ h_L A_{L,S}\left(T_L - T_a\right) + \frac{k_L A_{L,C}}{L_L}\left(T_L - T_b\right) + \frac{k_A A_{C,C}}{t_A}\left(T_C - T_b\right) \end{aligned} \quad (8)$$

http://dx.doi.org/10.5772/62570

In Eq. (8), T_L, T_b, and T_C are unknown, but we do not know the junction temperature (T_J) yet. Therefore, we need seek another control volume to get T_J.

2.5.2. Consider a control volume around the inside of the component

Assume a chip inside as shown in **Figure 7**, according to energy conservation

$$P_{tot} = Q_{C,R} + Q_{C,h} + Q_{C,J} + Q_{A,C} \tag{9}$$

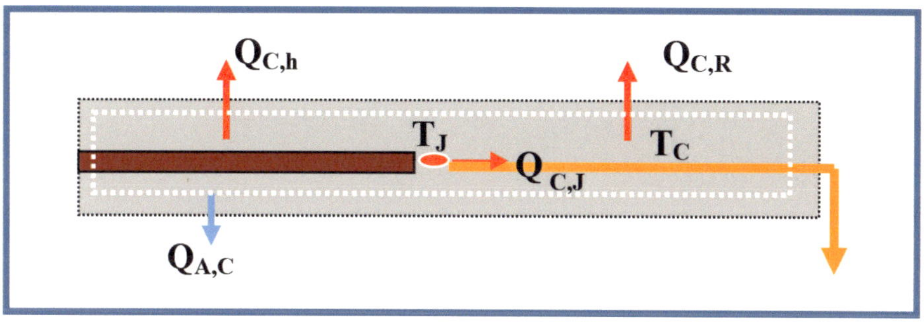

Figure 7. Case temperature and heat transfer diagram inside the chip.

2.5.2.1. Using Fourier's cooling law to change the inner thermal conduction of the chip into temperature

$$Q_{C,J} = (-\frac{k_L A_{L,C}}{L_L})_{eff}\left(T_C - T_J\right) = (\frac{k_L A_{L,C}}{L_L})_{eff}\left(T_J - T_C\right) \tag{10}$$

where $Q_{C,J}$=conduction heat transfer within the body of the component (W), $A_{L,C}$=effective lead cross-sectional area inside the component (m^2), $L_{L,eff}$=effective lead length inside the component (m), $k_{L,eff}$=effective thermal conductivity of the lead (W/m K).

2.5.2.2. Using Fourier's cooling law and Newton's cooling law to change the thermal conduction and thermal convection of the chip and lead into temperature

Compare Eq. (1) with Eq. (9).

$$P_{tot} = Q_{C,R} + Q_{C,h} + Q_{L,h} + Q_{L,C} + Q_{A,C} \tag{1}$$

$$P_{tot} = Q_{C,R} + Q_{C,h} + Q_{C,J} + Q_{A,C} \tag{9}$$

As shown in **Figure 8**, the conduction heat transfer within the body of the component $Q_{C,J}$ is the sum of the thermal convection from lead to ambient $Q_{L,h}$ and lead thermal conductance to board $Q_{L,C}$:

$$Q_{C,J} = Q_{L,h} + Q_{L,C}$$

Plugging all the thermal conduction equation and thermal convection into above equation, we obtain:

$$\left(\frac{k_L A_{L,C}}{L_L}\right)_{eff}(T_J - T_C) = h_L A_{L,S}(T_L - T_a) + \frac{k_L A_{L,C}}{L_L}(T_L - T_b) \tag{11}$$

Plug Eq. (11) into Eq. (8):

$$\begin{aligned} P_{tot} &= \sigma \in_C f_{C,ref} A_{C,C}\left(T_C^4 - T_{ref}^4\right) + h_C A_{C,C}(T_C - T_a) \\ &\quad + h_L A_{L,S}(T_L - T_a) + \frac{k_L A_{L,C}}{L_L}(T_L - T_b) + \frac{k_A A_{C,C}}{t_A}(T_C - T_b) \\ &= \sigma \in_C f_{C,ref} A_{C,C}\left(T_C^4 - T_{ref}^4\right) + h_C A_{C,C}(T_C - T_a) \\ &\quad + \left(\frac{k_L A_{L,C}}{L_L}\right)_{eff}(T_J - T_C) + \frac{k_A A_{C,C}}{t_A}(T_C - T_b) \end{aligned} \tag{12}$$

Solve for T_J from Eq. (12):

$$T_J = T_C + \left(\frac{k_L A_{L,C}}{L_L}\right)_{eff}^{-1} \left\{ P_{tot} - \left[\begin{array}{l} \sigma \in_C f_{C,ref} A_{C,C}\left(T_C^4 - T_{ref}^4\right) \\ + h_C A_{C,C}(T_C - T_a) + \dfrac{k_A A_{C,C}}{t_A}(T_C - T_b) \end{array} \right] \right\} \tag{13}$$

In Eq. (13), the junction temperature is what we need, but there are two unknown temperatures, such as T_b and T_C. Therefore we must seek another two equations to obtain T_b and T_C.

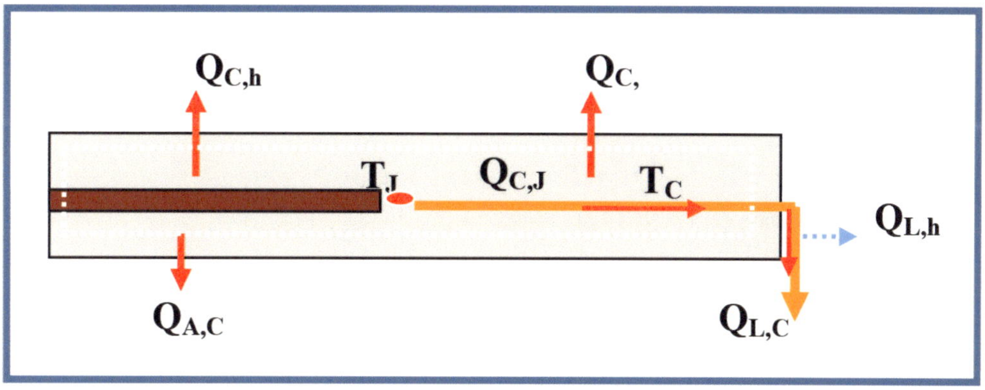

Figure 8. Junction temperature and heat transfer diagram inside the chip.

2.5.3. Consider a control volume around the air flow channel without considering adjacent heat source

Consider a control volume around the air flow channel as shown in **Figure 9**. The conduction heat transfer from component to board $Q_{C,C}$ is the sum of $Q_{L,C}$, $Q_{A,C}$, and $Q_{N,C}$, where $Q_{L,C}$=conduction heat transfer through lead, $Q_{A,C}$=conduction heat transfer through air gap under the component, and $Q_{N,C}$=adjacent heat input.

$$Q_{C,C} = Q_{L,C} + Q_{A,C} + Q_{N,C}$$

Neglect $Q_{N,C}$ heat conduction from neighbor and consider a control volume shown as in **Figure 9**. Chip heat conductance power $Q_{C,C}$ is then the sum of $Q_{b,h}$, $Q_{bb,h}$, $Q_{b,R}$, and $Q_{bb,R}$, where $Q_{b,h}$=convection heat transfer from board top surface, $Q_{bb,h}$=convection heat transfer from board bottom surface, $Q_{b,R}$=radiation heat transfer from board top surface, and $Q_{bb,R}$=radiation heat transfer from board bottom surface.

$$Q_{C,C} = \left(Q_{b,h} + Q_{bb,h}\right) + \left(Q_{b,R} + Q_{bb,R}\right) \tag{14}$$

From Eq.(1), with energy conservation of airflow channel:

……With energy conservation of air flow channel:

$$Q_{b,h} + Q_{b,R} + Q_{C,R} + Q_{C,h} + Q_{L,h} = m_{air} C_{p,air} \left(T_o - T_i\right) \tag{15}$$

Plug Eq. (15) into Eq. (1) and obtain Eq. (16):

$$\begin{aligned} P_{tot} &= Q_{C,R} + \left(Q_{C,h} + Q_{L,h}\right) + (Q_{L,C} + Q_{A,C}) \\ &= Q_{C,R} + [m_{air}C_{p,air}\left(T_o - T_i\right) - Q_{b,h} - Q_{b,R} - Q_{C,R}] + \left(Q_{L,C} + Q_{A,C}\right) \\ &= [m_{air}C_{p,air}\left(T_o - T_i\right) - Q_{b,h} - Q_{b,R} + \left(Q_{L,C} + Q_{A,C}\right) \end{aligned} \tag{16}$$

$$\text{Science } Q_{C,C} = Q_{L,C} + Q_{A,C} = \left(Q_{b,h} + Q_{bb,h}\right) + \left(Q_{b,R} + Q_{bb,R}\right) \tag{14}$$

Plug Eq.(14) into Eq.(16), and solve for it, i.e.,

$$P_{tot} = m_{air}C_{p,air}\Delta T + Q_{bb,h} + Q_{bb,R} \tag{17}$$

Assuming $Q_{bb,h}$ and $Q_{bb,R}$ can be ignored, Eq. (17) turns out to be:

$$P_{tot} = m_{air}C_{p,air}\left(T_o - T_i\right) \tag{18}$$

It is reasonable that all the power generation from the component should be carried away by the air flow. If not, the board temperature, the case temperature, and the junction temperature will be increased. However, Eq. (18) cannot help to solve the board temperature; therefore, we need to seek another control volume to solve $T_{b.}$

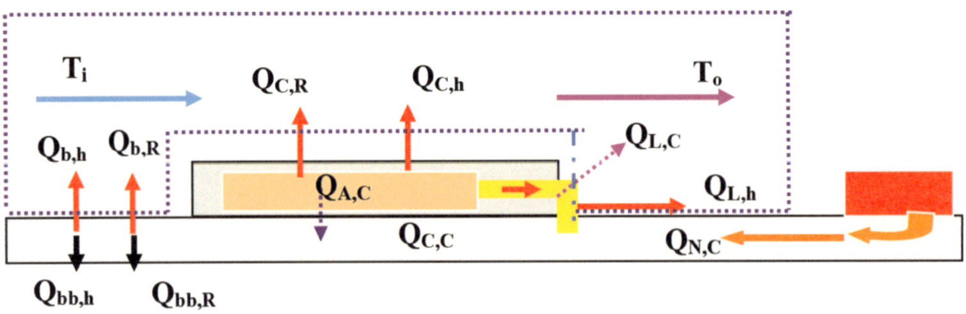

Figure 9. Schematic diagram for airflow channel.

2.5.4. Consider a control volume around the board

Consider a control volume around the board as in **Figure 10**, where T_b=board temperature (K), $Q_{C,C}$=conduction heat transfer from component to board (W), $Q_{b,h}$=convection heat transfer from board top surface (W), $Q_{bb,h}$=convection heat transfer from board bottom surface (W), $Q_{b,R}$=radiation heat transfer from board top surface (W), $Q_{bb,R}$=radiation heat transfer from board bottom surface (W), and $Q_{N,C}$=conduction heat transfer from neighboring component (W).

http://dx.doi.org/10.5772/62570

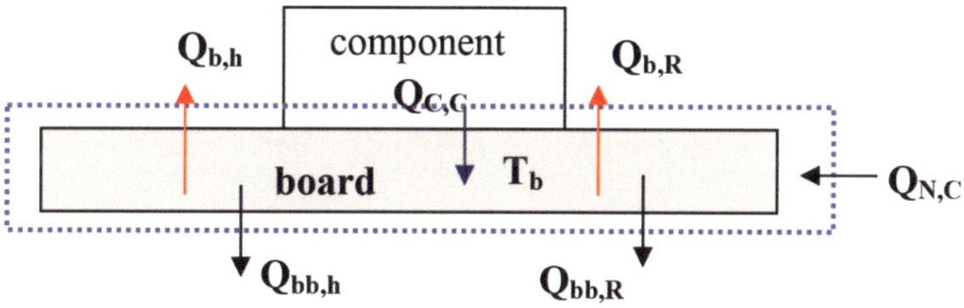

Figure 10. Schematic of chip on board.

Energy balance for the steady-state condition:

$$Q_{in} = Q_{out}$$

$$Q_{C,C} + Q_{N,C} = Q_{b,h} + Q_{bb,h} + Q_{b,R} + Q_{bb,R} \tag{19}$$

If neglect the bottom back board thermal convection and radiation effects, then $Q_{bb,h} = Q_{b,R} = 0$. Assume $Q_{N,C}$=0 and simplify Eq. (19) to be Eq. (20):

$$Q_{C,C} = Q_{L,C} + Q_{A,C} = Q_{b,h} + Q_{b,R} \tag{20}$$

where $Q_{L,C}$=conductance heat transfer from lead (W) and $Q_{A,C}$=conduction heat transfer through air gap under the component (W).

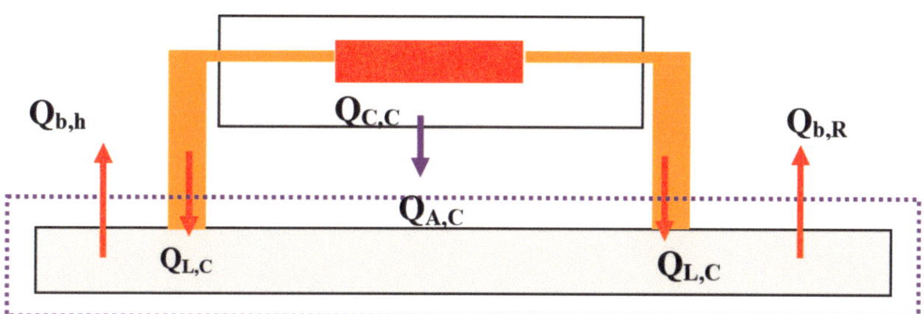

Figure 11. Schematic of heat transfer from lead to board.

In **Figure 11**, the conduction heat transfer from component to board $Q_{C,C}$ is the sum of the conductance heat transfer from lead $Q_{L,C}$ and the conduction heat transfer through air gap under the component $Q_{A,C}$. If we neglect the convection heat transfer from board bottom surface $Q_{bb,h}$ and the radiation heat transfer from board bottom surface, then the power $Q_{C,C}$ should also equal to the sum of convection heat transfer from board top surface $Q_{b,h}$ and radiation heat transfer from board top surface $Q_{b,R}$. Therefore,

$$P_{tot,board} = Q_{C,C} = Q_{L,C} + Q_{A,C} = Q_{b,h} + Q_{b,R}$$

$$= h_b\left(A_b - A_{C,C}\right)\left(T_b - T_a\right) + \sigma\grave{o}_b f_{b,ref}\left(A_{b-}A_{C,C}\right)\left(T_b^4 - T_a^4\right) \quad (21)$$

where h_b=heat transfer coefficient of air flow associated with the board, A_b=board upper surface area, and $A_{C,C}$=component top surface area=bottom surface area.

After obtaining a first estimate of the board temperature and assuming that the heat is uniformly distributed over the board, neglect $Q_{b,R}$ and thus obtain an initial average board temperature:

$$P_{tot,board} = h_b\left(A_b - A_{C,C}\right)\left(T_b - T_a\right) \quad (22)$$

Solve T_b from Eq. (22):

$$T_b = \frac{P_{tot,board}}{h_b\left(A_b - A_{C,C}\right)} + T_a \quad (23)$$

Hence, we have a first estimate of T_b.

where P_{tot}=total power generation from chip and $P_{tot,board}$=total power conduction to the board.

Remember, P_{tot} is different from $P_{tot,board}$. In general, under the forced convection condition, the heat conductance into the board is around 20–30%, $P_{tot,board}$=$0.2P_{tot}$ ~ $0.3P_{tot}$ whereas, under the natural convection condition, the heat conductance into the board is only 70–80%, $P_{tot,board}$=$0.2P_{tot}$ ~ $0.3P_{tot}$

2.5.5. *Solve for T_C, T_b, and T_J*

2.5.5.1. *Method 1*

2.5.5.1.1. *If $R_{th,JC}$ can be obtained from the vendor:*

$$R_{th,JC} = \frac{T_J - T_C}{P_{tot}} \quad (24)$$

Combining Eqs. (13), (23), and (24), T_J, T_b, and T_C can be solved.

$$T_J = T_C + (\frac{k_L A_{L,C}}{L_L})_{eff}^{-1} \left\{ P_{tot} - \left[\begin{array}{l} \sigma \in_C f_{C,ref} A_{C,C} \left(T_C^4 - T_{ref}^4 \right) + \\ h_C A_{C,C} \left(T_C - T_a \right) + \frac{k_A A_{C,C}}{t_A} \left(T_C - T_b \right) \end{array} \right] \right\} \tag{13}$$

$$T_b = \frac{P_{tot,board}}{h_b \left(A_b - A_{C,C} \right)} + T_a \tag{23}$$

2.5.5.1.2. *If* $R_{th,JC}$ *is unknown*

Assume that P_{up} is uniformly spread over the entire upper surface of the component. Therefore,

$$P_{up} = h_C A_{C,C} \left(T_C - T_a \right) \tag{25}$$

$$P_{tot} - P_{tot,board} = P_{tot} - h_b \left(A_b - A_{C,C} \right) \left(T_b - T_a \right)$$

$$T_C = \frac{P_{up}}{h_C A_{C,C}} + T_a \tag{26}$$

From Eqs.(13), (23), and (26), solve for T_J, T_b and T_c.

$$T_J = T_C + (\frac{k_L A_{L,C}}{L_L})_{eff}^{-1} \left\{ P_{tot} - \left[\begin{array}{l} \sigma \in_C f_{C,ref} A_{C,C} \left(T_C^4 - T_{ref}^4 \right) + \\ h_C A_{C,C} \left(T_C - T_a \right) + \frac{k_A A_{C,C}}{t_A} \left(T_C - T_b \right) \end{array} \right] \right\} \tag{13}$$

$$T_b = \frac{P_{tot,board}}{h_b \left(A_b - A_{C,C} \right)} + T_a \tag{23}$$

In the case of duct flow, from Eq. (26), we need to obtain T_a. Let us reconsider the airflow over the component in a channel. If we neglect the radiation effect, the heat transported by the air is obtained from

$$T_C = \frac{P_{up}}{h_C A_{C,C}} + T_a \tag{26}$$

$$Q_{up,C} = \dot{m}C_{p,air}\left(T_o - T_i\right) \tag{27}$$

T_o is air exit temperature of the flow channel, whereas T_i is the air inlet temperature of the flow channel. T_o can be obtained from Eq. (28):

$$T_o = \frac{Q_{up,C}}{\dot{m}C_{p,air}} + T_i \tag{28}$$

In duct flow, the ambient temperature is the average temperature of the air inlet temperature and air exit temperature:

$$\begin{aligned} T_a &= \frac{\left(T_o + T_i\right)}{2} = \frac{1}{2}\left(\frac{Q_{up,C}}{\dot{m}C_{p,air}} + 2T_i\right) \\ &= \frac{Q_{up,C}}{2\dot{m}C_{p,air}} + T_i = \frac{P_{up}}{2\dot{m}C_{p,air}} + T_i \end{aligned} \tag{29}$$

Plug Eq. (29) into Eq. (26) and then obtain chip case temperature T_C:

$$T_C = \frac{P_{up}}{h_C A_{C,C}} + T_a = P_{up}\left(\frac{1}{h_C A_{C,C}} + \frac{1}{2\dot{m}C_{p,air}}\right) + T_i \tag{30}$$

However, in Eq. (30), the heat transfer coefficient h_C is still needs to be obtained.

2.5.5.2. Method 2

If h_C is not readily available, let us use the junction-to-ambient and junction-to-case thermal resistance for the component as shown in **Figure 12**, the schematic diagram of thermal resistance in flow channel.

http://dx.doi.org/10.5772/62570

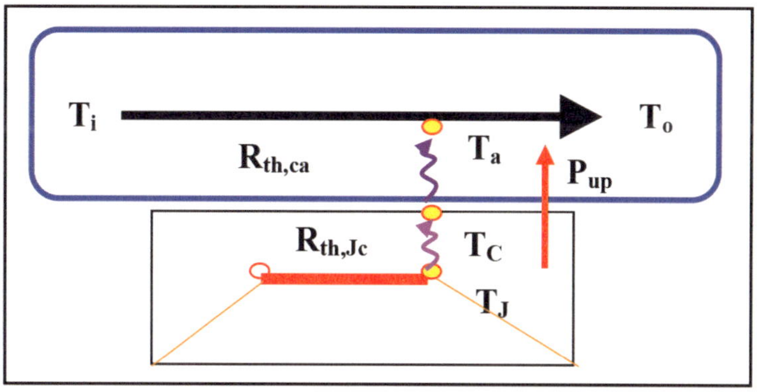

Figure 12. Schematic diagram of thermal resistance in flow channel.

The definition of thermal resistance $R_{th,JC}$ is the junction temperature (T_J) minus the chip case temperature T_C divided by power input as shown in Eq. (31):

$$R_{th,JC} = \frac{T_j - T_C}{P_{up}} \tag{31}$$

The thermal convection resistance from chip surface to ambient $R_{th,Ca}$ is shown in Eq. (32):

$$R_{th,Ca} = \frac{1}{h_C A_{C,C}} \tag{32}$$

Therefore, the total thermal resistance $R_{th,Ja}$ is the sum of $R_{th,JC}$ and $R_{th,Ca}$, shown as in Eq. (33):

$$R_{th,JC} + R_{th,Ca} = R_{th,Ja} \tag{33}$$

The thermal resistance $R_{th,Ch}$ (or $R_{th,Ca}$) can be represented by Eq. (34):

$$R_{th,Ch} = R_{th,Ca} = \frac{T_c - T_a}{P_{up}} = \frac{T_c - \dfrac{P_{up}}{2\dot{m}C_{p,air}} - T_i}{P_{up}}$$

$$= \frac{T_c}{P_{up}} - \frac{1}{2\dot{m}C_{p,air}} - \frac{T_i}{P_{up}} \tag{34}$$

The case temperature T_C can be represented by Eq. (35):

$$T_c = P_{up}\left(R_{th,Ca} + \frac{1}{2\dot{m}C_{p,air}}\right) + T_i \tag{35}$$

$$R_{th,Ch} = R_{th,Ca} = \frac{1}{h_C A_{C,C}} = \frac{T_c - T_a}{Q_{C,h}} \tag{4}$$

Plug Eq. (4) into Eq. (35) and obtain Eq. (36):

$$T_c = P_{up}\left(\frac{1}{h_C A_{C,C}} + \frac{1}{2C_p\left(\rho_{air}V_{air}A_{channel}\right)}\right) + T_i \tag{36}$$

Eqs. (36) and (30) are the same.

$$T_c = P_{up}\left(\frac{1}{h_C A_{C,C}} + \frac{1}{2\dot{m}C_{p,air}}\right) + T_i \tag{30}$$

Basically, we can solve for T_J, T_b, and T_C from Eqs. (13), (23), and (26).

2.5.6. Consider a control volume around the air flow channel with adjacent heat source

Now, if we want get a more accurate expression for the board temperature T_b, then we can reconsider the energy balance for the board, as shown in **Figure 13**. Because the value for T_C is known from Eqs. (26) and Eq. (30) from Eq. (17):

$$P_{tot} = m_{air}C_{p,air}\Delta T + Q_{bb,h} + Q_{bb,R} \tag{17}$$

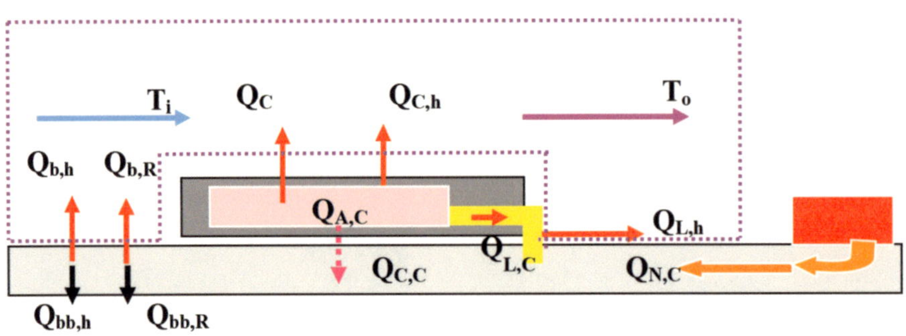

Figure 13. Schematic of chip thermal resistance and thermal resistance from adjacent heat source in the flow channel.

http://dx.doi.org/10.5772/62570

Total power P_{tot} thus can be represented in terms of temperature:

$$P_{tot} = \dot{m}C_{p,air}\left(T_o - T_i\right) + h_{bb}A_{bb}\left(T_b - T_{amb,bb}\right) + \left(\frac{1}{R_{th,bbR}}\right)\left(T_b^4 - T_{N,bb}^4\right) \tag{37}$$

where $T_{N,b}$=neighboring board temperature where the component top surface sees for radiation exchange (K),h_{bb}=heat transfer coefficient from the backside of the board (W/m K), A_{bb}=back surface area associated with above convection loss (m^2), $R_{th,b,R}$=radiation heat transfer resistance with respect to the board (K/W), $R_{th,bb,R}$=radiation heat transfer resistance with respect to the back of the board (K/W), and $T_{N,bb}$=board temperature of the neighboring board where the radiation exchange takes place with back of the board where the component of interest resides.

Solve for T_b in Eq. (37); theoretically, we need more accuracy equation such as Eq. (38). In fact, it is not easy to solve for Eq. (38); sometimes, we need numerical analysis. In addition, there are some variables that could affect its accuracy, such as h_{bb} and $T_{N,b}$.

$$\left(\frac{1}{R_{th,bbR}}\right)T_b^4 + h_{bb}A_{bb}T_b = P_{tot} + \left(\frac{1}{R_{th,bbR}}\right)T_{N,b}^4 + h_{bb}A_{bb}T_{amb,b} - \dot{m}C_p\left(T_o - T_i\right) \tag{38}$$

Because we have T_b, T_C, and T_a, T_J can be calculated from Eq. (13).

$$T_J = T_C + \left(\frac{k_L A_{L,C}}{L_L}\right)_{eff}^{-1}\left\{P_{tot} - \left[\begin{array}{l}\sigma\grave{o}_C f_{C,ref} A_{C,C}\left(T_C^4 - T_{ref}^4\right) + \\ h_C A_{C,C}\left(T_C - T_a\right) + \frac{k_A A_{C,C}}{t_A}\left(T_C - T_b\right)\end{array}\right]\right\} \tag{13}$$

Figure 14 shows the flow chart solution for T_J. (i) Consider a control volume around the outside of the component and lead pin for the first. Get a chip power P_{tot} as a function of (T_L, T_b, T_C, T_a). (ii) Consider a control volume around the inside of the component and get junction temperature (T_J) as the function of (T_b, T_C, T_a). (iii) Consider a control volume around the air flow channel, and the total power P_{tot} is equal to $mC_p(T_o-T_i)$. (iv) Consider a control volume around the board and assume that the power input to the board $P_{tot,board}$ is n times of the total power P_{tot}, $P_{tot,board}=nP_{tot}$. The average board temperature T_b obtained at this time is the function of $P_{tot,board}$ and T_a. (v) If the vendor can provide $R_{th,JC}$ data, then T_J, T_b, T_C, and T_a can be calculated. (vi) Calculate $Q_{L,C}$ and $Q_{A,C}$. Calculate $P_{tot,board}=Q_{L,C}+Q_{A,C}$, and $(P_{tot,board}/P_{tot})=n'$; if $(n'-n)/n>5\%$, take new n for $n=(n'+n)/2$, back to (iv) using iterative method, and recalculate until $(n'-n)/n<5\%$. Remember, the goal is to solve for T_J,Therefore, to ensure $\eta = \frac{\Delta T_{J,calc}}{\Delta T_{J,spec}} = \frac{T_{J,calc} - T_\infty}{T_{J,spec} - T_\infty} \leq 0.9$.

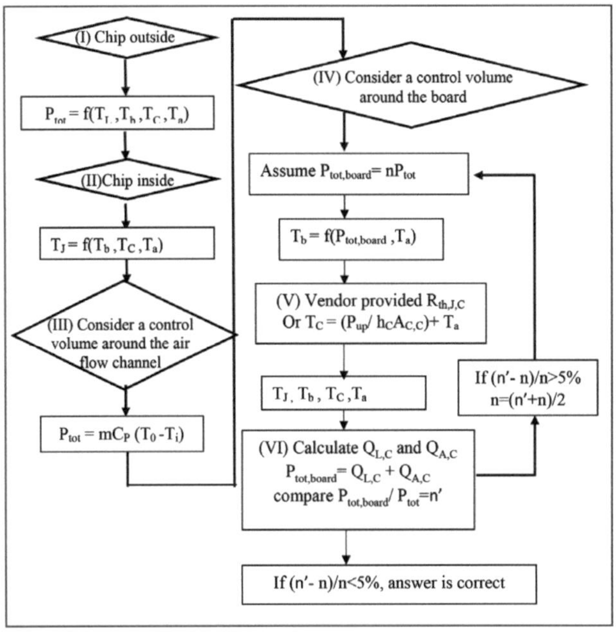

Figure 14. Flow chart of junction temperature calculation using the iterative method.

3. Summary

The goal of the thermal designer is to minimize the thermal resistance of the chip. Equations and analysis procedures are provided in this chapter to assist the designer in understanding the thermal characteristics of chip devices and the thermal performance of related materials. The methods are useful for the approximations of the chip junction temperature. In the meantime, the permissible dissipated powers of chip can be estimated as well.

Author details

Professor Wei-Keng Lin

Address all correspondence to: wklin@es.nthu.edu.tw

Engineering & System Science Department, National Tsing-Hua University, Hsinchu, Taiwan

http://dx.doi.org/10.5772/62570

References

[1] Bogatin E., Roadmaps of Packaging Technology. Chapter 6, In: Chip packaging: Thermal requirements and constraints, D. Potter and L. Peters, editors, Integrated Circuit Engineering Corporation, 1997, pp. 6-1. Available at: http://www.smithsonian-chips.si.edu/ice/cd/PKG_BK/title.pdf.

[2] Holman J.P., Heat Transfer, 7th ed., McGraw-Hill Publishing Co., Singapore, 1992, pp. 2–10.

[3] Rolle K.C., Heat and Mass Transfer, 1st ed., Prentice-Hall, Upper Saddle River, NJ/ Columbus, OH, 2000, pp. 205–228.

[4] Kern D.Q., Process Heat Transfer, McGraw-Hill Book Co., New York, 1976, pp. 62–84.

[5] Goldstein R.J., Fluid Mechanics Measurements, University of Minnesota, 1983, pp. 51–60.

[6] Byron Bird R., Stewart W.E., and Lightfoot E.N., Transport Phenomena, John Wiley Sons, Department of Chemical Engineering, University of Wisconsin, Madison, Wisconsin, USA, 1960, pp. 56–61.

[7] E. Benjamin Wylie Victor L. Streeter, "Fluid Transients Systems", Prentice-Hall Inc A Simon & Schuster Company, Englewood Cliffs, NJ, USA, 1993, pp.287–305.

[8] Whitaker S., Fundamental Principles of Heat Transfer, Library of Congress Cataloging in Publication Data, 1977, pp. 273–303.

[9] Holman J.P., Experimental Methods for Engineers, 7th ed. Mc-GRAW-Hill Book Co., Singapore, 2001. pp. 432–434.

[10] Schlichting H., Gersten K., Krause E., Oertel Jr. H., and Mayes C., Boundary-Layer Theory, 8th ed. Springer, 2004. ISBN 3-540-66270-7.